Diversity and Community
in the Academy

ISSUES IN ACADEMIC ETHICS

General Editor: Steven M. Cahn

DIVERSITY AND COMMUNITY IN THE ACADEMY

Affirmative Action in Faculty Appointments

CELIA WOLF-DEVINE

ROWMAN & LITTLEFIELD PUBLISHERS, INC.
Lanham • Boulder • New York • Oxford

ROWMAN & LITTLEFIELD PUBLISHERS, INC.

Published in the United States of America
by Rowman & Littlefield Publishers, Inc.
4720 Boston Way, Lanham, Maryland 20706

12 Hid's Copse Road
Cummor Hill, Oxford OX2 9JJ, England

British Cataloging in Publication Information Available

Library of Congress Cataloging-in-Publication Data

Wolf-Devine, Celia, 1942–
    Diversity and community in the academy: affirmative action in faculty appointments / Celia Wolf-Devine.
        p.   cm.—(Issues in academic ethics)
    Includes bibliographical references and index.
    ISBN 0-8476-8443-1 (cloth: alk. paper).—ISBN 0-8476-8444-X (alk. paper)
    1. College teachers—Selection and appointment—United States. 2. Minority college teachers—Selection and appointment—United States.   3. Affirmative action programs—United States.   4. Faculty integration—United States.   I. Title.   II. Series.
LB2332.72.W65   1997   96-48117
378.1'2—dc21   CIP
    ISBN 0-8476-8443-1 (cloth : alk. paper)
    ISBN 0-8476-8444-X (pbk. : alk. paper)

Printed in the United States of America

♾™ The paper used in this publication meets the minimum requirements of American National Standard for Information Sciences—Permanence of Paper for Printed Library Materials, ANSI Z39.48-1984.

Issues in Academic Ethics

Academic life generates a variety of moral issues. These may be faced by students, staff, administrators, or trustees, but most often the issues revolve around the rights and responsibilities of the faculty. In my book *Saints and Scamps: Ethics in Academia* (Rowman & Littlefield, revised edition, 1994), I set out to enumerate, explain, and emphasize the most fundamental of these professorial obligations. To do justice to the complexities of academic ethics, however, requires the work of many scholars focused on numerous areas of investigation. The results of such an effort are embodied in this series.

Each volume concentrates on one set of connected issues and combines a single-authored monograph with sources chosen by the author to exemplify or amplify materials in the text. This format is intended to guide readers while encouraging them to develop and defend their own beliefs.

In recent years philosophers have examined the appropriate standards of conduct for physicians, nurses, lawyers, journalists, business managers, and government policymakers but have not given equal attention to formulating guidelines for their own profession. The time has come to observe the Delphic motto "Know thyself." Granted, the issues in need of critical examination are not exotic, but as the history of philosophy demonstrates, self-knowledge is important to seek and difficult to attain.

Steven M. Cahn III

To Phil

Contents

Acknowledgments

I am grateful to Stonehill College for granting me a sabbatical during which I began work on this project. I also wish to thank the Carthage Foundation and the Earhart Foundation, whose generous assistance allowed me to take additional time off teaching to complete the book.

I am also indebted to the following people who read and commented on drafts of various chapters: Steven Cahn, Richard Capobianco, Violet Halpert, James Rachels, Robert Rafalko, Constance Rousseau, Ronald Tacelli, S.J., and Richard Velkley. I wish to thank Eleanore Devine for her help with proofreading. I am especially grateful to my husband, Phil Devine, who read and commented on the manuscript, allowed me to talk out ideas with him, bore generously all the stress inevitably generated by having a spouse in the throes of completing a book, and even helped with the index.

Introduction

This book is about affirmative action in faculty appointments. Affirmative action programs for student admissions are discussed in a separate volume of this series, and involve somewhat different issues. The appointment decision is particularly important because it is at this level that people are squeezed out of the profession; it is like a game of musical chairs with far fewer chairs than players. Once one has a foot in the door, at least if one's appointment is tenure track, one is accorded more legal protection. In addition, one has the advantage of insider information, unions or other professional organizations may be enlisted to help, one has time to cultivate allies among the faculty and administration, and sometimes student support can be mobilized to help if one is unfairly denied tenure. Those eliminated at the appointment stage have no protection, and quietly disappear from view. Thus the appointment decision is particularly crucial in determining the future shape of the professoriat.

My approach to affirmative action is philosophical rather than legal, and I do not take legal reasoning as philosophically paradigmatic as many writers in this area have done. The sorts of issues that arise in connection with faculty appointments are different from those that arise for hiring bank tellers or firefighters. Cultural politics and philosophical issues (such as epistemological relativism) are more central in faculty appointments, and therefore I highlight these more than is commonly done in books on affirmative action. The practice of affirmative action in faculty appointments will also have a particularly important cultural impact since universities are one of the primary institutions charged with the task of handing on our cultural tradition. Those seeking an in-depth discussion of the legal issues involved are referred to the supplementary essay by George Rutherglen.

In the early 1970s, when universities first came under serious pressure from government agencies to adopt affirmative action policies, this triggered a vigorous debate in the philosophical literature about the issue. But the stream of philosophical literature has gradually dwindled away to a trickle, and there seems to be a general perception that everyone has made up his or her mind about affirmative action and that it is hopeless to try to persuade people to change their minds.

1

Meanwhile, however, the external situation has changed dramatically since the early 1970s (and even more so since the early sixties, when affirmative action policies first began to take shape). To the extent that universities are under external pressure now, that pressure is more likely to be against affirmative action policies than for them. The recent decisions in *Adarand Constructors v. Pena* and *Texas et al. v. Cheryl J. Hopwood et al.* are only the most recent manifestations of an unmistakable trend toward increasingly strict scrutiny of affirmative action plans by the courts. In this changed legal climate, universities have a breathing space to step back and rethink their policies, taking into account the justifications that have been offered for affirmative action, the changed social context within which universities now operate, and the results such policies have had so far. That, then, is the purpose of this book.

The term "affirmative action" is a vague one and has been used to cover a very wide range of policies. At one end of the spectrum one might require national searches and encourage women and people of color to apply; at the other end it could involve outcome-forcing remedies such as quotas. One distinction that will be important for this book is the distinction between "procedural affirmative action" and "preferential affirmative action."[1]

Procedural affirmative action tries to ensure that all candidates, including women and people of color, receive fair consideration for the job. It is normally understood to include more than national searches and open advertising, but stops short of preference. Preferential affirmative action, by contrast, involves overriding the considered professional judgment of the search committee members or putting sufficient pressure on them to distort their judgment. Their judgment can be distorted, of course, by many other things, such as personality conflicts among committee members, and they may fail to obtain the best candidate in any case for extraneous reasons such as the loss of necessary documents. However, the fact that present procedures do not unfailingly result in the appointment of the best candidate does not justify deliberately introducing additional distortion into their deliberations—at least unless some version of the corrective argument can be made out.[2]

People's positions on this issue are, I think, strongly affected by their own personal experiences. A white man who has held a full professorship for twenty years, and who got tenure at a time when tenure was almost automatic, will think very differently from a hungry, young, white male gypsy scholar who haunts the placement tables at professional meetings and feels in imminent danger of being squeezed out of the profession. Likewise, those whose friends mostly resemble the former will think differently from those whose friends fall more into the latter category. Affirmative action is, however, an issue of serious moral importance, not only for those most directly affected by it, but for the university as a whole. It is therefore imperative that we reflect about it carefully and examine the arguments on both sides.

Chapter 1 provides a historical account of the evolution of affirmative action policies, emphasizing not only the law and the policies adopted by regulatory agencies such as the EEOC, but also the broader economic, political, and cultural context. Chapters 2, 3, and 4 analyze the arguments commonly given in support of affirmative action in faculty appointments. The compensatory arguments justify it as a way of making up for past discrimination. The forward-looking arguments (role models, mentors, and diversity) point to goods thought to be obtainable in the future by means of such policies. The corrective arguments defend affirmative action as a way of correcting for bias against women and people of color embedded in the procedures and standards of professional competence employed by search committees.

I do not find that any of these arguments justifies adopting affirmative action across the board for women and people of color. Nonetheless this does not mean that it is never justified, and I begin Chapter 5 with a discussion of the circumstances under which it might be legitimate.

I then step back and look at the affirmative action debate more broadly (not just in universities) and suggest some ways we may be able to get past the current impasse by disentangling affirmative action from other issues that have wrongly become entangled with it and by freeing ourselves from a faulty social paradigm that makes affirmative action look like a solution when it is not.

Finally, I offer some suggestions for developing a more adequate social paradigm, and conclude with a discussion of what universities ought to be doing. If I am right about the role universities ought to be playing, then affirmative action in faculty appointments as it is usually implemented and justified is part of the problem rather than part of the solution. People cling fiercely to affirmative action despite all the objections raised against it and assume without question that to support it is to be on the side of the angels, in large part because it appears to be the only game in town for those who are genuinely concerned about social justice. This is why serious thought needs to be given to developing a new social paradigm that will enable us to redefine the problem and more effectively get at the roots of the problems that affirmative action was designed to cure.

A Note on Terminology

In a project such as this, one's choice of terminology itself carries a message. I have attempted to refer to all those involved in terms that emphasize their common humanity. Thus I say "black people" rather than "blacks." Although I am unhappy with the term "people of color" (Pakistanis, for example, have far darker skin than most Asians or Hispanics), I have used it when a noun was needed to refer to Hispanics, Asians and Pacific Islanders, Native Americans and Alaskan Natives, and black people. For the related adjective I have followed the usual practice and used "minority." I also refer to "white men" rather than "white males." Women are standardly referred to as "women" rather than "females," and our usage should be symmetrical for the two sexes. "White male" has a degradingly zoological tone to it.[3]

I have also employed the common gender "he" sometimes when the text contains so many pronouns that constantly repeating "he or she" would make it too choppy.

Notes

1. Steven Cahn suggested these terms to me in conversation. Robert Simon also uses the terms in his article "Affirmative Action and the University: Faculty Appointment and Preferential Treatment," in Steven M. Cahn, ed., *Affirmative Action and the University: A Philosophical Inquiry* (Philadelphia: Temple University Press, 1993). My use of "procedural," however, differs from Simon's, and although my understanding of the terms is closer to Cahn's, it is developed in slightly different ways.
2. This argument is evaluated in Chapter 4.
3. This point was first called to my attention by Michael Lind in "Symposium: Affirmative Action," *Dissent* (Fall 1995), 470.

1

Historical Introduction

Affirmative action as it is now practiced has its roots in the civil rights movement of the 1960s, but enormous changes have occurred in the way such policies are conceived, justified, and implemented. A thorough analysis of these changes would require several volumes, since it would be necessary to struggle through a tangle of legislation, executive orders, and decisions made by a variety of courts and regulatory agencies that develop guidelines for enforcing such policies.[1] Besides the fact that such an extensive analysis cannot be undertaken here, it is not at all clear that a coherent narrative can be extracted from the mass of historical material, because the various players have often worked at cross-purposes (or at the very least have failed to coordinate their efforts), and political pressures have militated against any clear definition of the goals sought by affirmative action policies.

Politicians use vague language in order to enable them to please constituencies with conflicting interests, and are usually more concerned with image than with reality. Likewise, bureaucracies are known for their tendency to expand their power as much as possible, and promulgating murky and confusing rules (whose requirements are sufficiently ill-defined that they can be shifted from case to case) is an effective way to do so, since people cannot be sure whether they have adequately conformed to them, and are therefore constantly in fear of being penalized for violating them. Philosophers are, by the nature of their profession, required to seek clarification of such core concepts as equality, justice, discrimination, fairness, and merit, to reflect about what goals we should aim at, and to evaluate policies both in terms of their likely consequences and in terms of the principles involved. Their goals are therefore in serious tension (if not outright war) with the requirements of the political realm.

Philosophers tend to be more at home with the law since judges do things more like what philosophers do; they interpret and apply authoritative texts to particular disputes, and try to provide principled defenses for their decisions. However, a great many of the crucial decisions about how "affirmative action" was to be understood were first set forth in presidential executive orders (which have the force of law) as interpreted and amplified by various regulatory agencies (whose powers have been unclear and shifting and who have often been in serious tension with each other and with the congressional committees responsible for overseeing their work). People, therefore, have increasingly looked to the courts for guidance, but since what judges are given to work with is so often vague and reflective of deep conflicts within society, affirmative action has had a very troubled history in the courts and many of the legal issues it raises have not yet been resolved in a decisive way.

The goal of this chapter is to provide a brief history of affirmative action and to situate such policies in a broader historical, economic, and cultural context. This is necessary for understanding the point of affirmative action. And in order to evaluate the forward-looking arguments for affirmative action, we must try to predict what the consequences of such policies are likely to be now in the late 1990s, and this cannot be done without putting them in context. Policies that may have been appropriate twenty or thirty years ago are not necessarily appropriate now, or if they are justifiable now it may be for reasons very different from those originally advanced for them. Since the current state of the law is discussed in the supplementary essay by George Rutherglen, and since the history of affirmative action in the courts has been so complex and conflicted (and moreover has already been extensively discussed in the literature), most of my discussion (apart from my initial discussion of the Civil Rights Act of 1964) will focus on the changes in the economic, political, and cultural climate that frame the debate about affirmative action in universities.

I will also briefly discuss trends in the number of doctorates earned by women and people of color and their distribution among the professoriate. The philosophical arguments do not essentially turn on statistics, but some background information about the changing demographics of the academy will be helpful.

Our discussion begins with the period between 1964 and 1972, when affirmative action policies were first developed. We next consider developments between 1972 and 1980, when affirmative action began to have a significant impact on universities. Then we look at the Reagan-Bush years (1980–92), and finally at developments during the Clinton administration.

I. From Civil Rights to Affirmative Action: 1964–1972

Background

Economic Trends

The period from the passage of the Civil Rights Act in 1964 until 1972 saw the continuation of the economic boom that Americans had been experiencing since the end of World War II. The postwar boom, in turn, was itself a continuation of an unprecedented period of rapid economic progress beginning in the early 1800s, interrupted only by the Civil War and (to a lesser extent) the Great Depression. During the period 1947–73, large numbers of Americans were able to rise from poverty into the middle class. In 1947, 95 percent of Americans made less than $10,000 per year (in 1984 $), and one-third earned less than $2,500. By 1973, only 39 percent made less than $10,000 per year (1984 $), while those earning under $2,500 declined dramatically to only 4 percent.[2] One important reason for the increase in the size of the middle class was the growth in jobs in the core manufacturing industries of the economy; many workers were able to move to the suburbs and send their children through college on their union-protected wages. Gross domestic product grew at nearly 4 percent per year from 1948 to 1973,[3] and family incomes doubled between 1947 and 1973 alone.[4] During this period, gains were made by black people as well as white people, with a significant increase in the black middle class, many of whom were employed in core manufacturing industries. By 1973 the gap in pay between college-educated black and white Americans had narrowed to 3.7 percent, and for high school graduates the gap was 10.3 percent.[5]

Factional conflict increases when scarce economic resources pit groups against each other, but prosperity tends to smooth things over. Americans in the 1960s had come to regard their steadily rising standard of living as normal, and they were therefore for the most part willing to support temporary programs designed to provide a leg up for the poor, especially for the black poor who had been handicapped by discrimination, so long as these did not involve quotas.

Demographics on Earned Doctorates and Faculty Composition

During this period the proportion of doctorates being awarded to women began to recover from its lowest point of the century. In 1950–54 it had been 9 percent (down from its previous high of 15.2 percent in the 1920s); in 1955–59 it was 10.5 percent, in 1964–69 it was 10.8 percent, in 1965–69 it was 12.1 percent, and for 1970–72 it rose again to 14.9 percent.[6] These statistics, of course, cover up large variations among fields of concentration. Then, as now, women tended to gravitate toward fields like education and social work, and to avoid the hard sciences and engineering.

The total percentage of female faculty rose only slightly between 1968–69 and 1972–73, from 19 percent to 20 percent, but this covered an increase in their proportion at the more prestigious university level (14.8 percent to 16.5 percent) coupled with a decline at two-year colleges (25.6 percent to 21.9 percent) and four-year colleges (22.7 percent to 21.9 percent).[7] The fact that their proportion on faculties was larger than their proportion among Ph.D. recipients is presumably accounted for by more women obtaining teaching jobs without Ph.D.s, by their obtaining doctorates in fields where teaching is the main career option, and by their choosing teaching over nonacademic employment in fields where Ph.D. recipients can do either one. This pattern of overrepresentation relative to their proportion among doctorate recipients has been present throughout the century. In 1900, for example, women were awarded 6 percent of the doctorates and held 19.8 percent of the faculty positions, and it was only in 1980 that the proportion of Ph.D.s awarded to women caught up with their proportion among faculty (both were around 29 percent in 1980).[8]

The situation was considerably different for black people. The total number of black Ph.D. holders was far smaller than the number of women with doctorates. For example, between 1964 and 1968, black Americans received only 0.8 percent of the doctorates in arts and sciences. Whereas women held 13 percent of all Ph.D.s, black people held about 1 percent of them. A 1969 survey found that about 85 percent of the black faculty responding (of whom 80 percent were male) had received their undergraduate training at black colleges, and 80 percent of them were currently teaching at such colleges. Twenty-nine percent of them held Ph.D.s in education, 26 percent in the social sciences, 25 percent in biological and physical sciences, 12 percent in the humanities, and the remaining 8 percent in agriculture, business, engineering, home economics, and religion.[9] Starting from a lower base, the rate of increase in black faculty exceeded the increase for women. Between the academic years 1968–69 and 1972–73, it nearly doubled in universities (from 0.5 percent to 0.9 percent), tripled in two-year colleges (0.7 percent to 2.1 percent), and increased only slightly in four-year colleges (5.0 percent to 5.4 percent), Surveys indicated that black faculty at predominantly white, non-Southern schools received more job offers and were better paid than comparable white faculty.[10] This was at least in part a result of pressures on universities to increase their proportion of black faculty. Since black Ph.D.s were in short supply, schools had to offer them more money in order to attract black faculty away from other institutions.[11]

Changes in Political Culture: The Rise and Fall of the New Left

Many present defenders of preferential affirmative action think of themselves as heirs to the radical politics of the 1960s, and their opponents have readily concurred in this assessment. But the New Left and contemporary cultural radicals have very little in common, and at least if we confine ourselves to the radicalism of the early 1960s, they rest on completely different philosophical assumptions.

The Port Huron Statement, the manifesto of the early New Left, issued by Students for a Democratic Society (SDS) in 1962, drew on the theory of alienation developed in Karl Marx's *Economic and Philosophical Manuscripts of 1844*. In many ways its framers had an essentially Enlightenment vision of human beings, supplemented at important points by the influence of Judaism[12] and Christianity. For example, Tom Hayden, principal author of the Port Huron Statement took passages verbatim from Pope John XXIII's social encyclical *Pacem in Terris*.[13] "We regard men as infinitely precious and possessed of unfulfilled capacities for reason, freedom, and love . . . major social institutions . . . should be generally organized with the well-being and dignity of man as the essential measure of success."[14]

The framers were concerned that human beings were being depersonalized, manipulated into incompetence, and reduced to being mere cogs in the machinery of the vast social and economic institutions they had created.

Some would have us believe that Americans feel contentment amidst prosperity—but might it not better be called a glaze above deeply felt anxieties about their role in the new world? And if these anxieties produce a developed indifference to human affairs, do they not as well produce a yearning to believe there *is* an alternative to the present, that something *can* be done to change circumstances in the schools, the workplaces, the bureaucracies, the government? It is to this latter yearning, at once the spark and the engine of change, that we direct our present appeal.[15]

They appealed to people in the name of their common humanity, believed in human equality, and regarded ordinary people as capable of making intelligent decisions affecting the quality and direction of their own lives (through what they called "participatory democracy").

But how was society to be transformed? "Participatory democracy" threatened to turn life into an "endless meeting."[16] Marxism as a broad theory of social transformation had considerable appeal, but an essential ingredient was missing—namely a proletariat that could be mobilized to serve as the engine of social change. Although some of the more serious members of the New Left took jobs in factories and tried to raise the political consciousness of their co-workers, in fact the movement never caught on widely outside of universities and a few other small enclaves. The main activities of the New Left during the sixties were opposition to the Vietnam War and working for the civil rights of black Americans. Many were involved in the Mississippi Freedom Summer of 1964 and various drives to register black voters in the South, often at considerable danger to themselves. For example, two white civil rights workers, Andrew Goodman and Michael Schwerner, were killed in 1964. Like SDS, the movement in the early sixties for black civil rights was deeply influenced by Christianity. Black churches provided the organizational foundation and human resources for the civil rights movement,[17] and the leadership of the Reverend Martin Luther King Jr. was also important in this regard.

By the late 1960s, however, the New Left began to fall apart badly. The assassinations of Martin Luther King Jr. and Robert Kennedy destroyed the hopes of many leftists for access to mainstream political institutions. Angry black militants defected to form their own separate organizations, often with considerable bitterness against their former allies. A kind of pervasive demoralization verging on nihilism set in, drug use increased, and the movement itself began to splinter into sub-groups representing distinct interests—with feminists, Chicanos, American Indians, gays and lesbians following the lead of blacks in forming their own separate organizations. Such ideas as the human condition or the common good were now suspect, and as Todd Gitlin puts it: "The very language of commonality came to be perceived by the new movements as a colonialist smothering—an ideology to rationalize white male domination."[18]

By the end of the 1960s, then, the universalistic New Left of the early sixties was dead, and in its place were a variety of special interest groups, each pursuing its own goals. Thus when government pressures to attain proportional representation of women and minorities began to have a major impact on universities in the early seventies, the ground had been prepared for those who thought of themselves as people of the left to support such policies.

Laying the Foundation for Affirmative Action

Legislation

The major pieces of legislation pertaining to employment discrimination during this period were Title VII of the 1964 Civil Rights Act, and the amendments to it incorporated in the Equal Employment Opportunity Act of 1972. Universities were originally granted an exemption from Title VII, but this was eliminated in 1972. Title VI was also of importance for universities since it stipulated conditions that must be met by those receiving federal monies, and as of 1973, approximately 900 out of 2,500 institutions of higher learning did receive such monies and therefore came under federal contract compliance regulations.[19]

Title VI stipulated that "[n]o person in the United States shall, on the ground of race, color or national origin, be excluded from participation in, be denied the benefits of, or be subjected to discrimination under any program or activity receiving Federal financial assistance" (42 U.S.C. sec. 2000d).[20]

Title VII applied to all private employers (not only those with government contracts) with twenty-five or more employees, and stated that

It shall be an unlawful employment practice for an employer—(1) to fail or refuse to hire or to discharge any individual with respect to his compensation, terms, conditions, or privileges of employment, because of such individual's race, color, religion, sex, or national origin; or (2) to limit, segregate, or classify his employees in any way which would deprive or tend to deprive any individual of employment opportunities or otherwise adversely affect his status as an employee because of such individual's race, color, religion, sex, or national origin. (Sec. 703a)

Exactly what practices were forbidden was not entirely clear, but it was explicitly stated that religious institutions (Catholic colleges, for example) were permitted to select their employees based on their religious affiliation, bona fide seniority systems were declared permissible, and employers were also allowed to use tests to select from among potential employees, so long as they were not employed with discriminatory intent.[21]

At the time Title VII was adopted, some people feared that it might be used to justify race-conscious preferential policies or quotas. Therefore, a provision was added:

Nothing contained in this title shall be interpreted to require any employer . . . to grant preferential treatment to any individual or to any group because of race, color, religion, sex, or national origin of such individual or group on account of an imbalance which may exist with respect to the total number or percentage of persons of any race, color, religion, sex, or national origin employed by any employer . . . in comparison with the total number or percentage of persons of such race, color, religion, sex, or national origin in any community, State, section, or other area, or in the available work force in any community, State, section, or other area. (Sec. 703j)

To reinforce this point, language was added at section 706g emphasizing that the courts had to find that the respondent "has intentionally engaged" in an unlawful employment practice.[22]

Also important for our purposes were subsequent amendments to Title VII, otherwise known as the Equal Employment Opportunity Act of 1972. It extended Title VII to private employers and unions with fifteen or more employees or members, to public employers in state and local government, and to educational institutions. It also greatly increased the enforcement powers of the Equal Employment Opportunity Commission.

Presidential Involvement with Affirmative Action

Both Presidents Lyndon Johnson and Richard Nixon were active in the civil rights area, and played important roles in shaping affirmative action policies. Johnson believed that merely eliminating discrimination against black people was not enough. In his famous speech at Howard University in 1965, he said:

> You do not wipe away the scars of centuries by saying: Now you are free to go where you want, do as you desire, choose the leaders you please. . . . You do not take a person who for years has been hobbled by chains and liberate him, bring him to the starting line and then say, "You are free to compete with all the others," and still justly believe that you have been completely fair.[23]

He therefore sought to go beyond mere nondiscrimination to "affirmative action," although what he meant by "affirmative action" was unclear.

Johnson's Executive Order No. 11246 (1965),[24] as amended in Order No. 11375 (which became effective in 1968) to add sex discrimination, decreed that

> (1) The contractor will not discriminate against any employee or applicant for employment because of race, color, religion, sex, or national origin, and (2) The contractor will take affirmative action to ensure that applicants are employed, and that employees are treated during employment, without regard to their race, color, religion, sex, or national origin.

The task of spelling out what the term "affirmative action" was to involve then fell to the Office of Federal Contract Compliance (OFCC) set up within the Labor Department to oversee the federal contract program.

Order No. 11246 on its face did not seem to envision anything more than procedural affirmative action to guarantee equal employment opportunity for all individuals by doing things like publicizing openings and actively recruiting minority candidates. Yet in the course of implementing the executive order, the OFCC came to require contractors to submit affirmative action plans, to identify areas in which minorities were "underutilized," and to commit themselves to hiring goals and timetables for correcting that underutilization. The impact of these OFCC policies was considerable, since a large proportion of American businesses do business with the government (currently approximately 25 percent).[25]

Policies aiming at proportional representation of minorities gathered momentum under Nixon, who supported the controversial revised Philadelphia Plan in 1969,[26] requiring the construction industry in Philadelphia and three other cities to set goals and timetables for correcting racial imbalances in their workforce (relative to the composition of the available workforce). OFCC Order No. 4 in 1970 extended the goals and timetables requirement of the Philadelphia Plan to nonconstruction contractors, including universities, and Revised Order No. 4 (1971) added women to the list of protected groups.

Regulatory Agencies

The period from 1964 to 1972 saw the creation of seven large federal regulatory agencies (by comparison with only one between 1900 and 1964).[27] The agency responsible for handling complaints of employment discrimination under Title VII was the Equal Employment Opportunity Commission (EEOC). Its initial budget and powers were quite limited, and in light of the ghetto riots of 1965–66 and the resulting conservative turn in the 1966 elections, Congress was in no hurry to augment either its budget or its powers. It was authorized to investigate individual and commissioner-initiated charges, to make findings of reasonable cause to believe discrimination had occurred, and to conciliate disputes between the complainant and the employer. It could also issue procedural interpretations of Title VII and file amicus curiae briefs in individual discrimination cases.[28]

The EEOC, more than any other group, was responsible for the shift away from addressing employment discrimination on a case by case basis and toward focusing instead on broad patterns indicating "underrepresentation" or "underutilization" of minorities by particular firms or industries. Employers were required to conduct racial surveys and institute policies directed toward correcting their underutilization of minorities. This new direction emerged very quickly after the inception of the EEOC, and gathered momentum throughout the period culminating with the Title VII amendments in 1972. This shift was, and was perceived by many people to be, in tension with the original intent of Title VII—namely that individuals should not be subject to discrimination on account of their race, color, sex, religion, or national origin—since at least some of the remedies pursued by the EEOC required what amounted to racial preferences.

The Courts

The courts during this period were generally, although not universally, supportive of the direction civil rights policy was taking as a result of executive orders governing the federal contracts program and the policies adopted by the EEOC. Two key issues requiring clarification by the courts were defining illegal discrimination and determining what remedies were permissible.

(1) What was to count as illegal discrimination under Title VII? Was it necessary to establish that the employer *intended* to discriminate against specific employees or potential employees on grounds of race, color, religion, national origin, or sex? Or was it sufficient to establish a prima facie case against an employer that he engaged in employment practices that in fact had a disparate impact on members of different groups, absent a showing that such practices were justified on business-related grounds?

Those favoring the latter reading of Title VII pointed out that because of prior discrimination, practices that are on their face neutral between racial groups might in fact operate disproportionately against one group. If black employees had less seniority in some industry or department than white employees, then the last hired, first fired principle would operate disproportionately against them, and rules governing the transfer of seniority between departments might also operate to keep them from moving out of the lowest paid departments where they had mainly been employed. Or if, as a result of inferior, segregated schools, black people scored lower than white people on certain tests, then the use of these tests for hiring or promotion purposes would operate disproportionately against them. The fact that both seniority systems and testing had often been used deliberately in the South in order to maintain racial segregation gave a certain plausibility to the argument that employers should bear the burden of proof to justify continuing use of employment practices that in fact have significantly different impacts on black and white employees or job candidates. Title VII, however, had specifically protected bona fide seniority systems and professionally developed ability tests ("provided that such test, its administration or action upon the results is not designed, intended or used to discriminate because of race, color, religion, sex or national origin").

And, if the disparate impact of his employment practices were taken to be sufficient to shift the burden of proof to the employer, how heavy a burden of proof should he be asked to bear? Would it be enough to show that the tests bear some real relation to skills required by the job, or must the employer also prove that employing the tests in question is a "business necessity" and that there is no other test he could use that would predict success on the job equally well without having a disparate impact on white and black job candidates? The latter requirement would arguably place an unreasonably heavy burden on employers (especially small businesses). For proving a negative is next to impossible, and employers cannot spend unlimited amounts of time and money on validating their tests and investigating other possible tests (especially since the EEOC made this more difficult by insisting that a test validated in one company could not be used in another, even if used to select for the same job).[29] Should the plaintiff then bear the burden of showing that there is some other test or selection procedure that would serve the employer's purpose equally well without having a disparate impact?

The Supreme Court, in the widely cited *Griggs v. Duke Power and Light* (1971), upheld the disparate impact interpretation, and required employers to prove that tests or other selection devices that had a disparate impact were justified by "business necessity." The traditional interpretation of Title VII as requiring discriminatory *intent* was dropped.[30] Duke Power and Light was a vulnerable target, since it was located in North Carolina, where overt racism was rampant, and had suddenly introduced high school diploma requirements and intelligence and ability tests (so demanding that half the high school graduates in the country would fail them)[31] when it was forced to eliminate its Jim Crow policies.[32]

The *Griggs* decision was widely interpreted as a broad approval of the disparate impact theory of discrimination and the assignment of a heavy burden of proof to the employer to justify any employment practices having a disparate impact on black and white workers. Although other cases set some limits to the application of disparate impact theory, *Griggs* continued to dominate fair employment policy well into the 1970s. As a result, increasingly many employers adopted informal hiring quotas in order to protect themselves against litigation or loss of federal contracts.

(2) What sorts of remedies were permissible under the law? Attempts were made to distinguish sharply between quotas (which were highly unpopular) and the goals and timetables required of federal contractors. Goals were said to be more flexible, and the contractor, it was argued, need only demonstrate good faith efforts to attain

them. However, this distinction was not as sharp as people pretended (the crucial fact is that success is defined in numerical terms), and no matter what label one employed, requiring contractors to correct for the underutilization of minorities certainly looked on the face of it as if it necessitated treating employees differently on the basis of their race. This, however, would be a violation of Title VII, and reverse discrimination suits under Title VII were soon filed by white employees who claimed that their rights had been trammeled. No decisive case on this issue was decided at the Supreme Court level during this period.

Underlying Causes of the Trend Toward Proportional Representation

The overall trend during this period, then, was from a focus on individual rights and fair procedures toward fairly aggressive policies aiming at proportional representation of minorities. This was accomplished by using a disparate impact theory of discrimination to shift an increasingly heavy burden of proof to the employer. The reasons for this shift were complex. It did not take place because merely publicizing positions and recruiting qualified applicants failed to increase significantly the number of minorities (or as one author put it: "the reason that policy evolved from outreach to preference was that outreach was not working").[33] The shift toward racial preferences occurred so quickly that the removal of formal barriers to black advancement and purely procedural affirmative action had hardly been given a chance to work.

Certainly political factors played a significant role. The ghetto riots, the assassinations of Malcolm X and Martin Luther King Jr., and the rise of the Black Power movement generated fears of increased racial violence unless something was done quickly to help black people, whose expectations had been raised faster than they were able to be satisfied. The Moynihan report (1965) sounded the alarm about the disorganization of black family structure, warned against the deteriorating status and authority of the black male, and recommended that "we must not rest until every able-bodied negro male is working."[34] The analogy between American black people and hobbled runners employed by Johnson in his 1965 speech at Howard University had real moral force, and the case for some sort of temporary programs to provide a leg up for poor black people deserved serious consideration.

The international situation increased the concern of American leaders to do something quickly to resolve our racial crisis. American leaders were acutely conscious of the fact that our racial tensions might undermine our international image and hence our leadership role in the Cold War—especially in light of the rising power of the newly liberated African former colonies and the important U.N. initiatives on human rights that coincided with the race riots.[35]

In a climate of mounting racial tensions no president could politically afford to be perceived as opposed to civil rights, and so Presidents Johnson and Nixon tended to go along with the demands of the civil rights lobby and to allow the new regulatory agencies a free hand. The Vietnam War drained away resources just at the time when a number of very ambitious social programs were launched. It also eroded the moral and political capital of the presidency, thus weakening the president's power to curb the rising power of the burgeoning federal bureaucracy.

The requirements of bureaucratic efficiency also seemed to favor a more wholesale approach to correcting discrimination, since the EEOC quickly acquired an unmanageable backlog of cases (30,000 in 1971).[36] Understandable though it may be that the regulatory agencies were impatient for results, the EEOC, in particular, behaved in high-handed and overzealous ways. For example, it pursued racial preferences in hiring its own staff to such a degree that the EEOC *itself* was found guilty of violating Title VII in a reverse discrimination suit brought by a group of displaced white male regional directors in 1978.[37]

Finally, there are difficulties with trying to enforce a law requiring a finding that an employer *intended* to discriminate on the basis of race, color, religion, sex, or national origin—difficulties that naturally drive the would-be enforcer in the direction of requiring results. In requiring discriminatory intent, the framers of Title VII were trying to steer a middle course between the libertarian solution of allowing the market to correct for employment discrimination[38] and actually requiring employers to attain some particular proportion of minority or female employees.

But people's intentions are not open to inspection,[39] and discriminatory intent is difficult to prove except in very blatant cases. Philosophers generally ackowledge that statements about someone's intentions are conceptually connected with that person's behavior. I cannot simply insist at 5:30 that it is my intention to walk to Joe's house for a 6:00 dinner engagement and that I intend to be on time while vigorously walking in the opposite direction for 15 minutes.

Thus the foreseeable consequences of an employer's behavior (in this case the disparate impact of his employment practices on black and white job applicants or employees) must be taken into account when trying to determine whether he acted with discriminatory intent, and his denial that he did so need not always be taken at face value. But to drop all talk of intent and simply press for numerical hiring goals aiming at proportional representation, or to place such a heavy burden of

proof on employers that the only practicable way they can establish
that they are not engaging in illegal discrimination is by attaining specific numerical results, is to abandon the search for a middle ground
and embrace one of the extremes.

Adding Women: Linking Race and Sex

Since the opening salvos in the affirmative action battles in the universities (in the early seventies) were fired largely by women and
women's advocacy groups, a closer look at their inclusion in Title VII
is in order. The issues of racial and sexual discrimination in employment have become so closely linked in many people's minds that it is
difficult to disentangle them. Their connection, however, is by no
means as natural and obvious as it might seem, and their conjunction
in Title VII was the result of something of a fluke.

Sex discrimination was added to Title VII (but not to any of the other
sections) at the last minute by Howard Smith, a conservative Southern
opponent of civil rights legislation. His motives appear to have been
mixed. In part he hoped to secure the defeat of the bill itself by adding
sex discrimination, or at the very least to throw a monkey wrench into
its enforcement by bringing in a whole new protected class. (All but
one of the men who spoke in favor of Smith's amendment voted
against the bill itself.)[40] He is reported to have said privately that the
amendment was a joke (certainly some of the floor debate on the
amendment had a rather jocular tone), but he also claimed at other
times to have been sincere. He was a supporter of an Equal Rights
Amendment (ERA) and personal friend of Alice Paul, head of the
National Women's Party (NWP), which was lobbying hard for the
inclusion of sex in Title VII, having met with obstacles in its pursuit of
the ERA.[41] He also believed, as a chivalrous Southern gentleman, that
it was only fair that white women be accorded the same legal protections black men were.[42]

Since sex discrimination was added at the last minute, very little
serious debate took place about the reasons for its inclusion in a bill
aimed at black civil rights, or for that matter about whether this sort of
legislation was truly in the interests of women. Women themselves
were sharply divided on this issue, and many influential women
opposed Smith's amendment. Some women (e.g., Esther Peterson)
feared it would impede passage of the civil rights bill. Many women
(especially Democratic women influential in the labor unions) were
concerned that it would endanger women's protective legislation,
which they believed provided an important protection to working class
women. They therefore preferred the "specific bills for specific ills"

approach to women's problems (e.g., the Equal Pay Act of 1963) instead of sweeping remedies like the ERA or Title VII. Some women believed that sexual discrimination, although real, involved sufficiently different problems from racial discrimination that it ought to be addressed separately.[43] Finally, some women were concerned that the inclusion of women would divert attention and resources from the more pressing needs of black people.[44] This concern was shared by many high-ranking people in the NAACP, although they hesitated to say this too publicly.

The division among women was roughly along class lines. The NWP was a small group of affluent, business-oriented, politically conservative women (sometimes called "the tennis-shoe ladies"), while opposition to Smith's amendment and the ERA came from politically liberal, Democratic, union-oriented women. The lack of hearings and committee reports on Smith's amendment had prevented the AFL-CIO and the dominant women's protectionist groups from testifying in favor of exempting women's protective laws.[45] Thus the NWP women won the day, and after some initial confusion about what impact it would have on women's protective legislation, Title VII ultimately was held to invalidate such laws. Section 708, invalidating any state laws conflicting with Title VII, had been directed against Jim Crow laws in the South, but when considered along with Section 703, it logically entailed the elimination of laws forbidding night work or limiting working hours for women (but not men), or imposing limits on such things as the amount of weight a woman (but not a man) could be required to lift.[46]

Once the bill was passed with Smith's amendment included, those women who had supported its inclusion were not sufficiently united, organized, or prepared to press for its enforcement. No one at first took their inclusion very seriously; both Johnson's Order No. 11246 and the Labor Department's Order No. 4 omitted women entirely, and had to be amended to include them. The EEOC was at first very lukewarm about enforcing the provisions of Title VII for women, in part because it was already overburdened with problems of racial discrimination, and in part because women's groups were exerting pressure on the EEOC in contradictory directions. The Women's Bureau tried to dissuade the EEOC from using Title VII to invalidate women's protective legislation, and since it had more than enough to do already, it did not at first move against such laws.

Eventually, however, the EEOC's waffling on the issue of sex-segregated help wanted ads angered enough women that they buried their differences and united against the EEOC to demand that sex discrimination be taken more seriously. The National Organization for Women (NOW) was formed in 1966 and took a leading role in pressing for an end to employment discrimination against women.[47] By the end of the 1960s the dominant protectionist wing of the women's movement rooted in the Democratic Party's traditional blue- and pink-collar constituency had been superseded by a bipartisan coalition of business and professional elite women, and women's protective legislation was quickly swept away.[48]

The unplanned effect of adding women to Title VII was that as affirmative action policies became increasingly oriented toward promoting proportional representation for minorities (mainly at this time black people, although Hispanics were becoming increasingly vocal in their demands), it seemed that if women were included on the same footing with other groups, they too should be entitled to proportional representation. But adding women to a list of groups who must, as individuals, be protected against illegal discrimination and accorded fair access to jobs was one thing, and pursuing proportional representation for women in all occupations and at all levels was quite another. Women, after all, are over half the population, and achieving sex-based proportional representation would involve massive changes in family structure and sex roles that were (and still are) controversial among the electorate.[49]

Finally, adding women cushions the class impact of affirmative action. The job lost by the middle-class man may go to his wife (or another middle-class woman) with no net gain for the most economically disadvantaged.

II. The Entrenchment of Bureaucracies: 1973–1980

Background

Economic Trends

Beginning in 1973, the economy began to falter in ways that gradually became more apparent to the average worker. Growth in worker productivity dropped sharply to 0.9 percent per year. Productivity growth had averaged 2 percent since the Civil War, and immediately after World War II had climbed to 2.7 percent per year. The oil crisis of 1973 triggered a serious recession, and led to an inflationary spiral accompanied by two other serious recessions in the next seven years. Real wages (adjusted for inflation) began to stagnate, and for many workers (especially nonmanagerial ones who make up 80 percent of the workforce) they began to decline. This period also saw the rise of what has been called the postmodern economy. Whereas previously most people were engaged in actual production of goods and services, fewer and fewer jobs had any discernible connection with producing tangible goods and services, and a new international class of symbolic analysts rose to positions of power and wealth. Companies sprang up and disappeared with alarming frequency, and capital began to move across national frontiers more quickly. One result of these changes was a growing sense that we really didn't understand how our economy worked, and were caught in a complicated web of global social and economic forces beyond our control.

The gap in pay between black and white workers began to rise again, especially in the Midwest. Since the heavy manufacturing industries were no longer thriving, and large numbers of black people had been working in them, black workers were particularly hard hit, and a strong trend toward polarization among black people got under way, with the black middle class continuing to make gains while the plight of the black urban poor deteriorated rapidly.[50]

The economic downturn hit universities hard, enrollments were declining, competition for teaching jobs intensified, and many of those coming out of graduate school during this period either had to take badly paying temporary jobs (if lucky enough to find them) or else retrain in some other profession. As a result of diminished employment opportunities in teaching, affirmative action pressures naturally generated more bitterness than they would have in a better job market.

Demographics on Earned Doctorates and Faculty Composition

During this period the number of female Ph.D. recipients grew rapidly, while the number of men hit its peak in 1972 and then began to decline. The number of women receiving Ph.D.s rose by 79 percent between 1972 and 1980, going from 16 percent of the total to 30.3 percent, while the number of men obtaining the Ph.D. declined by 22 percent.[51] Women's greatest numerical gains were in life sciences, social sciences, and education (the areas in which they were most heavily concentrated already). For all racial and ethnic groups the number of women grew more rapidly than the number of men. As a proportion of total faculty women increased from 22.3 percent in 1972–73 to 26.7 percent in 1980–81, with their proportion among new appointments rising rapidly during the 1970s to a level of 24.5 percent in the late seventies.[52]

Black Americans obtained 3.7 percent of the doctorates awarded to U.S. citizens in 1975, and 4.1 percent in 1979 (only a 5.6 percent increase in total number).[53] In 1976–77 Hispanics obtained 1.6 percent of the Ph.D.s granted, Asians or Pacific Islanders 2 percent, and Native Americans/Alaskan Natives 0.3 percent, while nonresident aliens obtained 11.3 percent.[54] Asians have consistently tended toward the sciences and engineering, while other people of color are concentrated in education and the social sciences. Not surprisingly in light of the small number of Ph.D.s earned by members of these groups, their representation on faculties was not large, and black faculty remained concentrated at predominantly black colleges, although this pattern was beginning to change.

Changes in Political Culture

The 1970s saw an acceleration of the trends that got under way in the late 1960s. The crushing defeat of George McGovern in 1972 led many left-of-center intellectuals to despair of having any significant impact on the broader society, and to retreat into elite enclaves, chief among which were the universities. The various subgroups who had split off from the early New Left because they thought its leadership was deaf to their concerns and interests quickly caught on and took root there. Black Studies (then called Afro-American Studies) and Women's Studies programs spread rapidly, and Chicanos, gays, lesbians, and physically handicapped people all began increasingly to insist (sometimes quite stridently) that their voices be heard as well. In order to have intellectual credibility in the academy, however, they had to develop beyond the merely reactive phase—beyond just saying "What you mean *we*, white man?"[55]

The theoretical underpinning for the identity politics that became increasingly entrenched during the 1970s and 1980s was taken largely from the French philosopher Michel Foucault, whose lectures in New York and San Francisco during the 1970s and early 1980s attracted enormous numbers of people. He wrote in a brilliant, erudite, and highly arcane style that carried an aura of academic respectability. Besides that, his theory offered a heady mixture of sex, power, and politics that seemed to dovetail nicely with the direction in which the heirs of the New Left were already moving.

Sexual politics was already central to the concerns of the gay and lesbian movements as well as to the feminists who had coined the slogan that "the personal is the political" in the 1960s.[56] This slogan had originally been intended to convey their conviction that anyone who was seriously interested in improving the political and economic situation of women could not ignore the impact of practices within the "private" or familial sphere, such as who does the housework and childcare, or marital rape (to take a more dramatic example). Through the influence of Foucault, however, this slogan took on a new and wider meaning.

For Foucault, politics was everywhere. Like Friedrich Nietzsche, he held that the will-to-power pervades all human relationships and institutions; everything, from one's clothing, language, and sexual behavior to culture or knowledge itself, was transformed into a kind of battleground to be understood in terms of power and dominance. Culture, on this view, was constituted by discourses that determine who or what is to be central or important and who or what is, by contrast, marginal and unimportant. Feminist, Afro-American, gay, and lesbian groups who thought that their concerns had been marginalized by their former allies and friends in the New Left now saw a possibility that they might join together and expose the ways in which the dominant culture had been constructed to rationalize the dominance of white, heterosexual men. This sort of undertaking could be done within the sheltered environment of universities, but at the same time allowed professors to feel that they were still being faithful to their radical political commitments.

Foucault's influence on left-leaning intellectuals thus contributed to a growing tribalization in American universities. His rejection of the Enlightenment ideal of a common human nature and his claim that difference cannot be bridged seemed to justify each group's insistence on the distinctiveness of its own experience and perspective (or as the T shirt puts it: "It's a black thing. You wouldn't understand"). This way of thinking lent a certain plausibility to the demand for affirmative action. For if women, black people, gays, lesbians, Chicanos, etc., represented not merely interest groups in the traditional political sense, but were also viewed as each possessing its own distinctive *culture* (comprehensible only to insiders), and if it was important to combat the hegemony of white, male, heterosexual culture by asserting the claims of formerly marginalized cultures, then it would stand to reason that universities ought to be encouraged, or if necessary pressured, to appoint members of these groups.

In fact, the embrace of Foucault by academic leftists was a bad move from the point of view of any seriously left politics. If politics was everywhere, it was also nowhere, and actual constructive political engagement with the world declined as more and more time and energy went into intrauniversity politics. As Todd Gitlin put it: "The more their political life was confined to the library, the more their language bristled with aggression."[57]

And the problem was not just that other commitments left no time for political activity. Foucault's theory philosophically undercut the very possibility of collective social action; his denial of human communality went considerably further than his American admirers realized. His vision was ultimately an individualistic one; each individual's experience (and even each individual moment of experience) was radically incommensurable with every other. This, in turn, undermines the basis for the sort of solidarity within groups required by identity politics.

Foucault said, "I do not appeal to any 'we.' "[58] But invoking some sort of "we" is indispensable for politics. In fact his philosophy ultimately undermines the possibility of even a stable self. Finally, leftists under the influence of Foucault tended to write in a language unintelligible to the ordinary person, and that itself was a serious political handicap.

These sorts of fissiparous forces acted within universities at a time when they had grown increasingly dependent on federal grant money, were under pressure from declining enrollments and cuts in federal and state funding,[59] and had largely lost any sense of having a shared purpose or mission. The vast majority of private four-year colleges had originally been founded under the auspices of religious denominations, but their distinctively religious character had been increasingly attenuated.[60] Nor had any coherent secular alternative emerged. Thus universities were in danger of becoming institutions whose only purpose was to serve the needs of those in a position to exert pressure on them—predominantly those who paid the bills, but also those who threatened internal disruption (e.g., sit-ins or strikes) if their demands were not met.[61]

The Regulatory Agencies and the Universities

During this same period, universities were subject to increasing affirmative action pressures from the rapidly growing federal regulatory agencies. Between 1966 and 1979, the budget of the EEOC had risen from $3.25 million to $111.4 million, while that of the OFCC had climbed from $570,000 to $43.2 million, and together they covered about half of American workers.[62] Universities with large research contracts had already been covered by Executive Order No. 11246 (amended in 1968 to include women), and the Department of Labor had delegated the authority to enforce this for universities to the Office for Civil Rights within the Department of Health, Education, and Welfare (HEW), who required them to submit data regarding their employment of women and minorities, and to devise affirmative action plans to correct for any underutilization of these groups.

In October 1972, HEW issued a set of affirmative action guidelines for universities, along much the same lines as those already employed in dealing with other federal contractors. Also in 1972 the exclusion of universities from Title VII was revoked, so that they now also came under the jurisdiction of the EEOC whether or not they had federal contracts. The EEOC (or the attorney general in the case of public institutions) could bring civil actions in the federal courts against an institution alleging patterns of discrimination as well as charging unlawful employment practices bearing on individual complaints. The result of these changes was that universities were caught in a complicated web of overlapping jurisdictions of several federal agencies, in addition to that of the Fair Employment Practices Commissions that existed in most states. The agencies had different data requirements and sometimes operated with differing criteria for determining the existence and extent of discrimination.[63] Between December 1969 and January 1974, twenty large universities had temporary blocks imposed on new contracts or renewals for failure to submit data or acceptable affirmative action plans.[64]

The majority of the suits brought against universities in the early seventies were on the grounds of sex discrimination, and by mid-1973 pattern complaints of sex discrimination had been brought against 500 of the 2,500 institutions of higher education (including most of the major ones). Many of these had been brought by women's advocacy groups such as NOW and Women's Equity Action League (WEAL). Individual complaints had also been brought by 350 women.[65] No doubt this is because there was a larger supply of qualified women (many of whom already had faculty positions and thus were in a better position to sue) than of people of color, and because they were backed by women's organizations who were highly motivated to press their demands in the university setting.

Affirmative action pressures from regulatory agencies provoked a storm of protest. Many faculty were sympathetic to the goals of such policies,[66] but the intrusion of government agencies into the daily workings of universities was troubling to many. For these agencies had hitherto only dealt with businesses, and universities were different in important ways from businesses.[67] Heated debate took place among academics over the issue, and the 1970s saw the publication of an impressive amount of philosophical literature on both sides of the controversy.[68]

One of the more troubling things about the way affirmative action policies were put into effect was the way in which they put universities under contradictory pressures. For example, at the same time that the University of Washington was fighting the *DeFunis* case (a reverse discrimination suit dismissed as moot in 1974) in the courts in order to be able to continue considering race in admissions, it was also under pressure from federal officials threatening to cut off its funds unless it adopted more aggressive policies for minority recruitment and advancement.[69]

Affirmative Action and the Courts: *Bakke* and *Weber*[70]

The decision in *Regents of the University of California v. Bakke* (1978), which outlawed rigid quotas but allowed universities to take race into consideration as one consideration among others in the admission of students, was widely viewed as a compromise. There is at the present writing considerable speculation about whether the Supreme Court will continue to espouse the position set forth in *Bakke* in the wake of its increasingly critical stance toward preferential affirmative action policies, and it declined in *Hopwood* (1996) to recommit itself to those aspects of *Bakke* that supported affirmative action.[71]

The other major Supreme Court decision during this period for our purposes was *Kaiser Aluminum and Chemical Corporation v. Weber* (1979), in which the court permitted *voluntary* affirmative action plans that took race into account, but only under certain conditions— namely, that they must be "designed to break down old patterns of racial segregation and hierarchy," and do not "unnecessarily trammel the interests of the white employees."[72] This went part way, at least, toward protecting employers from being caught in the cross fire in the way the University of Washington had been, but the underlying tension remained between increasing the representation of women and minority members and avoiding reverse discrimination against white men.

III. The Reagan–Bush Years: 1980–1992

Economic Context

Under President Ronald Reagan, attempts were made to stimulate economic growth. Although these met with some success, productivity growth continued to lag. The economy was only slightly ahead of its 1979 level by 1989, and even the slow level of growth of GDP attained under Reagan petered out under President George Bush. The federal deficit increased dramatically, and most of the economic gains went to the richest sector of the population. The distribution of wealth between rich and poor became more polarized, giving America, by some measures, the largest gap dividing the top fifth and the bottom fifth of any major industrialized country.[73] The number of millionaires doubled between the late seventies and the late eighties, and the number of billionaires rose from less than five in 1980 to more than fifty in 1988.[74] The top 1 percent of the population (in terms of family income) increased their income 74.2 percent over the decade, while the income of the lowest 10 percent went down 10.5 percent.[75] International competition became tougher as other countries began to catch up in terms of technology and productivity. The flight of capital began to take a large toll in terms of basic manufacturing jobs, with many firms moving abroad to take advantage of lower wages.

Polarization between rich and poor was more marked among women and minorities.[76] Thus, if affirmative action was having an economic impact, it was helping those with the highest level of skills and education while doing very little for the poorest members of the target groups.

Changes in Political Culture: The PC Wars

During the late eighties and early nineties, universities suddenly began to attract the notice of the popular press, who sounded the alarm about what came to be called "political correctness." Most readers are, no doubt, familiar with the controversy over PC,[77] but the philosophical issues underlying the debate are perhaps less well known. At the heart of the identity politics that had been gathering momentum in many universities during the Reagan years (especially in the humanities and social sciences) was a commitment to recognizing and respecting diversity. The groups characterized as diverse, however, did not just insist that they had legitimate concerns overlooked by the dominant culture. They became increasingly hard-edged, and each group came to regard its culture as something only insiders could understand. This strategy locked them into a kind of cultural relativism in which different cultures were incommensurable and all were regarded as equally valuable. Another word for this view is "strong multiculturalism"—by contrast with "weak multiculturalism," which claims only that other cultures have valuable things to teach us. (When I use the term "multiculturalism" from here on, I mean "strong multiculturalism.")[78]

But what could hold together the "Rainbow Coalition" of marginalized groups? A commitment to relativism and diversity certainly, but this left open the possibility that another group might come along and assert that its way of thinking was true or right. The Rainbow Coalition groups could not say that those claiming truth were wrong, since that would imply that it is possible to talk about a truth or falsity transcending the cultures of the different groups. Nonrelativists were therefore the one group that could not be tolerated, and this fact provided multiculturalists with a common enemy to unite against. Since they could not argue rationally with their opponents (since different cultures are incommensurable and there is no truth) all they could do was to fight them in other ways—emotional pressure, guilting, shunning, silencing, speech codes, and trying to keep opponents out of those parts of the university where multiculturalists had sufficient power to do so. The best-known defender of the resulting politics of "political correctness" is Stanley Fish, as is clear from the title of his book *There's No Such Thing as Free Speech, and It's a Good Thing Too*.

To the extent that multiculturalists had control of the curriculum, they allotted more space to the history, literature, and more generally the perspectives of previously marginalized groups, and less space to the work of dead white males. They also sought to introduce pedagogical methods founded upon relativistic assumptions, and strongly supported preferential affirmative action in order to increase the representation of marginalized groups in the universities.

Many people were strongly critical of "political correctness," including New Rightists, communitarians, maverick welfare liberals, paleoconservatives, and libertarians. Within the universities, however, the strongest opposition came from those commonly labeled "neoconservatives."[79] Neoconservatives were united in opposing preferential affirmative action, but there were several different (but overlapping) strands of thought among them, and most individual neoconservatives exemplified more than one of these strands.

Those who had been strongly anticommunist, and hostile to the radicalism of the sixties (seldom distinguishing between the early sixties and the late sixties), saw in the academic left of the late 1980s and early 1990s a recrudescence of sixties radicalism (the radicals, they reasoned, had ensconced themselves in universities and were subverting them from within). With the collapse of the Soviet Union in 1989, they now had more time and energy to direct against internal enemies, and the hostility of the academic left toward the whole liberal Western tradition galvanized them into action. Many of them advocated introducing a core curriculum centered around the Western tradition and designed to give students an appreciation of what was unique and valuable about the American ideal. An example of this sort of neoconservative would be Midge Decter.

Another strand was composed of people who had long regarded themselves as liberals, had strongly supported black civil rights in the sixties, and believed in free speech, individual rights, fairness, and equal opportunity. They often supported procedural affirmative action but regarded preferential affirmative action as a betrayal of the ideals of the civil rights movement, since it perpetuated racial and other unfair discrimination in a new form (in other words, reverse discrimination). Some of them had fought hard against anti-Jewish quotas, and were horrified to find racial preferences suddenly introduced by people they thought of as their allies. An example of this type of neoconservative would be Nathan Glazer.

A third theme that was present in neoconservative thought was their commitment to the merit principle. They believed that social benefits should be distributed according to merit, which in turn was a function of both ability and effort. Many of them had managed to succeed by merit in the face of significant discrimination, usually based on ethnicity or national origin. Within the academy they were committed to academic excellence, both in scholarship and in teaching, and were strongly opposed for this reason to preferential affirmative action, since it involved allowing considerations of race, gender, or ethnicity to override the considered judgments of search committees about the relative merits of candidates. An example of this line of thinking would be the late Barry Gross.

Finally, many neoconservatives were primarily concerned to defend free market capitalism. They often did this because they saw it as part of the American way of doing things as they understood it, and thus their defense of it blended with their more general defense of American values against radical critics. Michael Novak is one example of this school of neoconservative thought.

Other conservatives had been (and still are) prepared to defend capitalism as just, rational, conducive to virtue, and especially compatible with freedom and democracy. But neoconservatives characteristically were reluctant to ask ultimate questions about social justice, arguing at most that the alternatives to the American way of doing things were totalitarianism and chaos.[80] To the extent that they celebrated capitalism as simply the way we do things in America rather than defending its merits in comparison with those of alternative types of economic systems, they, in effect, embraced a conservative form of relativism, and thus had a certain philosophical affinity with their politically correct adversaries.

Neoconservatives of this type opposed preferential affirmative action because it sanctioned government encroachment on the freedom of employers to make decisions about hiring and promotion in accord with their own perceptions of who would do the best job. While they agreed that we should tirelessly combat racial discrimination, they were hostile to any attempt to prescribe the "correct" racial or ethnic composition of an institution a priori, since this sort of thing smacked strongly of the kind of social engineering they abhorred. The undemocratic way in which racial and ethnic preferences were introduced (through federal bureaucracies and the courts) confirmed all their worst suspicions of such programs.[81]

The culture wars in academia go on, and no resolution of the conflict appears to be in sight. The result of all the sound and fury has been a hardening of the battle lines. To the extent that the academic left has embraced postmodernism and takes rational dialogue to be impossible, or dismisses any arguments made against them as merely attempts to preserve white male privilege, its only option is to nail the flag to the mast and go down with the ship. And their opponents are not about to quietly go away. Meanwhile, the vivid portrayal of the campus culture wars in the popular media has had important political consequences, which will be discussed below.

The Courts

In the late 1980s, the tide began to turn against preferential policies at the Supreme Court level. *Wards Cove Packing Co., Inc. v. Atonio* (1989) shifted much of the burden of proof from employer to employee in disparate impact cases. Plaintiffs cannot rely solely on statistics to establish a prima facie case of discrimination, but must identify a particular practice and causally link it to the statistics, and show that the employer's claimed justification for the practice was spurious. And in *City of Richmond v. J. A. Croson Co.* (1989), the Court insisted on strict scrutiny, and rejected a 30 percent minority set-aside requirement for public contractors at the state and local government level. (Strict scrutiny requires that the policy must serve a compelling state interest and must be a necessary means to that end.)

The Changing Demographics of the Academy

Since the seventies, when affirmative action pressures began to be applied seriously to universities, some significant demographic changes have occurred. It is, of course, impossible to determine just how much affirmative action policies themselves caused this shift, and how much was due to changing preferences of the groups in question[82] or other factors unconnected with affirmative action policies (such as, for example, the large influx of foreign students—most of them Asians). It is easy to lose the forest for the trees when discussing statistics, so I will confine myself to the broad trends since 1976–77 when statistics first became available for the groups currently targeted by affirmative action policies.

In terms of Ph.D.s awarded, the proportion of men receiving Ph.D.s has been declining in education and the social sciences since 1972, while in the humanities it hit a low in 1984 and has risen slightly since then (although it continues to drop precipitously in some fields such as English and foreign languages and literature). Women and men receive roughly the same number of Ph.D.s in humanities and social sciences, and women receive more than men in education. In the life sciences the number of men receiving degrees has remained more or less the same since 1969, and the number of women has risen steadily and is now approaching parity with men. In physical sciences and engineering (which together account for over half of the Ph.D.s awarded) men continue to outnumber women by large margins, although the number of women receiving Ph.D.s in these areas has risen steadily. In 1994 women received 20 percent of the degrees in physical sciences and 11 percent in engineering.[83] However, in light of the fact that foreign students earned a third of the Ph.D.s granted in 1994 (approximately one-fourth of the Ph.D.s in the life sciences, nearly half of those in the physical sciences, and 61 percent in engineering)[84] and that these foreign students are predominantly male (78 percent),[85] American women are actually doing considerably better relative to American men than would appear from simply looking at the numbers.

The number of Ph.D.s awarded to black people rose slightly between 1976–77 and 1992–93 to a total of 1,352. Of these 45 percent were in education, and there was also a heavy concentration (about 20 percent) in the social sciences. Doctorates conferred upon Hispanics rose 42.3 percent during the same period to a total of 827, and were concentrated in education, social sciences, and humanities. Native Americans and Alaskan Natives received a roughly constant but small share of Ph.D.s, earning 106 in 1992–93. The number of Asian Americans earning doctorates increased by roughly 140 percent to a total of 1,582, and they were concentrated in engineering and physical sciences.

In interpreting these sorts of statistics, it is necessary to keep in mind the underlying demographics of the groups in question. If one thinks in terms of proportional representation, Asians are doing significantly better than black people and Hispanics since there are nearly four times as many black people and roughly three times as many Hispanics as there are Asian Americans in the general population.

The largest growth between 1976–77 and 1992–93 was in nonresident aliens, who nearly tripled the number of Ph.D.s they obtained during this period, to a total of 11,454 in 1992–93.[86] In the wake of the 1989 Tiananmen Square uprising, mainland Chinese studying here were offered the opportunity to obtain permanent visas, and tens of thousands of them took advantage of the offer (now expired). This naturally has a large impact on the job market in fields like physics, where half those who obtain Ph.D.s are from China.

The shifts in faculty composition since affirmative action policies first began to be enforced in universities show significant increases in the percentage of faculty positions held by women (from 24.7 percent in 1975–76 to 31.8 percent in 1991–92), Asians and Pacific Islanders (from 2.2 percent in 1975–76 to 5.1 percent in 1991–92), and Hispanics (from 1.4 percent in 1975 to 2.2 percent in 1991–92). Native Americans and Alaskan Natives gained very little (up from 0.2 percent to 0.3 percent) during the same period, as did black people (from 4.4 percent to 4.7 percent).[87]

Faculty composition, of course, changes slowly as a result of the tenure system. But if one looks at recently appointed faculty, it is evident that changes are already occurring. According to a recent survey, one-third of all faculty are in the first seven years of their academic careers, and this faculty cohort differs significantly from their senior colleagues.

Only 43 percent of the newly appointed faculty are native-born white men (compared with 59 percent of the senior cohort), one-quarter of them were not born in the United States (compared with 16 percent of the senior cohort), 41 percent are women (relative to 28 percent of the senior cohort), and 17 percent are minorities (relative to 11 percent of the senior cohort)—with the biggest gains made by Asian men. The newly appointed men more often have their doctorates than the women (59 percent compared with 41 percent). Many of the newly appointed faculty included in the survey do not hold tenure-track positions, and fewer women than men hold tenure (16 percent versus 28 percent). Newly appointed women outnumber newly appointed men at both liberal arts and community colleges. Only a third of the new appointments at doctoral institutions are women, but women are making gains at research institutions; 46 percent of the women at research institutions have been in academia less than seven years.[88]

IV: Where We Are Now

The Clinton administration chose to support affirmative action despite the rift this policy caused with many traditional Democratic Party constituents. However, the sort of ringing moral appeal found, for example, in Lyndon Johnson's famous shackled runners speech is notably lacking in Bill Clinton's rhetoric. In part this is because, with the addition of new groups demanding preference, it has become increasingly difficult to provide a justification for the choice of beneficiaries. The administration's brief to the Supreme Court asking them to review the *Hopwood* case illustrates this problem. It argued that blacks and Hispanics deserve preference in college admissions because they have "experience[d] . . . racial minority status" (regardless of whether they come from affluent families). In short, people of color are to be preferred because they are people of color, and racial differences are more important than other differences because they are racial differences.

The current state of the law regarding affirmative action is discussed in the supplementary essay by George Rutherglen, so I will focus in this last section on the economic, cultural, and political context of the current debate over affirmative action. Not only have the types of programs put forward under the name of "affirmative action" shifted since the mid-1960s, and not only has the list of beneficiaries undergone significant changes since then, but changes in American society since the sixties have resulted in a climate increasingly hostile to preferential (as opposed to merely procedural) affirmative action. Of course the fact that many people oppose a policy does not necessarily prove it is a bad policy, but it does mean that continuing the policy will have significant social costs. In making a decision about affirmative action policies, then, it is important to understand why such policies have become so unpopular.

Economic Context

In examining the contemporary economic context of affirmative action, the appropriate comparison is not with other countries, most of whom are doing equally poorly or even worse in many ways; it is with our past performance. The issue is not national pride, but the influence frustrated expectations have had on attitudes toward affirmative action (and racial issues generally). The postwar boom that petered out in the early seventies remains fresh in people's minds, and that boom itself was a continuation of an extraordinarily long period during which our standard of living had been (with a few interruptions) steadily rising.

Although there are indications that the overall strength of the economy is improving, productivity gains have not led to an increase in real wages for most American workers during the 1990s.[89] The same trends at work in the Reagan-Bush years have continued unabated: the flight of capital across national borders in search of cheaper labor, stiffer international competition, the decline in manufacturing (80 percent of Americans now work in service industries), and polarization of rich and poor. The ratio of the average CEO's salary to that of the average worker rose from about 40 to 1 in 1975 to roughly 150 to 1 in 1990, with some estimates of the current ratio being as high as 225 to 1,[90] by contrast with 16 to 1 in Japan and 21 to 1 in Germany.[91] At the lower end of the spectrum, the percentage of workers employed full-time who earn less than what the Commerce Department defines as a living wage ($13,091) rose to 16 percent of all workers in 1992.[92]

The woes of the middle class have received considerable attention from the press, but very little has been done to ease them. In more and more families both parents must work in order to maintain a middle-class level of income,[93] fewer jobs offer medical benefits,[94] and the growing economic polarization of American society has made a college education harder and harder for middle-class students to afford.[95] In 1990 over half of America's freshmen attended community colleges, where they get very little in the way of a liberal education,[96] and even these options are increasingly out of the reach of the truly disadvantaged. For example, in California, community college fees rose 290 percent between 1990–91 and 1994–95.[97] Meanwhile the leading colleges and universities are becoming more and more the preserve of the affluent.[98]

Growing job insecurity has created waves of fear on the part of large numbers of workers. The "lean production" methods employed by our international competitors have been making major inroads in the United States. More people have lost their jobs than at any other time in the postwar era, and in the 1990s those who lost jobs and found new ones took an average pay cut of 23 percent.[99] Seniority no longer offers protection, and unions have declined sharply in power.[100] Reengineering teams can suddenly descend on companies and eliminate whole categories of workers, and American workers have fewer protections than those in Europe or Japan. There is a far stronger communal tradition in Europe, for example, so that when there are cutbacks, unions frequently agree to share the burden by all employees taking a cut in hours. When work is outsourced in Japan (Toyota now farms out 70 percent of its components in this way), the employees of the privileged suppliers often belong to unions and have life-long job security, but when U.S. companies outsource their work, it is done by low-paid nonunion workers with little or no job security.[101]

As a result of the new leaner economy, middle-class college graduates (who now graduate increasingly in debt) are anxious about their futures and worried that they will never be able to afford a house like the one they grew up in, or provide adequately for their own children. Since the costs of affirmative action fall disproportionately on younger and more vulnerable white males, their economic anxieties fuel their resentment of preferential policies.

Among the hardest hit workers have been white men. The unemployment rate of the two million college-educated white men between the ages of forty-five and fifty-four has risen sharply, and their average earnings fell by 17 percent between 1988 and 1992.[102] White men serving as their family's only breadwinner had been losing out particularly badly (with their inflation-adjusted median income falling 22 percent between 1976 and 1984), and well-paid male blue-collar union members (of all races) lost the most, especially young ones with only a high school education.[103] These economic trends have far-reaching political consequences, since the Democratic Party has traditionally been allied with labor unions and found its strongest support among blue-collar workers. Since white male workers perceive affirmative action as worsening their already precarious position, they have become increasingly disaffected from the Democratic Party.[104]

One reason for opposition to affirmative action, then, lies in the economic stresses and insecurity generated by the postmodern economy.

People are likely to blame affirmative action, whether or not it was actually involved, reasoning: "I didn't get the job because they had to hire a minority member who was less well qualified." The ubiquity of forms requiring job applicants to indicate their racial or ethnic status[105] easily leads people to suspect that the information is being used against them. And to the extent that women and people of color are actually hired and promoted noticeably beyond their skill level, this will confirm the suspicions of those passed over for the jobs. In this explosive climate, the danger of black people being set up as scapegoats for white middle-class anger and frustration is not to be taken lightly.[106]

It is extremely difficult to measure just how much impact affirmative action policies have actually had. The most rigorous studies indicate that the gains made by black people as a result of affirmative action in the federal contract program have been very modest. It is, however, hard to distinguish between the effects of merely enforcing antidiscrimination laws and the effects of racial preferences, and it is possible that increases in the proportion of black workers in companies under federal contract compliance requirements are mirrored by corresponding decreases in those employed by other firms (in other words, the same workers may simply have shifted from noncontractors to contractors).[107]

Cultural Conflict

Economic issues, however, are by no means the only important ones. The 1990s have been a time of intensifying cultural conflict. The battle over homosexuals in the military at the beginning of Clinton's presidency is only one example. The abortion controversy continues to fester, and more and more people have begun to express concern that our democratic institutions may not be able to survive our growing economic inequality and lack of cultural consensus.

Books are appearing with titles like *Before the Shooting Starts: Searching for Democracy in America's Culture War, Democracy on Trial, Democracy in Peril,* and *Democracy's Discontent* (to name only a few). Disaffection from all public institutions is on the rise, and people manifest their anger in a variety of ways, ranging from blowing up federal buildings to simply not taking the trouble to vote (the percentage of registered voters casting ballots declined from 55 percent in 1992 to only 49 percent in the November 1996 elections).[108] Another manifestation of the erosion of a sense of the common good is the increase in taxpayers revolts. People are less willing to pay taxes if they perceive the government to be engaging in favoritism toward groups of which they are not members. And to the extent that affirmative action policies undertaken by government support this perception, they will undermine people's willingness to participate in the political process and make sacrifices for the common good.

The fact that preferential policies have been instituted largely by regulatory agencies and the courts has especially provoked the ire of voters. A grassroots reaction against them is picking up momentum, as manifested, for example, in the easy victory of the California Civil Rights Initiative (CCRI) in the 1996 elections,[109] and similar movements are under way in other states. In fact, racial and gender preferences are not even supported by members of the groups that benefit from them. In two recent Gallup polls (1987 and 1990), two-thirds of the black people surveyed rejected racial preferences for blacks.[110] And a recent survey found that 70 percent of women favored a law forbidding the government from granting racial and gender preferences.[111]

The Crisis in Education

Education is a key area in which cultural conflicts have been played out. One of the main functions of schools is the transmission of culture from one generation to the next, and the question of what sort of people we want the next generation of Americans to be is one that engages all of the deepest issues that divide us. Battles have raged over the abolition of school prayer, the content of sex education courses, the teaching of evolution in biology courses,[112] and finally the way in which American history should be taught. The portrayal of Christopher Columbus in textbooks arouses enormous controversy, religious believers are disturbed by the textbooks' neglect of religion,[113] feminists object to women being omitted or depicted in ways that reinforce traditional sex roles, homosexuals are angered by the absence of people who loved others of the same sex,[114] and every ethnic and racial group wants more recognition. It seems impossible to piece together any unified narrative, particularly since combatants show little willingness to compromise. The battle over textbooks in the Oakland, California, public schools, which surfaced in 1991, for example, was so savage, and proved so intractable, that three years later the fourth-, fifth-, and seventh-grade classes still had no history textbooks.[115]

One measure of parental discontent is the sudden growth in homeschooling (up approximately 2,500 percent since the early 1970s).[116] Taking into account the sacrifices of time and income involved in a commitment to school one's children at home, this remarkable growth bespeaks a deep dissatisfaction on the part of parents who feel their values are not being reflected in the public school curriculum. Another sign of this is the rapid growth of fundamentalist Christian academies, which had only a handful of students in the early sixties, but approximately 1.45 million students in 1986.[117]

The same sorts of conflicts are at work in postsecondary education as well, and more and more people are expressing concern about declining academic standards. Businesses are understandably upset to discover that more and more college graduates lack basic verbal and analytical skills and require on-job remedial training. At a recent national summit on education (at which only state governors and business leaders were present as a result of growing public suspicion of Washington), Louis Gerstner Jr., the chairman of IBM, bewailed the fact that "Our educational system is broken—we all know that. I could stand here for hours reading the grim statistics. We are behind other countries . . . and in an increasingly global economy, I'm not liking our chances."[118]

The publicity given the PC wars has also fed into the current widespread discontent with the way our colleges and universities are performing. There has always been a deeply entrenched suspicion of high culture among Americans, and the PC wars have done a lot to confirm their suspicions. Leading professors of humanities say that the whole Western cultural tradition is corrupt, and their critics, in turn, trumpet the horrors of multiculturalism. The press, of course, highlights all that is most repugnant to the moral sensibilities of the general public. The situation is rather like a dirty political campaign in which both parties come out totally discredited.[119] This sort of thing makes public higher education increasingly vulnerable to budget slashing by politicians who are already more interested in vocational education than in the liberal arts or in pure scientific research.

Affirmative Action and the Crisis in Education

The direct economic impact of preferential affirmative action in the appointment of college professors is limited to a fairly small number of people (although its impact on those directly affected is great), but its impact is magnified by its effects on the enormous numbers of students enrolling in institutions of higher education[120] and by the visibility of the campus culture wars in the media. The kind of impact that preferential appointment of women and people of color for faculty positions can be expected to have on the broader society is discussed in Chapter 3, section II, so I will merely touch on a few points here.

First, those worried about declining academic standards may worry that preferential policies will result in the appointment of women and people of color who are less qualified than available white male candidates. Parents, taxpayers, and students will fear that they are not getting the best education possible for their money.

And second, since affirmative action has become so entangled with multiculturalism and battles over the curriculum (or, as it is sometimes called, "the canon"), people with no particular prejudices against women or people of color may quite reasonably oppose preferential appointment of women and people of color to faculty positions if they believe it is being used to promote programs with which they disagree.

While trustees and administrators who are pushing for affirmative action are usually concerned only to increase the number of women and people of color on the faculty, those faculty members and students who are most vocal in their support for affirmative action would not be satisfied with the appointment of large numbers of women who thought like Phyllis Schlafly or of black people who thought like Clarence Thomas. They are concerned to advance a particular cultural and political program—namely multiculturalism[121]—and this has the effect of linking affirmative action with the sorts of bitter and intractable cultural conflicts described above.

V. Conclusion

Several things of importance for the rest of this book have emerged from this chapter.

(1) In the 1970s, universities were under increasing pressure to increase the representation of women and people of color among the professoriate. However, the prevailing winds have now changed, and to the extent that universities are under external pressure at all it is more likely to be operating against affirmative action than for it. Universities thus have breathing space in which to reflect about their existing policies and decide what policies would be most beneficial for them to adopt, taking into account both their educational mission and the message their actions communicate to those outside the academy.

(2) Although the Civil Rights Act of 1964 was designed to benefit black Americans, women are the ones who have gained most in terms of their proportions among doctoral candidates and among the professoriate. Asians have also made marked gains.

(3) In the current political climate, preferential affirmative action has costs of a kind that it did not have in the 1960s when such programs were introduced.[122]

Preferential affirmative action is likely to increase people's disaffection from, and hostility to, the federal government, since it has been instituted in ways insulated from scrutiny by voters, and reinforces a widespread perception that the government is under the thumb of whatever group squawks most loudly. Preferential affirmative action has also been important in fueling the growing tribalization of America. Even procedural affirmative action can have this effect unless it is very carefully designed and implemented.[123] And, finally, preferential affirmative action is likely to contribute to the already dangerous level of free-floating anger, not only for economic reasons, but because of the way it has been linked (in academia especially) with cultural conflicts.

The possible social costs of preferential affirmative action do not necessarily imply that such policies should not be undertaken, but such costs must be taken into account when deciding what to do. To the extent that there are persuasive arguments showing such policies to be necessary—for example, on the grounds of compensatory justice, to attain diversity, or to provide role models for female or minority students—then these reasons might be sufficiently important to outweigh the risks involved. We turn, in the next chapter, to one of the most important arguments for preferential affirmative action—the argument from compensatory justice.

Notes

1. Several studies that are valuable for helping thread one's way through the historical material are Hugh Davis Graham's *The Civil Rights Era: Origins and Development of National Policy, 1960–1972* (New York: Oxford University Press, 1990), and Herman Belz, *Equality Transformed: A Quarter-Century of Affirmative Action* (New Brunswick, N.J., and London: Transaction, 1991). John Skrentny's book *The Ironies of Affirmative Action* (Chicago: University of Chicago Press, 1996) provides a good account of the evolution of affirmative action policies in their political and cultural context, and Terry Eastland's *Ending Affirmative Action: The Case for Colorblind Justice* (New York: Basic Books, 1996) gives an up-to-date history of affirmative action that is more legal in focus.

2. William E. Hudson, *Democracy in Peril: Seven Challenges to America's Future* (Chatham, N.J.: Chatham House, 1995), 234.

3. Jeffrey Madrick, *The End of Affluence: The Causes and Consequences of America's Economic Dilemma* (New York: Random House, 1995), 13.

4. Madrick, *End of Affluence*, 125.

5. Madrick, *End of Affluence*, 135.

6. Richard Lester, *Antibias Regulation of Universities: Faculty Problems and Their Solutions* (New York: McGraw-Hill, 1974), 37.

7. Lester, *Antibias Regulation*, 50–51.

8. Figures cited by Harold Orlans, "Affirmative Action in Higher Education," *Annals of the American Academy of Political and Social Science* 523 (September 1992), 154.

9. Lester, *Antibias Regulation*, 48–49. The 1969 survey involved a sample of 2,280 black Ph.D. holders, of whom 1,096 returned their questionnaires—a response rate of about 50 percent.

10. Lester, *Antibias Regulation*, 49–50.

11. This finding about higher salaries for black professors was corroborated by Thomas Sowell's 1975 study *Affirmative Action Reconsidered: Was It Necessary in Academia?* (Washington, D.C.: American Enterprise Institute for Public Policy Research, 1975), especially 15–23, where he shows that Asian faculty are actually the most underpaid relative to their qualifications and fields of concentration.

12. Both their message and their style owed a great deal to the Hebrew prophets. This was particularly true, of course, of the Rev. Martin Luther King Jr., whose famous "I Have a Dream" speech of 1963 powerfully evoked the passage from Isaiah about how every valley shall be exalted, and the glory of the Lord will be revealed. *A Testament of Hope: The Essential Writings of Martin Luther King, Jr.*, James Washington, ed. (San Francisco: Harper & Row, 1986), 219.

13. E. J. Dione, *Why Americans Hate Politics* (New York: Simon and Schuster, 1991), 38.

14. From the Port Huron Statement, reprinted in James Miller, *Democracy in the Streets: From Port Huron to the Siege of Chicago* (New York: Simon and Schuster, 1987), 332–33.

15. Miller, *Democracy*, 330–31.

16. A valuable discussion of the breakdown of the New Left, to which I am indebted in this chapter, is found in Todd Gitlin, *The Twilight of Common Dreams: Why America Is Wracked by Culture Wars* (New York: Metropolitan Books, Division of Henry Holt, 1995), esp. ch. 3.

17. See James Jackson, ed., *Life in Black America* (London: Sage, 1991), 106.

18. Gitlin, *Twilight*, 100.

19. Lester, *Antibias Regulation*, 9.

20. Sex discrimination was thus not originally included under Title VI as it was under Title VII. The story of its last-minute inclusion under Title VII is given below.

21. " . . . it shall not be an unlawful employment practice for an employer to apply different standards of compensation, or different terms, conditions, or privileges of employment pursuant to a *bona fide* seniority or merit system . . . provided that such differences are not the result of an intention to discriminate because of race, color, religion, sex, or national origin, nor shall it be an unlawful employment practice for an employer to give and to act upon the results of any professionally developed ability test provided that such test, its administration or action upon the results is not designed, intended or used to discriminate because of race, color, religion, sex, or national origin."

22. As Hubert Humphrey explained to his Senate colleagues, "The express requirement of intent is designed to make it wholly clear that inadvertent or accidental discriminations will not violate the title or result in the entry of

court orders. It means simply that the respondent must have intended to discriminate." Graham, *Civil Rights Era*, 192.

23. *Public Papers of the Presidents: Lyndon B. Johnson, 1965* (Washington: U.S. Government Printing Office, 1966), I, 636.

24. This order was modeled on John F. Kennedy's Executive Order No. 10925 (issued in 1961).

25. U.S. Department of Labor, Fact Sheet No. ESA 95-17: Executive Order No. 11246 (Washington, D.C.: U.S. Government Printing Office, 1965).

26. The Philadelphia Plan, initiated during the Johnson administration, had come under severe attack in Congress, the Senate, and by the Comptroller General, and was rescued from defeat by aggressive action on the part of Nixon, who saw it as a way of dividing the Democratic Party and forcing the Democrats to choose between alienating their labor union allies or maintaining their image as favoring civil rights. Belz, *Equality Transformed*, 37, and Graham, *Civil Rights Era*, ch. 13. See also Skrentny, *Ironies*, ch. 7, on Nixon's role.

27. Graham, *Civil Rights Era*, 464.

28. Belz, *Equality Transformed*, 27.

29. Belz, *Equality Transformed*, 125.

30. Interestingly, the EEOC itself, in its official *Administrative History* acknowledged that under the "traditional meaning" which was the "common definition of Title VII," an act of discrimination "must be one of intent in the state of mind of the actor." Graham, *Civil Rights Era*, 388. Therefore the EEOC hoped to get Congress to reconsider the Dirksen amendment (sec. 706g) that contained the clearest language about the need for discriminatory intent. However, the *Griggs* decision obviated the need for this sort of reconsideration by giving them more than they had hoped for.

31. Graham, *Civil Rights Era*, 390.

32. Graham, *Civil Rights Era*, 389.

33. Stephen Steinberg, cited in Dinesh D'Souza, *The End of Racism* (New York: Free Press, 1995), 218.

34. Graham, *Civil Rights Era*, 210.

35. For example, the International Convention on the Elimination of All Forms of Racial Discrimination (1965). I am indebted to Skrentny's *Ironies*, ch. 4, for pointing out the importance of the international situation.

36. Belz, *Equality Transformed*, 77.

37. Although in 1971 blacks represented 11 percent of the population and 12 percent of the workforce, 49 percent of the EEOC staff were black, and by 1978 the percentages of female and Spanish-surnamed employees had also increased until white males were only 20.6 percent of EEOC staff. Graham, *Civil Rights Era*, 459–60.

38. For an intelligent defense of this option, see Jan Narveson's essay in Marilyn Friedman and Jan Narveson, *Political Correctness: For and Against* (Lanham, Md.: Rowman & Littlefield, 1995).

39. Indeed, as psychologists and religious teachers have frequently insisted, people's intentions are often opaque even to themselves.

40. Cynthia Harrison, *On Account of Sex: The Politics of Women's Issues, 1945–1968* (Berkeley: University of California Press, 1988), 179.

41. Their attempt to append it to the civil rights bill was in part a kind of revenge against the President's Commission on the Status of Women, headed by Esther Peterson, who had recently come out against the ERA. Carl Brauer, "Women Activists, Southern Conservatives, and the Prohibition of Sex Discrimination in Title VII of the 1964 Civil Rights Act," *Journal of Southern History* 49, 1 (February 1983), 41.

42. Brauer, "Women Activists," 45. Many members of the NWP were themselves no friends to civil rights legislation and some of them were outright racists.

43. This position was taken by Esther Peterson, director of the Women's Bureau in the Department of Labor, and head of the President's Commission on the Status of Women. She advocated equal economic opportunity for women, but opposed blanket sorts of measures like the ERA and Title VII because they would threaten women's protective legislation. The other members of the PCSW agreed with her, concluding that sex discrimination "involves problems sufficiently different from discrimination based on the other factors listed to make separate treatment preferable." Brauer, "Women Activists," 46. (The quotation refers to an executive order relating to federal employment, but the point is equally applicable to Title VII.)

44. Edith Green, for example, argued that "For every discrimination that has been made against a woman in this country, there has been 10 times as much discrimination against the Negro of this country." The amendment, she said, "would clutter up the bill and it may later—very well—be used to help destroy this section of the bill by some of the very people who today support it." Brauer, "Women Activists," 50.

45. George Meany wrote to Congressman James Roosevelt (who fashioned what was to become the heart of Title VII), urging him not to include sex discrimination. Graham, *Civil Rights Era*, 208.

46. It was not entirely clear at the time that Title VII would have this effect, although Everett Dirksen offered this as one reason for his opposition to adding sex discrimination to Title VII. Brauer, "Women Activists," 52, 54.

47. For an excellent account of the early battles between the EEOC and various women's groups, see Graham, *Civil Rights Era*, ch. 8.

48. I am indebted to Graham's insightful analysis of this shift. *Civil Rights Era*, esp. 472–74.

49. An illuminating discussion of some of the differences between the structural implications of equal employment opportunity for women and black people is found in Paul Burstein, *Discrimination, Jobs, and Politics: The Struggle for Equal Employment Opportunity in the United States Since the New Deal* (Chicago: University of Chicago Press, 1985), esp. 174–77.

50. See Thomas Byrne Edsall and Mary D. Edsall, *Chain Reaction: The Impact of Race, Rights, and Taxes on American Politics* (New York: Norton, 1991), esp. chs. 6 and 11.

51. Mariam Chamberlain, ed., *Women in Academe: Progress and Prospects* (New York: Russell Sage, 1988), 257–58.

52. Chamberlain, *Women in Academe*, 260, 263.

53. *Summary Report 1994*, computed from Table B2, p. 78.

54. National Center for Education Statistics, *Digest of Education Statistics, 1995* (Washington, D.C.: U.S. Department of Education, 1995), Table 262.

55. As Tonto is reputed to have said to the Lone Ranger, when the latter exclaimed in alarm, "We're really in trouble now! We are surrounded by Indians."

56. Such concerns were understandably less central to the groups representing people of color, and the influence of Foucault on Black Studies programs or Chicano (or Hispanic) Studies was considerably weaker than on Women's Studies and Gay/Lesbian Studies.

57. He makes this point in a chapter delightfully entitled "Marching on the English Department While the Right Took the White House." Gitlin, *Twilight*, 147.

58. Paul Rainbow, ed., *The Foucault Reader* (New York: Pantheon, 1984), 385.

59. Federal funding for higher education fell 14 percent between 1981 and 1986, and between 1980 and 1989, spending for higher education at all levels of government declined by 24.3 percent in constant dollars. Gitlin, *Twilight*, 187.

60. For an excellent account of how and why this happened, see George Marsden's *The Soul of the University: From Protestant Establishment to Established Nonbelief* (New York: Oxford University Press, 1994).

61. For example, Clark Kerr, in his influential book *The Uses of the University* (Cambridge: Harvard University Press, 1963), says, "The university started as a single community—a community of masters and students. It may even be said to have had a soul. Today the large American university is, rather, a whole series of communities and activities held together by a common name, a common governing board, and related purposes." A university, thus understood, functions mainly to meet whatever demands the broader society may choose to make upon it.

62. Edsall and Edsall, *Chain Reaction*, 117, 127.

63. Lester, *Antibias Regulation*, 6–7.

64. Lester, *Antibias Regulation*, 4.

65. Lester, *Antibias Regulation*, 5.

66. Actually, only about a third of them supported preferential appointment policies according to a 1972–73 survey. Of the faculty surveyed, 32 percent of the males and 42 percent of the females supported giving preference to women, while 35 percent of the males and 36 percent of the females supported it for members of minority groups. Lester, *Antibias Regulation*, 2.

67. For an extended defense of the claim that it is inappropriate to apply affirmative action policies designed in a business setting to universities, see Lester, *Antibias Regulation*.

68. *Philosophy and Public Affairs* devoted 10 percent of its pages between 1973 and 1978 to the issue (figure from Steven Cahn's introduction to *Affirmative Action and the University* [Philadelphia: Temple University Press, 1993], 2). See also Barry Gross, ed., *Reverse Discrimination* (Buffalo: Prometheus Books, 1977); Alan Goldman, *Justice and Reverse Discrimination*

(Princeton: Princeton University Press, 1979); Nathan Glazer, *Affirmative Discrimination* (New York: Basic Books, 1975); and Thomas Nagel, Thomas Scanlon, and Marshall Cohen, eds., *Equality and Preferential Treatment* (Princeton: Princeton University Press, 1977).

69. R. M. O'Neil, "The Case for Preferential Admissions" in Gross, *Reverse Discrimination*, 79.

70. See George Rutherglen's essay for an in-depth discussion of the legal issues involved.

71. *Texas et al. v. Cheryl Hopwood et al., cert. denied*, July 1, 1996.

72. 443 U.S. 208 (1979).

73. Kevin Phillips, *The Politics of Rich and Poor* (New York: Random House, 1990), 8.

74. Phillips, *Politics*, 10.

75. Phillips, *Politics*, 14.

76. Phillips, *Politics*, 203, 207.

77. Dinesh D'Souza, *Illiberal Education* (New York: Free Press, 1991), and Roger Kimball, *Tenured Radicals: How Politics Has Corrupted Our Higher Education* (New York: Harper and Row, 1990), for example, provided extensive documentation of the excesses of the politically correct.

78. I do so because that is usually what is meant by the term.

79. Political labels are always a bit touchy, but this one is more controversial than most, and a fair number of those usually characterized as "neoconservatives" refuse to accept the label. The classic study of neoconservativism is Peter Steinfels, *Neoconservatives: The Men Who Are Changing America's Politics* (New York: Simon and Schuster, 1979). For a more recent study of neoconservative thought, see Mark Gerson, *The Neoconservative Vision: From the Cold War to the Culture Wars* (Lanham, Md.: Madison Books, 1996).

80. See, e.g., Irving Kristol, "A Capitalist Conception of Justice," in Richard T. DeGeorge and Joseph Pichler, eds., *Ethics, Free Enterprise, and Public Policy* (New York: Oxford University Press, 1978), and Roger Scruton, *The Meaning of Conservatism* (Totowa, N.J.: Barnes and Noble, 1980), 86–90.

81. My discussion here is indebted in part to Mark Gerson's discussion of affirmative action, *The Neoconservative Vision*, 146-154.

82. The increase of women in academia, for example, is part of a more general influx of women into all the professions; the number of women receiving law and medical degrees has also skyrocketed during this period.

83. *Summary Report 1994: Doctorate Recipients from United States Universities*, 8.

84. *Summary Report 1994*, 9.

85. *Digest of Education Statistics, 1995*, Table 262.

86. Statistics in the paragraph are from *Digest of Educational Statistics 1995*, 289, and from the *Summary Report 1994*, 11.

87. *Indicators of Equal Employment Opportunity—Status and Trends* (Washington, D.C.: Equal Employment Opportunity Commission, 1991).

88. Denise Magner, "New Generation of Professors Is Changing the Face of Academe," *Chronicle of Higher Education*, Feb. 2, 1996, A17.

89. See Simon Head, "The New Ruthless Economy," *New York Review of Books* (Feb. 29, 1996), 47.
90. *Washington Post National Weekly Edition* (Mar. 4–10, 1996), 15, cites the 40 to 1 figure for 1975 and says that current estimates range as high as 225 to 1.
91. Figures for Germany and Japan are for 1990. See Robert Frank and Philip Cook, *The Winner-Take-All Society* (New York: Free Press, 1995), 70.
92. Gitlin, *Twilight*, 225.
93. The number of two-earner families rose 20 percent in the 1980s. Madrick, *End of Affluence*, 138.
94. Sixty-one percent according to Madrick, *End of Affluence*, 141.
95. For example, whereas in 1979 a student from the top quarter of American families had four times the chance of getting a B.A. by age 24 as one in the bottom quarter, in 1992 it was 19 times the chance. Gitlin, *Twilight*, 225.
96. *Digest of Education Statistics 1995*, 185.
97. Gitlin, *Twilight*, 30.
98. For example, 60 percent of the entering freshmen at UCLA in 1991 came from families with incomes over $60,000 a year. Of those, 40 percent came from families with incomes over $100,000 a year. Russell Jacoby, *Dogmatic Wisdom* (New York: Doubleday, 1994), 21.
99. Madrick, *End of Affluence*, 136.
100. On the decline in union power, and its connection with the rise of identity politics, see Gitlin, *Twilight*, 226.
101. Head, "The New Ruthless Economy."
102. Madrick, *End of Affluence*, 137.
103. Phillips, *Politics*, 18.
104. Only 37 percent of white men voted for Clinton in 1992 (Gitlin, *Twilight*, 233). In the November 1996 elections, 39 percent of white men voted for Clinton (National Exit Poll, World Wide Web, Nov. 8, 1996, http://www.politicsnow.com).
105. My four-year-old nephew's report card from pre-kindergarten has a spot to fill in his racial or ethnic status.
106. A recent study by Paul Sniderman and Tom Piazza showed that respondents were far more likely to express negative attitudes toward black people if the interviewer mentioned affirmative action before getting to questions on racial attitudes. *The Scar of Race* (Cambridge, Mass.: Belknap Press of Harvard University Press, 1993), ch. 4, esp. 97–104.
107. George Rutherglen, "After Affirmative Action: Conditions and Consequences of Ending Preferences in Employment," *University of Illinois Law Review* (1992), 350.
108. Voter News Service exit polls, Nov. 9, 1996.
109. The CCRI is an amendment to the state constitution stipulating that "(a) The state shall not discriminate against, or grant preferential treatment to, any individual or group on the basis of race, sex, color, ethnicity, or national origin in the operation of public employment, public education, or public contracting."

110. Gallup asked the question in 1987 and 1990 in the form "We should make every effort to improve the position of blacks and other minorities even if it means giving them preferential treatment." When the question was asked about tie-breaking in favor of the black person over the white one when both were equally qualified, 42 percent of blacks still opposed it. Seymour Martin Lipset, "Equal Chances or Equal Results?" *Annals of the American Academy of Political and Social Science* 523 (September 1992), 67.

111. The question was "Do you strongly support, somewhat support, somewhat oppose, or strongly oppose a federal law that would prevent the federal government from discriminating against or granting preference to any person based in whole or in part on race or gender?" Fifty-four percent of women put strongly support (compared to 51 percent of men), and 16 percent put somewhat support (compared to 14 percent of men). Polling Company data, 1996.

112. Creationism has gained an able advocate in Phillip Johnson, professor of law at University of California, Berkeley, and former law clerk to Chief Justice Earl Warren.

113. Paul Vitz, cited in James Davison Hunter, *Culture Wars: The Struggle to Define America* (New York: Basic Books, 1991), 205.

114. Gitlin, *Twilight*, 28–29.

115. Gitlin, *Twilight*, 32.

116. In 1990 it was estimated that there were 250,000 to 300,000 home-schooled children in America by comparison with only about 10,000 to 15,000 in the early 1970s. Jane Galen and Mary Anne Pitman, eds., *Home Schooling: Political, Historical, and Pedagogical Perspectives* (Norwood, N.J.: Ablex Publishing Co., 1991), 20–21.

117. Edsall and Edsall, *Chain Reaction*, 132. It is hard to disentangle how much the growth of such schools is a function of "white flight" in the face of the movement toward integration in southern schools, and how much it is a function of other factors such as their perception that "secular humanism" was what was being taught in public schools.

118. *Providence* (Rhode Island) *Journal-Bulletin* (Mar. 27, 1996), 10.

119. I am indebted for this analogy to a conversation with Joseph Ryshpan.

120. In 1994, 61.9 percent of those graduating from high school in the last 12 months were enrolled in college in October. *Digest of Educational Statistics, 1995*, Table 178.

121. For example, students at a leading law school who had been sitting-in, demanding the appointment of more black and Hispanic professors, objected to one Hispanic candidate on the grounds that he was a Republican.

122. These are discussed in greater detail in Chapter 3, section II.

123. For example, sending a candidate an affirmative action form to fill out immediately upon receipt of his or her application is the sort of thing that is likely to increase tribalization. Relatively unobtrusive monitoring of the work of search committees by a dean or provost in order to ensure fairness is, by contrast, considerably less likely to do so.

2

Compensatory Arguments

One important argument in favor of preferential treatment of women and people of color relies on the notion of compensatory justice. This argument is powerful because it appeals to an intuitively clear and widely accepted moral principle that the one who wrongs another owes the other compensation. Although no argument about social policy decisions can ignore empirical questions entirely, those who employ compensatory arguments do not appeal to consequences to justify preferential policies, and therefore need not become mired in the morass of conflicting and incomplete evidence regarding the effects preferential policies have already had or might be expected to have in the future. To assess the force of the compensatory argument, I begin by setting up what I take to be the most plausible version of it, considering it as a justification for according preferential treatment to black job candidates. I then consider how far the argument can be extended to include other groups.

There are several reasons for proceeding this way. First, black people have the strongest case for compensation. Second, most discussions of the compensatory argument in the literature focus on the compensation owed black people as a kind of paradigm case, and then add the other groups with remarks like "and a similar argument could be constructed also for . . ." or "this argument could be extended [perhaps with a few unspecified modifications] to apply also to. . . ." Third, the case of black people is central because a great deal of the moral capital supporting the demand for preferential policies in general flows from the oppression and sufferings of black people. Had it not been for slavery, and had Africans simply come here as one group of immigrants among others and done less well economically than other groups, it is very unlikely that affirmative action programs in their present form would have been instituted.

And finally, the way in which other sorts of arguments have been developed has been deeply influenced by the compensatory argument.

47

For one thing the compensatory argument stands in the background and serves to identify the groups that corrective or forward-looking policies are designed to benefit. Thus, when we Americans aim at greater social equality, we think in terms of equality between racial groups rather than, say, narrowing the gap between rich and poor. And when preference is extended to other groups, there is a tendency to think of such groups as like races[1] and to assimilate the difficulties they face to those experienced by black Americans in a way that sometimes obscures important differences.

I. The Argument

Premise 1. Black people are owed a debt of compensation.

What makes the position of black people in America unique is the fact that their ancestors were brought here against their will as slaves. In addition to having their labor expropriated, their human dignity was affronted in a deep way by their being treated as property to be bought and sold at will. Moreover, the institution of slavery was, until the Civil War, sanctioned by law at all levels of government. Being deprived of the fruits of their own labor, the slaves were unable to advance in the world in the way other immigrant groups did, so that when they were freed they had nothing to hand on to their children. Furthermore, to move on to rather more sensitive and controversial ground, the culture developed by black people in America was deeply marked by the experience of slavery in ways that arguably make it particularly difficult for them to be successful in our current highly competitive and individualistic economy. And since black people have tended to be segregated from the larger society, their material and cultural disadvantages have been passed down from generation to generation, so that black people now living still suffer from the harmful effects of slavery. And wrongs against black people did not end with the abolition of slavery, so that compensation is owed them for these wrongs also.

Premise 2. This debt is owed by "society" (or alternatively "the community").

Supposing, then, that black people are owed compensation, it is necessary to specify someone who owes it to them. We cannot apply the principle that one who wrongs another owes the other if the perpetrator of the wrong and the one who must pay are not the same person. Since the strongest argument that compensation is owed to black people must include the wrongs inflicted by slavery, I focus on the version of the argument that employs the term "society" or "the community,"[2] understood as a transgenerational entity that bridges the gap between slavery and the present day.

Premise 3. Being awarded jobs is a particularly appropriate way of compensating black people for the wrongs they have suffered.

Black people were wronged not only materially but also by being denied full membership in the community, and the respect that goes with it. They have not been given an equal chance at the benefits generated by what the community owns, nor have they felt they even had a right to it. Being awarded a job provides a remedy for both sorts of wrongs. It provides both a stable income and a recognized place in the community. Furthermore, in the absence of the injustices they have suffered, there would be more black people holding prestigious and lucrative jobs; we are, thus, only giving them what would be theirs but for the wrongs they have suffered.

Premise 4. In order to compensate black people for their injuries, search committees may justifiably override any rights to equal consideration that other applicants might have (to simplify the argument, let us assume that the other applicants are white) and the rights of any other people affected by the appointment.

In defense of this premise, it is often argued that just as the black candidate has been unjustly disadvantaged because of past wrongs, the white candidate has been correspondingly given an unjust advantage as a result of past injustices perpetrated against black Americans, so that what is taken away from him is not really something he has a right to.

Conclusion: Assuming then that the black candidate for a job possesses at least the basic or minimum qualifications to perform the job, he or she ought to be appointed.

II. Evaluation

This type of argument draws its inspiration from legal practice. The compensatory argument is essentially modeled on the law of torts—which is unfortunately the most incoherent branch of American private law. It is therefore beset by many of the same problems that beset tort law. Assessing damages is particularly difficult, especially in cases that involve emotional distress. The standard of liability is contested, ranging from culpability to mere causation (or strict liability, as it is called). It is hard to know what would make the plaintiff whole, since to do so we would need to know what his condition would be but for the accident. For these reasons, it is tempting to use tort law as a way of helping out the unfortunate—should they be "fortunate" enough to be damaged by a wealthy defendant or one with generous insurance coverage. The problem of social cost is thus easily evaded, at least for a while.

The objections raised against the compensatory argument by philosophers, then, are deeply connected with the sorts of difficulties that lawyers struggle with in applying tort law to cases; expanding the scope of the argument to justify compensation for damages suffered by one's parents and ancestors (as many philosophers have done) exacerbates the difficulties. Since the law itself is in an unsatisfactory state, seeking guidance from legal practice will not take us very far toward resolving our difficulties.

Premise 1. Black people are owed a debt of compensation.

That slavery both wronged and harmed[3] the slaves, and that this has resulted in at least some harm to their descendants, is generally conceded. It may of course be the case that some individual slaves were materially better off under slavery than they would have been otherwise. Perhaps many of the slaves who were brought to America would have died young from famine or been slaughtered in tribal warfare had they remained in Africa; thus we can't know that in every case they were worse off under the conditions they faced as slaves in America. Furthermore, most Africans brought to America as slaves were already enslaved in Africa, and were purchased by slave traders from Arabs or other Africans.[4] But it seems safe to say that being a slave is bad for any human being; being bought and sold as property is violative of human dignity (in addition to the material exploitation involved).

Jim Crow laws denied black people the normal rights and respect accorded white people and are likewise agreed to have harmed black people. The current generation of black people have also been the victims of more informal racial prejudice at a variety of different levels, including not only personal relationships, but also employment discrimination and even racially discriminatory policies of government agencies. Supposing, then, that we concede that black people have been unjustly harmed in all these ways, does it follow that they are owed a debt of compensation? Not necessarily.

First, it is impossible to compensate all the victims of social injustice. It is not even possible in practice to compensate all victims of individual injustice through tort law. And the problem is even worse for injustice that is embedded in our institutional structures.[5] Even assuming, optimistically, that we could manage to arrive at a shared understanding of just what "social injustice" *is*, many groups have been and still are victims of this sort of injustice, and to compensate only some of these groups is to penalize others and thus to generate a further injustice that will in turn require compensation. If we cannot compensate all those who have been similarly injured, it is wrong to compensate only some and thus perpetuate injustice. Why should those to be compensated be selected on the basis of the color of their skin?

At this point the special history of black people in America becomes relevant. Although many groups have been subjected to severe prejudice and systematic discrimination, only black people were enslaved. Japanese Americans who were held in camps during World War II have been compensated for their losses, and the slavery endured by generations of black Americans surely inflicted far more serious injury on them than that suffered by the Japanese Americans who received compensation.

When we take the effects of slavery into account, then, the situation of black Americans does seem unique. If the claim that they are owed compensation for the injury they suffered as a result of slavery can be successfully established, then this would justify special treatment for them. But there are serious practical and conceptual difficulties with claims to recover damages for injuries suffered by one's parents and ancestors. If one takes tort law as a model (as the compensatory argument inevitably does), the law has been reluctant to allow people to collect for damages to their parents or ancestors (with a very few exceptions such as "wrongful death" actions, or laws requiring the return of stolen property by the heirs of the thief). In part, of course, the reason for this is a practical one.[6] But the problem of ancient wrongs[7] raises deep philosophical problems as well.

In the case of slavery, the slaves cannot be made whole for their injuries, being no longer alive. And supposing that black people now living have been injured by the wrongs committed against their ancestors, exactly what is the nature of their injury and what sort of compensation, if any, would make them whole? Even in relatively simple tort cases, assessing how much compensation is appropriate requires what philosophers call "counterfactual knowledge."[8] In other words, we need to know what would have happened *if* the wrong had not been inflicted. This is difficult enough when the damage was done to the person now seeking compensation (and even when the damages sought are purely monetary), but the amount of counterfactual knowledge required increases exponentially as one moves to the intergenerational case, especially when several generations have elapsed. Had it not been for slavery, the slaves would have remained in Africa. But had they miraculously been transported as immigrants to the same region where they in fact lived as slaves, what would have become of them and their descendants? Is there any reason to assume that they would now hold high-paying and prestigious jobs in greater numbers than the rural southern white people who held small plots of land in the same area? The whole economy of the region would have been so different that it is hard to know how to even begin to answer the question.

Paying compensation to someone for the damages suffered by an ancestor generates a further conceptual problem because in some cases the present individual seeking compensation would not in fact exist in the absence of the wrong committed against the ancestor. Being compensated for the damages inflicted by slavery is a case of this sort, since in the absence of slavery, the present American Negro population (almost all of whom have some white ancestors) would not exist as the biological individuals they are.

Perhaps a more fruitful line of argument would be to focus on the nonmaterial damages suffered by the slaves and passed on to their descendants. Being deprived of the fruits of their labor was not the only harm suffered by the slaves, and taking into account the emotional and psychological effects of slavery gives us a far fuller understanding of the damage inflicted on them. The ways in which the slaves managed to adapt to their situation and cope with the horrors of slavery left a deep mark on the culture developed by black people in America, and since that culture has been passed down to their descendants, they too have been affected by slavery. Although slave culture may have been admirable in many ways,[9] it is sometimes argued that as a result of the slave experience, black culture has developed in ways that make it hard for black people to succeed in a competitive and individualistic society like ours.[10] Are they, perhaps, owed compensation for this?

Seeking to be compensated for damage to one's culture, however, runs into difficulties fairly quickly. How could such damage be measured, and what would count as making the victims whole? Supposing that there are some features of black culture that make it especially difficult for black people to succeed in an individualistic and competitive society, this would seem to imply that to be made whole from their injuries they need to be somehow freed from these features of their culture. But at least some of the features of their culture that supposedly hold them back economically are likely to be integrally connected with other features of their culture that they treasure deeply and that are in fact quite admirable. A culture that maximizes one's capacity to succeed in an individualistic and competitive society is not necessarily better than one that does not. Must black people abandon their entire cultural heritage? (For that matter, can cultures be changed at will?) And if they do wish to affirm and retain their own distinctive culture while acknowledging that some features of that culture place them at a disadvantage in an individualistic and competitive society, is it reasonable to ask for compensation? Above all, is it reasonable to ask to be preferentially hired for the sorts of jobs they have just admitted that their culture disables them from performing successfully?

And at a deeper level, does it really make sense to separate oneself from one's culture in the way this argument requires? Is there a disembodied and ahistorical self that stands wholly outside the cultural tradition that has shaped it and is entitled to claim compensation for having been shaped by that culture?[11] Does it make sense to seek compensation for being the person that one is? The metaphysical issues involved here are connected with those we encountered above when we noted that in the absence of slavery the current generation of black Americans would not exist as the biological persons they are. Had they been transported at birth to Tibet and brought up in Buddhist monasteries, there is also a sense in which they would not be the persons they now are. In any case, no social policy can make it be the case that we are not the persons our biology and culture have made us. As Agathon said, "one thing alone is lacking to the gods, to make undone that which has been done."

Shelby Steele has said, "If all blacks were given a million dollars tomorrow it would not amount to a dime on the dollar for three centuries of oppression, nor would it dissolve the residues of that oppression that we still carry today."[12] He may well be right. But if it is impossible to calculate the amount of damages, or articulate a defensible notion of what would count as making the victims whole from their injuries, how can we employ the compensatory model in practice? It seems, then, that when we try to expand the tort law model to cover wrongs that span many generations and include a large element of nonmaterial damages, as is done by those who defend preferential hiring of black people as a compensation for past wrongs, the conceptual difficulties that arise are so severe that the model begins to crack under the strain. I am not maintaining the absurd thesis that only small wrongs count (as Stalin once said, "one death is a tragedy; a million is a statistic"). But the conceptual framework that helps us deal with automobile accidents may be hopelessly inadequate in dealing with the displacement of peoples that makes up so much of history.

Finally, there has been considerable migration of black people into the United States since the immigration laws changed in 1965 (before that, black immigration was negligible). In 1970 there were 253,458 foreign-born black people in the United States (1.1 percent of the black population). In 1990 there were 1,455,294 foreign-born black people (4.9 percent of the black population).[13] Given that immigrants characteristically enter the country when they are young adults, the impact of roughly 1,200,000 of them on the labor market will be larger than one would expect from their mere numbers. On the face of it, at least, there is no reason to give recent black immigrants preference on compensatory grounds.

Premise 2. This debt is owed by "society" (or alternatively "the community").

Against this premise, it has been objected that there is no such entity as "society" that spans the time period between the infliction of wrongs by slave masters and the present day. It will not work simply to equate society with all those now living in the United States. People now living bear no responsibility for the harms inflicted on black people by slavery, so there is no reason why they should have to pay compensation. If something more than the current generation of Americans is meant, then this needs to be explicated.

One way of making "society" more concrete is to say that the U.S. government owes black people compensation. This seems appropriate for the damages inflicted by slavery after all, since the U.S. government did legally sanction slavery until the Civil War, and it is the sort of transgenerational entity that is needed to bridge the gap between the wrongs done the slaves and the present-day black population. Those who have not themselves harmed black people are nonetheless obliged to bear their share of any debts incurred by the federal government, and immigrants who choose to become citizens arguably commit themselves to doing this also. Narrowing down what is meant by the term "society" in this way has the advantage of identifying clearly an entity that is obligated to make compensation to black people. Its disadvantage, however, is that neither the injury caused by Jim Crow laws that existed only in southern states nor the harm black people have suffered from the racist attitudes and actions of individuals or groups of a more informal sort can be laid at the door of the federal government—or at least not without further argument.

It is possible that some understanding of "society" that is richer than simply the federal government can be articulated in a way that goes beyond mere hand-waving (and I will say more about this problem in Chapter 5). But when one is thinking in terms of compensatory justice it is essential to be precise about who exactly it is who is obligated to pay the compensation owed the victim and why. And the alternative that each non-black American directly owes compensation to the black community turns out to be extraordinarily difficult to defend. The reasons why this is so will be discussed under premise 4 below.

Premise 3. Being awarded jobs is a particularly appropriate way of compensating black people for the wrongs they have suffered.

Being awarded jobs is a more appropriate way of compensating people than giving them money, it is argued, because they give the person both a source of income and a stable place in society. Judith Jarvis Thomson puts the point as follows: "Financial compensation (the cost of which could be shared equally) slips through the fingers; having a job and discovering you do it well, yields—perhaps better than anything else—that very self-respect which blacks and women have had to do without."[14] A number of arguments have been offered against premise 3.

First, we ought not to regard jobs primarily as benefits to those who receive them. Each job carries with it responsibilities and an opportunity to make a contribution to the good of society in some way. It is in the interest of society that all jobs be done by those best able to perform the tasks involved, and selecting a candidate who is less qualified than other available candidates is therefore undesirable. Furthermore, to the extent that preferential hiring policies encourage job recipients to regard their jobs primarily as plums or as a payback for past wrongs, this will generate a sense of entitlement and undermine their motivation to perform them well. It is true that jobs are, among other things, benefits to their recipients in at least some ways, but we ought not to regard them primarily in this way. This objection is ultimately an objection to the whole idea of employing a compensatory model to jobs at all—except of course in cases where what the person is claiming is that he was unjustly deprived of a specific job.

Second, jobs are not owned by "society" or the U.S. government, and therefore businesses or universities are under no obligation to assume whatever debts of compensation are owed to black people. This point seems well taken in the case of private colleges, and especially that of religious universities that cannot under American law be instruments of the state. Let us, therefore, limit the scope of the argument to the case of state universities. However, since this argument assumes that it is appropriate to regard jobs as benefits or plums to be awarded as compensation, it is vulnerable to the first objection above.

Third, preferential hiring is a poorly chosen tool for compensating victims of social injustice because it compensates those who have been least harmed. Jobs go to those who are best qualified, leaving the most severely damaged (black ghetto residents, for example) uncompensated.[15] Black ghetto residents are not compensated or made whole from their injuries by the appointment of middle-class black people to the professorate. No doubt it is true that even those black people who are least damaged or who have been most successful at overcoming their injuries have still been harmed by racism in some ways,[16] but nonetheless a method of compensation that systematically compensates those least injured by the wrong that is being compensated to the exclusion of those most badly injured should certainly not be chosen as our primary mode of compensation.

Fourth, if part of our purpose in awarding jobs as compensation is to give the person a stable place in society and the self-respect that goes with having a job and finding out that he can do it well, then preferential hiring would seem to be an ineffective way of achieving this goal. Although such people's place in society may be stable if affirmative action pressures continue long enough for them to get tenure or other seniority privileges, it is questionable whether the desired effect on their self-respect will be attained by this route. If the recipient of the job believes he or she was hired because of race rather than qualifications, this militates against the sort of pride in one's accomplishment that helps build self-respect. And if colleagues perceive someone as "an affirmative action hire," this will undermine their respect for him or her and generate resentment. Promoting people to jobs they are poorly qualified for is more likely to lead to frustration and lowered self-respect than anything else. Defenders of preferential appointments do not, of course, advocate appointing poorly qualified people, but when universities are put under heavy pressure to increase the number of black teachers at a time when there are not enough well-qualified ones out there, the appointment of poorly qualified people is a likely result. Thomson, who originally formulated this argument, limited the scope of her argument to the case of tie-breaking affirmative action, so that these particular adverse effects upon one's self-respect would have been minimized.

In response to this fourth objection, it has been argued that the recipient of the job can, after all, believe that although he is less qualified, he nonetheless deserves the job for other reasons (as compensation for past wrongs, for example), but to the extent that these other reasons are that he has been damaged by being a victim of social injustice and thus cannot be judged by the same standards white people are, this does not seem terribly likely to promote self-respect either. One who feels he got a job only because the standards were lowered will certainly not gain as much self-respect from this as one who feels he genuinely achieved something excellent.[17] If the job in question is one that requires only fairly low-level skills that can be easily acquired on the job, so that the preferentially hired person can be expected to perform them as well as anyone else within a short period of time, this problem will not be so severe. But college teaching is not a job of this sort. Higher education is a field in which reputation is very important, both for schools and for individual professors, so anything that would lower the status of black professors in the eyes of others should be avoided if possible.[18]

One other argument that is sometimes offered in support of premise 3 is that in the absence of the wrongs black people have suffered in America, more of them would now hold prestigious and well-paying jobs, so that preferentially awarding such jobs to black people is only making them whole from their injuries. One writer argues thus, "We can . . . think of preferential treatment . . . as aiming at picking out candidates who would be deserving of the positions on grounds of competence, were it not for the present effects of past injustice."[19]

This sort of counterfactual meritocracy,[20] however, is suspect on a number of grounds. The arguments offered under premise 1 apply here—that to ascertain what proportion of American black people would now hold prestigious and lucrative jobs in the absence of slavery requires an impossible amount of counterfactual knowledge—and they apply more strongly still if we claim to know which candidate in particular would be most qualified in the absence of past injustice. Then there is the problem of which past injustices we are supposed to correct for[21]—namely, do we favor those who would have been most qualified in a perfectly just world or those who would have been most qualified in the absence of certain specific injustices? Finally, the problem of the unsituated self arises again. Who is the (hypothetically best-qualified) self who is entitled to preferential treatment (since the conditions under which this individual would have come into existence never obtained), and how is he or she connected with the self who is actually asserting a right to the job?

Premise 4. In order to compensate black people for their injuries, society may justifiably override any rights to equal consideration that other applicants might have (to simplify the argument, let us assume that the other applicants are white) and the rights of any other people affected by the appointment.

I have considered the question of whether compensation is owed before considering who must pay it because I am trying to construct the most persuasive compensatory argument possible, and rhetorically this strengthens the case for preferential hiring of black people (this strategy is frequently followed by plaintiff's attorneys in tort law cases).[22] Let us thus concede for the sake of argument that black people are owed a debt of compensation by society (understood as the U.S. government). But the question of who is to be made to bear the costs of compensation can now no longer be evaded.

If we also concede that jobs are the most appropriate form of compensation, we have a problem on our hands. Preferential hiring, even if it is the best way to make the victims of injustice whole, is in conflict with the white job candidate's right to fair (or equal) consideration for the position in question—the right to be judged only on the basis of criteria that are relevant to one's ability to perform the job.

The existence of such a right to fair consideration would seem to be something the defenders of preferential hiring are committed to by their own argument, since past job discrimination is one of the things for which they believe black people deserve compensation. If people did not have a right to fair consideration for jobs, then discrimination of the sort black people have suffered (being denied fair consideration for jobs) would not be wrong. Furthermore, if one adopted the utilitarian line of reasoning and argued that jobs should be filled on the basis of social utility alone, then it would be legitimate for employers to refuse to hire black people when, in their judgment, doing so would generate racial tensions that would diminish the efficiency of their workforce. Some people regard the right to fair consideration for jobs as so important that it cannot be overridden by black people's claim for compensation, and argue therefore that some second-best mode of compensation must be chosen instead of preferential hiring.[23] Others regard it as less important and more easily overridden. But even if other considerations justify overriding this right, its existence is generally conceded.

Not surprisingly this is the point at which the debate has become particularly heated, since people's careers are on the line. If preference were claimed only by black people, its practical impact in academia would be relatively small in most fields, but at this point the issue is one of principle. Preferential appointment to faculty positions, by its very nature, assigns the cost of compensation to a small number of individuals (rather than distributing it evenly as could be done if financial compensation were being made out of tax monies, for example), and the white candidate passed over (after investing considerable time, effort, and money in obtaining a Ph.D.) for a less qualified black candidate so that society may pay its debt of compensation owed to the black community may quite justifiably ask, "Why me?"

Justice is best served, of course, when it is possible to exact compensation from the person or persons who perpetrated the wrong. But when, as in the case of black people in America, what we are talking about includes wrongs going back hundreds of years, this avenue is not open. Slave owners, slave traders, and large numbers of those most responsible for these wrongs are long dead. To the degree that we can identify particular living individuals who have in fact unjustly discriminated against black people, there is nothing morally problematic about asking them to make some sort of amends. And if discriminatory practices could be firmly proved against a specific department within the university, then it would be appropriate to require that department to make some compensation to those injured. But no one believes that the rejected candidate who must bear the cost of compensation is particularly likely to have been guilty of perpetrating serious wrongs against black people. Indeed, the rejected candidate, usually being fresh out of graduate school (or worse yet, having been shunted around for years from one nontenure track or part-time job to another), has had very little power so far to harm or benefit anyone very much.

Why, then, is it legitimate for society to override the white candidate's right to fair consideration for the job and to demand this sacrifice of him or her? The usual answer is that the white job candidate has somehow benefited from wrongs done to black people, and that therefore being deprived of a job he would otherwise have received is merely being asked to repay some of the benefits he has unfairly reaped as a result of being white. At this point, critics of preferential policies have usually adopted one of two strategies.

(1) Concede that white people have benefited from unjust social practices that have caused harm to black people, but argue that for the most part they have benefited innocently from such practices (and perhaps have even opposed them) and therefore should not be obligated to make compensation to those who have been harmed.[24] They point out that the unjust advantages white people have received are usually something they have no choice about accepting (they were not, after all, offered the option of living in a fully just society—they had to live in the one we have), and in fact such advantages are often not the sort of thing that they could hand over to someone else even if they wanted to—their superior education, for example, or their self-confidence.

Some ingenious analogies have been advanced here. Robert Fullenwider compares the case of the young white applicant who has benefited from racist social arrangements to the following case. My neighbor contracts to have his driveway paved and tells the contractor to come to his address, where they will find a note describing the driveway to be paved. An enemy of his substitutes a description of my driveway, and they come while he is at work and pave my driveway. Even though I have benefited, I am not obligated to compensate my neighbor, since I am wholly innocent of the wrong. Just so, he says, the benefits enjoyed by white men are accepted for the most part involuntarily, and are ineradicable in that I cannot just hand them over to someone else (any more than I can remove the pavement from my driveway).

Bernard Boxill attempts to answer this argument by extending the analogy and asking whether, if the neighborhood had a prize for the best driveway on the block, Fullenwider would be entitled to insist that he deserves it, or whether if someone wanted to rent a driveway on the block he could insist that his driveway most deserves to be chosen (Boxill's answer to both questions is "no"). Thus, although he concedes to Fullenwider that the white candidate is not morally obligated to pay back to the black community the cost of the unfair advantages he or she has received, he denies that the white candidate "deserves" the benefits that would normally accrue to him or her as a result of those advantages (namely, in this case, the job).

Analogies are always imperfect, as becomes apparent when one tries to ascertain who is right in this debate. A paved driveway is radically unlike the allegedly unjust advantages enjoyed by the white candidate, in that what we are talking about is the sort of person he or she has become through the complex interaction of biology, nurture, education, culture, and innate (or at least very deeply ingrained) character traits—at least insofar as these have an impact on his or her potential performance as a teacher. Nor is a job like a prize (since it involves duties as well as benefits, and other people are affected by how well one performs those duties), and the analogy with someone renting a driveway is so weak as to be a nonstarter. The other problem is that on disputed points appeals to intuition often do not settle things, since people's intuitions are likely to differ on such issues. It may be obvious to Boxill that Fullenwider would not deserve to have his driveway chosen for the prize, but others would assert with equal conviction that it is obvious he would deserve it.

Some very thorny issues in social philosophy about the basis of desert underlie these conflicting intuitions, and the conflict cannot be resolved without an in-depth excursion into the theory of justice, which cannot be undertaken here.[25] Certainly, the law would not require Fullenwider to make compensation to his neighbor in such a case, since he is not liable for "unjust enrichment."[26] And if he is not guilty of any injustice, then the law, at least, would not debar him from receiving any benefits that might accrue to him as a result of having a particularly high-quality driveway.

(2) Concede that all white people have benefited from practices that have unfairly disadvantaged black people, and therefore owe them compensation even though they are for the most part "innocent" beneficiaries, but argue that even so, preferential hiring is not a morally permissible way of exacting that compensation because it allocates the costs of compensation in an unfair way.

It is unfair in three ways. (1) It distributes the burden unevenly, in that only a few individuals are made to bear all the costs of compensation. If all white people have benefited from the wrongs, all should pay. (2) It is also unfair in that this way of doing it lays the heaviest burden on those who are least likely to have been perpetrators of the wrongs being compensated. (3) Those made to bear the cost of compensation are not only innocent in the sense of not having perpetrated injustices against black people, they also have had the least opportunity to benefit from these wrongs.

Just as on the black side of the ledger it is those least damaged who receive compensation, it is the young white academic who is asked to pay the compensation instead of the older white academic who may well have perpetrated injustice against black people, or at least has had longer to benefit from it. A former colleague of mine called the philosophy behind this method of compensation "Mea culpa, you-a pay-a."

In her defense of preferential hiring, Thomson acknowledges the justice of this complaint, and says, "[I]t seems to me in place to expect the occupants of comfortable professorial chairs to contribute in some way, to make some form of return to the young white male who bears the cost, and is turned away."[27] To my knowledge, no attempt has been made to ask tenured professors to do this. And in any case, what could make up to someone for being prevented from pursuing his chosen career? Retraining in another profession? Several years' salary? A lifetime salary? Many teachers view their work as a vocation central to their identity and therefore nothing could adequately make up for being denied the opportunity to practice it.

Although both of these lines of argument have some validity, it is, I think, important to examine a bit more carefully the prior claim that all white people have benefited from unjust social institutions that disadvantage black people. One argument for this claim focuses on the wrongs inflicted on black people by slavery. The other one focuses instead on the benefits the white candidate has received in his lifetime through the operation of unjust social institutions that disfavor black people.

The first argument was formulated by Boxill in his article "The Morality of Reparation," published in 1973. In it he argued that each white person has, in fact, benefited from the wrongs inflicted on black people by slavery—an institution universally accepted as unjust—and that therefore the benefits white people have received as a result of this are unjust in the sense that they have their source in an unjust institution. His argument is suggestive but rather sketchy. He envisions the "white community" as like a corporation or a company, whose members (whether or not they joined voluntarily as immigrants did) must help bear the costs of any debts incurred by the company. The wealth generated by the unpaid labor of slaves was passed on by the slave owners to their descendants to the relative exclusion of the descendants of slaves (this argument thus focuses on the material rather than the cultural damage inflicted on the slaves). Since this wealth was diffused within the white community rather than being limited to the descendants of slave owners, white people generally have been recipients of benefits to which the descendants of the slaves have "at least partial rights." They therefore now owe compensation to the black community.

The first difficulty with this argument concerns whether it is legitimate to regard "the white community" as like a company or corporation in the way his argument requires. First, the "white community" lacks a formal unifying institutional structure. An Indian tribe or a nation state has institutions set up for joint decision making by members of the community and designed to pass on a way of life to future generations. The "white community" does not have such institutional structures. Second, and relatedly, to think of the "white community" in this way is to overlook the extraordinary diversity that exists among "white" people. It is easy to think of the WASPs who inhabit the boardrooms of major corporations and the corridors of government power as "the white community" and totally forget the poor WASPs in Appalachia or the Minnesota Iron Range, and the large number of immigrant groups who currently face severe prejudice themselves, such as Portuguese, Poles, Arabs, and Italians. In addition to severe ethnic tensions there are also class conflicts and regional tensions (for example, between Northerners and Southerners) among white people.

Boxill's argument is also suspect on purely historical and economic grounds. The image of a stream of wealth generated by slavery being handed down from generation to generation within the white community is highly questionable. It is hotly disputed among historians whether slavery was an economically profitable institution.[28] And even if it was profitable, slaves were held only in the South, only 25 percent of free Southerners had any connection with slavery either through family ties or direct ownership (and of these only 12 percent had five or more slaves in 1860),[29] and the large slave owners (the ones who had made the most profit) were for the most part ruined by the war. Many had their plantations burned, and those who had made money had invested heavily in Confederate war bonds that were worthless after the war, so that after the war they had very little to hand on to their children. Granted, there were Northerners who had made money in the slave trade and were not ruined by the war, but the slave trade was outlawed in 1808, and the wealth generated by it was not large relative to other sources of wealth such as manufacturing.[30] Furthermore, not all white people gained from slavery even during its heyday; the wages of the white poor were forced down by their having to compete economically with slave labor.

Thus if a river of wealth has been passed along within the white community over the generations since the Civil War, the wealth generated by the unpaid labor of slaves was a very small tributary. This is especially true when we consider the magnitude of immigration during this period. In 1860 the Negro population was 2,216,744 and the white population was 13,811,387.[31] In 1995 the black population was 32,672,000, and the white population was 216,470,000.[32] Almost 12 million immigrants have come in between 1971 and 1990 alone,[33] and 40 million between 1861 and 1970.[34] Many of these immigrants arrived with only the clothes on their backs, and whatever wealth they amassed was not based on the unjust gains from slavery. Boxill's argument that all white people owe compensation to the black community as a consequence of slavery, therefore, turns out not to be very persuasive.

If it can't be shown that each member of the white community has benefited from the wrongs inflicted on black people by slavery, can it be shown that he or she has benefited from presently existing social institutions that unjustly harm black people? Probably the reason why this point has not been discussed more in the literature is because it is formulated in such a vague way that it is hard to know how to approach the question. What institutions in particular are involved, and why should a search committee assume automatically that any white candidate has benefited from institutions that unjustly harm black people and that his or her advantages are therefore somehow "unfair"? What is the standard of fairness? A society in which everyone has exactly the same advantages? A society in which black and white people are represented in the same proportion in all economic classes or in all professions? A society in which each person gets what he deserves on the basis of his own efforts? A society in which prejudice never interferes with anyone's life prospects? No doubt it is unreasonable to expect arguments in social philosophy to have the sort of precision we aspire to in logic or metaphysics, but more is required than the mere assertion that the white candidate has benefited from injustice to black people and that therefore his or her advantages are unfair.

Even if, other things being equal, having white skin is an advantage (in many contexts), it is only one among many unchosen traits that are advantageous, and whatever positive effect it might have can easily be offset by others that are just as apparent as skin color—say, being ugly, or having an accent and manner that identifies one as lower class,[35] as from a different region (say, having a Brooklyn accent in West Texas, or a southern drawl in Cambridge, Massachusetts), or as a member of an ethnic group widely disliked in the area where one lives. Society is bitterly divided along all sorts of lines. Regional hostilities, religious antagonisms, class tensions, a variety of inter-ethnic prejudices, and ideologically motivated hatreds may well be more important in the 1990s than white on black racial prejudice.[36] To cast the whole dispute in terms of whites versus blacks involves a dangerous oversimplification of social reality. White people are not a unified group and not all of them have benefited from wrongs suffered by black people.

But even if racial prejudice were as major a factor in our society as defenders of preferential hiring believe it is, black people would not be the only losers from it. The classical Marxist argument that racism is harmful to the white working class because it divides workers, and thereby weakens their position vis-à-vis the ruling class, has considerable force. Casting our social problems, as this argument does, exclusively in terms of race impedes cooperation and crowds out other issues of common concern to both black and white working-class people—such as structural shifts in the economy that eliminate blue-collar jobs, plant closings, and the flight of capital to Third World countries.

And if we focus our attention on academia, the situation has changed greatly in the past twenty-five years. Colleges are presently competing fiercely with each other for qualified black students[37] and faculty, so the white candidate may well have been harmed already by preferential programs favoring minority students sometime earlier in his or her academic career.

I conclude, then, that no persuasive argument has been offered justifying the overriding of the white candidate's right to equal consideration for the job. If one accepts premises 1–3, the fairest way to award black people compensation would be to have the government fund (out of tax money) special set-aside professorial chairs to be awarded only to black Americans.[38] There is, however, the likelihood that those holding such positions would bear the stigma of being second rate (for if they had been as well qualified as the white candidates they could presumably have been appointed to regular positions). It would be fairer than what we now have, although it would still have the implication that students would be receiving less good instruction than they otherwise could have.

The rights and interests of students are, after all, also infringed by preferential appointment of female and minority faculty, since they receive poorer-quality instruction than they otherwise would have. The main reason why Thomson advocates only tie-breaking is because she believes the university has a responsibility to provide its students with the best teachers it can afford (after all, students are paying customers), and that failure to do so is a violation of their rights. The injury to students is less severe (every student has a few bad teachers during his college career) than that inflicted on rejected applicants. But although the injury is less severe it is spread over a very large number of people—namely, all the students who will be taught by the professor in question.

Conclusion. Assuming, then, that the black candidate for a job possesses at least the basic or minimum qualifications to perform the job, he or she ought to be appointed.

Defenders of preferential appointment policies do not wish their argument to be taken to justify appointing people unqualified to perform the duties associated with the job. Hence they qualify their position by stipulating that the preferentially appointed person must have at least the basic qualifications needed for the job. But how widely is this principle to be extended? The point is often made that in some professions it is important to hire only the most qualified. Common examples are airplane pilots and surgeons. But if a grocery clerk is preferentially hired over another job applicant who is faster at ringing things up, this may be irritating, but people would not become nearly so upset over this as they would if they knew they were to be operated on by a preferentially hired surgeon.

The more important a service is perceived to be, the less likely it is that the recipient will be satisfied with anything less than the best-qualified person. To the extent that we are willing to accept the minimally or basically qualified over the better qualified as college teachers, this then seems to carry with it the unfortunate implication that we don't really regard the services performed by teachers as all that important. If, however, it can be shown either that our current criteria for teaching excellence are biased in ways that lead us to systematically overlook the types of teaching excellence characteristically manifested by black people, or that being black is itself (for one reason or another) a positive qualification for being a good teacher or a good teacher for certain students, then this objection will have been successfully answered. These points will be addressed in Chapters 3 and 4.

III. Application to Other Groups

Native Americans

The case for preferential hiring of Native Americans is closest to the case for black people in that it includes ancient wrongs and a significant element of damage to their traditional culture and way of life. The case is weaker in that they were not enslaved. But it is more manageable in that their material damage claim is more clearly defined because often they were unjustly deprived of identifiable pieces of land, and can point to specific treaties made and broken by the U.S. government. Also, since Native Americans are organized into tribes, there is a representative body to whom compensation can be paid. For these reasons, many Indian tribes have already been awarded compensation by the U.S. government. There are some particularly thorny legal questions that arise in connection with rights to land, however, and since the number of Native Americans seeking employment as college teachers is so small, I will not go into all the fine points here. Suffice it to say that although their case for being awarded land is stronger, and their tribal structure makes the mechanics of compensation easier than in the case of black Americans, their claim to preferential hiring for skilled jobs (for example, as college teachers) is not significantly stronger and is open to the same sorts of problems discussed above in relation to compensation to black people.

Hispanics and Asians

Ethnic groups that have suffered discrimination resemble black people and Native Americans in that their distinctive culture is to some degree passed down from parents to children; if one generation has been seriously disadvantaged by discrimination, this will affect the next generation. The groups most commonly proposed as beneficiaries of preferential treatment are Hispanics and Asians. On compensatory grounds, at least, their case for preferential treatment is weaker than that for black people and Native Americans.

First, discrimination against them has for the most part not been officially sanctioned by the government (with the exception of Japanese interned during World War II). They were not enslaved, nor was their land stolen (with the possible exception of the Mexican American War, which would imply benefits only to Mexican Americans and not to Hispanics generally).[39]

Second, both groups are composed largely of fairly recent immigrants (over half of our Asian population in 1991, for example, entered the country during the preceding twenty years, and the population of Hispanic origin increased from 14 million to 23 million between 1980 and 1991),[40] so that much of the oppression they have suffered is not something Americans are responsible for.

Third, and most important, the selection of Hispanics and Asians (in addition of course to black people and Native Americans), and only these groups, appears arbitrary from a moral point of view. Ethnic prejudices are extremely widespread and various. In some regions Poles are hated, in others it is Portuguese, Greeks, Italians, or Arabs. Skin color cannot be the criterion for selecting those who deserve compensation, since Indians and Pakistanis frequently have very dark skins, and members of many other groups are at least as dark-skinned as many Hispanics. Is there any reason to suppose that Hispanics and Asians have suffered more unjust discrimination than other groups?

Jews have been subjected to discrimination based on descent, which is often of an intense and visceral character not unlike that suffered by black people and yet no one proposes that they be preferentially hired for prestigious and lucrative jobs. The most obvious reason for this is that large numbers of them already hold such jobs.

But just because someone has managed to overcome the damaging effects of discrimination, this does not imply that he is not deserving of compensation. Boxill argues that middle-class blacks who have overcome their injuries are not what they would have been had they never been injured, and that "though I may be a better person for prevailing over unfair obstacles, this does not absolve my injurers from the obligation to compensate me."[41] It would certainly seem that this argument applies equally to Jews. Perhaps in the absence of discrimination a still larger proportion of doctors, lawyers, and professors would be of Jewish descent.

Women

The compensatory argument is weakest for women. Like black people they were at one time denied the right to vote, and there have been some restrictions on their right to own property. But they are unlike black people and ethnic groups in that they are neither economically marginalized[42] nor bearers of a distinctive culture. They and the men with whom their lives are intertwined in various ways share the same language (including regional accent), for the most part have similar religious, political, and moral values, and are members of the same social class as their fathers (when they are children) and husbands (when married). And unlike being black, being a woman is not hereditary, since women have sons as well as daughters, and fathers as well as mothers.

In light of these differences, one of the motivations for according preferential treatment to black people and ethnic minorities does not hold for women. Having black skin is hereditary, and black people tend to live in areas apart from white people.[43] The economic and educational disadvantages suffered by black parents are handed on to their children. Black people now living have thus been harmed by injustices done to their parents and ancestors, and will pass them on to generations of black children yet unborn even if discrimination were ended today.[44] The same is true, although to a smaller degree, of at least some ethnic groups. But since being a woman is not hereditary, and women do not usually live in self-contained communities, the disadvantages suffered by one generation of women, qua women, are not necessarily handed on to their daughters. Therefore, in their case, simply abolishing discrimination would enable women to compete on equal terms with men.

It might be objected that the disadvantages of women are in fact handed on from one generation to another. For women model themselves on their mothers, who modeled themselves on their mothers, and so on, and thus they have developed a conception of what it is to be a woman—an understanding of the proper role for women—that disadvantages them in a variety of ways. They are, for example, encouraged to center their lives more around their families and children than men are, and this penalizes them in their careers and leaves them vulnerable to exploitation by men.[45] Thus although women do not have a separate culture, they tend to be socialized into certain roles within the common culture they share with men, and these roles are obstacles to their success in the competitive world of careers.

The argument here is akin to the cultural damage argument discussed above, and is vulnerable to the same objections. Being socialized in such a way that one's motivation and capacity to succeed in an individualistic and competitive society are maximized is not necessarily an unmixed blessing. And to the extent that a woman is seeking compensation for being the sort of person she is, the problem of the unsituated self again presents itself. Who is the self who stands outside the presently existing woman with her actual values and preferences and who is entitled to be compensated for her socialization?

Not only is the case for according compensation to women as a group weaker than it is for black people, but doing so would have very far-reaching consequences. Women make up over half the population, so including them creates a new minority—white men. This greatly exacerbates the problem of distributing the costs of affirmative action fairly. As the list of groups to be compensated grows and the class of persons being asked to pay therefore shrinks, the burden upon each of them necessarily grows, whatever method of compensation we employ, and preferential hiring makes the burden heavier still because it singles out an even smaller group (white men who lack tenure or other seniority protections) to bear the entire cost of compensating wronged groups.

Furthermore, assuming for the moment that compensation is an appropriate approach to social problems, adding half the human race to the list of groups deserving compensation will diminish the amount of compensation received by the black community and Native Americans (since neither jobs nor resources are infinite), and these groups clearly have a prior claim to that of women. No doubt this is one of the reasons why proportional representation is an attractive goal; each group is accorded its proper share.

I will conclude by briefly considering the most frequently cited argument for preferential appointment of female faculty—that given by Thomson in 1973. She does not defend the claim that women in general are deserving of compensation (although she tends to assume this), but she does give some reasons why academic women in particular deserve it. Female job candidates will, she says, have suffered discrimination earlier in their careers, while white males will have enjoyed unfair advantages already. Men have often been

> direct beneficiaries of policies which excluded or down-graded blacks and women—perhaps in school admissions, perhaps in access to financial aid, perhaps elsewhere; and even those who did not directly benefit in this way had, at any rate, the advantage in the competition which comes of confidence in one's full membership, and of one's rights being recognized as a matter of course.[46]

The female candidate will have been correspondingly disadvantaged. Women, she argues, have often not been taken seriously intellectually, and even if they have not themselves been downgraded for being women, they have seen other women downgraded and have therefore lost self-confidence and self-respect.

In light of these facts, she argues that it is legitimate to award the job to a woman in cases where the candidates are equally qualified in the opinion of the hiring officer. There are, however, some difficulties with her argument.

For one thing, her rhetoric appears to justify more than her argument actually supports. She constantly uses the term "preferential," and the sort of evening-the-score rationale she employs could easily be used to support preference of a stronger sort than mere tie-breaking. In fact she virtually invites the reader to do so, saying that she thinks her argument could be appealed to, to justify preferential hiring outside the narrow range of cases in which the candidates are equally qualified (although she herself will draw no conclusions beyond the tie-breaking case).[47] It is not surprising, then, that many people seem unaware that she defends only tie-breaking and appeal to her argument to defend stronger forms of preference. (Her reason for not defending more than tie-breaking is her conviction that students, and taxpayers at state schools, have a right to the best-quality instruction the school can afford to offer.)

Another problem is that Thomson's argument appears to assume that women are fungible. This is just false. Awarding a job to one woman does not compensate another. Unlike being black, being a woman is not hereditary; younger female academics have not been directly disadvantaged by discrimination against older ones. All too often search committees believe themselves to have righted past wrongs against women by appointing a woman fresh out of graduate school. They are likely to prefer to appoint younger women because their employment records do not contain awkward gaps, because they are believed to be more familiar with recent developments in their fields, because they are willing to work for lower salaries, or because they are perceived as less threatening to men who are not at ease with regarding a woman as an intellectual equal. But surely, if compensation is owed, it is older women unfairly kept back by discrimination who ought to receive it rather than women just out of graduate school.

Furthermore, in light of the fact that women are now doing considerably better in academia, and in education at all levels, than they were twenty-five years ago when Thomson was writing, one can no longer assume that every female candidate will have been disadvantaged in the ways she mentions. In 1994, 65.4 percent of women compared to only 59.7 percent of men went on to college from high school (up from 37.9 for women and 54 percent for men in 1960).[48] While in 1976–77 423,476 women and 494,424 men obtained bachelor's degrees, in 1991–92 the figures were 612,857 women and 516,976 men.[49] And the statistics on earned doctorates and first professional degrees presented in Chapter 1 show an even more dramatic improvement for women. These figures may not show that academia is a bed of roses for women, but they are not indicative of the sort of pervasive downgrading of women alleged by Thomson.

The situation of white men has also changed in the past twenty-five years, and one can no longer assume that they have received unfair advantages earlier in their careers. Indeed they are more likely to have been disadvantaged in terms of admissions and financial aid at least. Nor, in light of the present cultural and political climate, can they be fairly described as having confidence in their full membership (in the community), and of their rights being recognized as a matter of course.

It may be objected that the improved situation of women in academia is the result of affirmative action policies and that if they were discontinued things would return to their previous condition. Whether this would happen is, however, doubtful. Women are not, I believe, less able intellectually than men. Their relative scarcity among the professoriate had many causes other than discrimination.[50] Hence, once the ice has been broken and women have begun to prove themselves in various fields, no further intervention is needed. One should not simply assume that white men are irredeemably prejudiced and incapable of learning.

IV. Conclusion

The results of our examination of the compensatory argument are rather troubling. Clearly black people do seem to have the strongest case for compensation. Their ancestors were brought here as slaves, and since voluntary immigration by black people has been small relative to the American black population as a whole (at least before 1965), having black skin marks one as having had ancestors who were slaves. (This is not true in the countries of Western Europe, for example, who have black immigrants but never had slavery on their own soil.) And the harms inflicted on them by slavery have been passed on to subsequent generations of black people. Slavery has left deep marks not only on the descendants of the slaves, but on our whole society, and the way in which we think about issues of poverty and class.

Analyzing and addressing the problems of black people in terms drawn from tort law, however, does not work very well. It is impossible to quantify the damages owed. An important element in the damages is nonmaterial. Also, we lack the necessary counterfactual knowledge about what would have happened in the absence of the wrongs in question, and therefore we can't determine what would count as making the victims whole. In the absence of slavery, the current generation of American black people would not exist as the biological individuals they now are. Nor would they exist as the individuals they now are insofar as they have been shaped by a culture itself affected by the slave experience of their ancestors. In the absence of slavery they, therefore, would not be the people they are, and there is no pure transcendent self who can stand outside of the history that has made them who they are to claim compensation.

But the fact that it seems inadequate to capture the moral claims of black people is not the only problem with trying to apply tort law categories to social problems in this way. Many of the difficulties that philosophers have raised against the compensatory argument stem from trying to fit complex historical facts into a plaintiff-defendant structure—for example, the problems that arise when we try to apply the principles of compensatory justice to groups (instead of individuals), which have been so often noted in the literature, or the difficulty with pinning down who precisely it is who is obligated to make compensation and why. Since it is impossible to identify or locate most of the actual perpetrators of injustice, someone else must be found to pay, which leads to new injustices. Treating jobs as a form of compensation is inevitable when we employ the tort law model to justify preferential hiring, but this practice is open to all sorts of serious objections.[51]

We seem to be moving toward a tort law model of society as made up of victims and perpetrators who can be made to pay—that is, plaintiffs and defendants. But making the tort law model so central to one's way of thinking about social problems has deep and dangerous consequences. First, it is bound to encourage the breakdown of society into competing tribes who think primarily in terms of grievance and entitlement. This has the effect of undermining any sense that we all belong to one community and are therefore obligated to contribute to the common good. When this happens, those claiming compensation can no longer rely on the existence of a "society" or "community" willing to assume the burden of compensation; the compensatory argument thus cuts the ground out from under itself.

Second, thinking in these terms leads the different groups to form shifting political alliances in search of a vulnerable defendant with deep pockets (as occurs in tort law). This has a corrupting effect on public discourse, for it becomes necessary for political reasons to lump together groups that have, in fact, very different bases for their claims. Thus people concerned mainly about the problems of women in the academy (e.g., Thomson) simply tack on blacks, or those concerned mainly about black people (e.g., Boxill) tack on women, and soon a kind of formulaic list of oppressed groups deserving compensation develops and is repeated by everyone. When dissimilar claims are thus combined, what tends to be used to hold it all together is vague allegations of injustice intended to generate feelings of guilt. Given that the compensatory argument does not yield any clear answer to how much is owed, demands threaten to become endless, and to the extent that guilt is used as a political weapon, a great deal of anger is generated that could easily become very socially destructive.

V. Transition: A Cross-Temporal Argument

In light of the difficulties with the compensatory argument, perhaps we can defend affirmative action by reconceptualizing the point of such policies, and not thinking too rigidly in terms of making reparation for past wrongs. In his book *Autonomy and Self-Respect*, Thomas Hill argues that the point of preferential policies is to restore a relationship of trust and respect that has been damaged by past injuries. It is thus backward-looking because it is past wrongs that make such policies necessary, but the compensation offered is viewed more as a gesture meant to communicate that we genuinely deplore and wish to dissociate ourselves from the evil social practices of which they have been victims than as a payback for past wrongs. In fact, to think in terms of something that can be paid back is, he argues, to be silent about the insulting nature of racism and sexism and the way in which "prejudicial attitudes damaged self-esteem, undermined motivations, limited realistic options, and made even 'officially open' opportunities seem undesirable."[52]

The message that affirmative action is intended to communicate, then, is this:

> We acknowledge that you have been wronged—if not by specific injuries which could be named and repaid, at least by the humiliating and debilitating attitudes prevalent in our country and our institutions. . . . We welcome you respectfully into the university community and ask you to take a full share of the responsibilities as well as the benefits.[53]

More than mere words is needed to convey this message, and thus "positive efforts, even at considerable cost, may be needed to express appropriately and convincingly what needs to be said."[54]

Recognizing that the kinds of wrongs that affirmative action is intended to remedy are not merely material or quantifiable, and that it is important to think about how to rebuild a relationship of mutual trust and respect, is, I think, a good first step toward rethinking the justification for such policies. But there are some features of Hill's argument that are troubling upon closer examination.

First, he fails to distinguish adequately between affirmative action of a basically procedural sort—wider outreach, communicating a welcoming attitude toward female and minority applicants, etc.—and actually giving such candidates preference over equally or better qualified white men. The message communicated will differ in the two cases.

Second, like Thomson, he treats women and black people as fungible. He refrains from falling into regarding jobs as "goodies" to be distributed in the way she does. But nonetheless he seems to believe that appointing and welcoming one woman or black person will somehow heal the damaged relationship with others. In this regard his argument resembles the "morality play" view of affirmative action which I discuss in Chapter 3.

Third, the wounded-puppy image of women and black people that emerges from his argument is one that members of both groups may find demeaning.

Fourth, there is some unclarity about just which attitudes and practices the search committee is deploring and dissociating itself from. If the wrong to be deplored and acknowledged is slavery, virtually no one believes it was a morally defensible institution. That Americans do not condone slavery has already been proved by the fact that the Union fought an extraordinarily bloody and costly war, at least in large part to bring slavery to an end, and that a special amendment was added to the Constitution forbidding it. Perhaps it would have been better if at the end of the Civil War each freed slave had been given forty acres and a mule, as some people suggested at the time. But we can't do that now.

If the problem is the current racist and sexist attitudes prevalent in our society, there does seem to be something odd about making amends for wrongs committed by others. As I understand Hill, he is saying that it is necessary to do this because women and black people have, as a result of insults and injuries inflicted by others, become distrustful and skeptical about the good intentions of white men generally. Hence white men must prove their sincerity by actions and not just words.

But more is involved than merely the racist and sexist institutions and attitudes prevalent in the broader society. This is clearest in the two-person analogue to the hiring case, in which he speaks of two people, John and Mary. Other people have been abusive and insulting to Mary. "If the insults were deep and it is not entirely clear whether or not he really associated himself with them, then mere words may not be enough to convey the message *or even to assure himself of his own sincerity*" (emphasis added).[55] By analogy, then, the search committee members are trying not merely to dissociate themselves from the evils of sexism and racism. They are also concerned to make amends for possible traces of racism and sexism that may linger (unbeknownst to themselves) in their own hearts, and to prove to themselves and others that they are really sincere.

Once the message to be communicated is spelled out in this way, the morality of using preferential appointment policies as a way of conveying it appears very questionable. Making a serious effort to reach out to formerly excluded groups and being genuinely welcoming to them would be entirely appropriate. But when actual preference is given, Hill's argument presents a rather less benign face. For it condones sacrificing the interests of innocent third parties (the white male candidates) in order to allow older tenured academics to dissociate themselves from the evils of sexism and racism, to make amends for whatever traces of these may still linger in their hearts, and to assure themselves of their own sincerity.

Should they wish to make sacrifices out of what is their own, this might be admirable. (Even here, to the extent that they are motivated by a need to defend themselves against their own feelings of guilt, this does not bode well for the future of their relationship with those to whom preferences are extended.) Moreover, since the evils of racism and especially of sexism are so vague and open-ended, and extend well beyond the university, the possibilities for generating guilt are virtually endless, and there is a danger that both parties will slip into an unhealthy relationship based on the manipulation of guilt, constantly expiated at the expense of innocent third parties.

Notes

1. In using the term "race" as I have done, I do not mean to beg any questions about the reality of race above and beyond the fact that some social distinctions have historically been made on the basis of skin color. I am, myself, inclined to agree with Barbara Fields that there is no biological basis for racial classifications. Barbara Fields, "Race, Politics, and Education" (lecture delivered at Providence College, February 13, 1993).

2. This is the version most frequently offered in the literature. See, e.g., Judith Jarvis Thomson, "Preferential Hiring," *Philosophy & Public Affairs* 2, 4 (1973), and Robert Fullenwider, "Preferential Hiring and Compensation," *Social Theory and Practice* 3 (Spring 1975), 307–20. These articles are reprinted in Steven M. Cahn, ed., *The Affirmative Action Debate* (New York: Routledge, 1995).

3. Wrong and harm are different. I can wrong someone without harming him; for example, a doctor who prescribes John an experimental medication that carries with it serious health risks and does not inform him of this fact wrongs him. I can also harm Mary without wronging her, as for example if I am (unbeknownst to myself) coming down with a serious contagious disease and go to her house for dinner the night before I get sick and she catches it.

4. Slavery in Africa, however, was less harsh than slavery as practiced in the South.

5. Defenders of affirmative action tend to pass very quickly from individual injustices such as my stealing your bicycle or hitting you with my car to social injustice as though there were no difference between the two sorts of cases. But the whole notion of social injustice is a far more complicated one, and not everyone even acknowledges that there is such a thing. See, e.g., Irving Kristol, "A Capitalist Conception of Justice," in Richard DeGeorge and Joseph Pichler, eds., *Ethics, Free Enterprise and Public Policy* (New York: Oxford University Press, 1980), and Roger Scruton, *The Meaning of Conservatism* (Totowa, N.J.: Barnes and Noble, 1980), 86–90.

6. If the law courts are now overcrowded with cases, imagine what would happen if people were allowed to collect for damages to their parents and ancestors!

7. I borrow the term "ancient wrongs" from George Sher, who has an interesting discussion of some of the problems raised by trying to right ancient wrongs in "Ancient Wrongs and Modern Rights," *Philosophy & Public Affairs* 10, 1(1981).

8. Philosophical accounts of counterfactuals involve possible worlds, and judgments of relative similarity among them, that quickly become intellectually unmanageable. For a sophisticated account, see David Lewis, *Counterfactuals* (Cambridge: Harvard University Press, 1973).

9. For a valuable account of the controversies raging among historians over the cultural impact of slavery, see Peter Novik, *That Noble Dream: The "Objectivity Question" and the American Historical Profession* (Cambridge: Cambridge University Press, 1988), 472–91.

10. Bernard Boxill in his 1978 defense of preferential hiring, for example, considers the argument that black people are underrepresented in desirable

positions because of cultural traits such as a lack of appropriate work habits and discipline. He argues that these sorts of deeply ingrained traits may in fact inhibit the success of black people, but that black culture has evolved in the way it has because blacks have been driven to these sorts of behavior patterns by impossibly unjust situations, and that therefore such traits can legitimately be classed as "unjust injuries." Bernard Boxill, "The Morality of Preferential Hiring," *Philosophy & Public Affairs* 7, 3 (1978), 255. Reprinted in Steven M. Cahn, *The Affirmative Action Debate.*

11. Particularly powerful criticisms of the whole notion of the disembodied or "unencumbered" self have been developed by Alasdair MacIntyre in *After Virtue* (Notre Dame: University of Notre Dame Press, 1984) and Michael Sandel in *Liberalism and the Limits of Justice* (New York: Cambridge University Press, 1982).

12. Shelby Steele, *The Content of Our Character* (New York: St. Martin's Press, 1990), 119.

13. *Census of Population*, ch. C, "General Social and Economic Characteristics," part I, PC80-1-C1. Tables 43 and 77. U.S. Department of Commerce, December 1983.

14. Thomson, "Preferential Hiring," 383.

15. This argument is made, for example, by Alan Goldman in *Justice and Reverse Discrimination* (Princeton: Princeton University Press, 1979), 91.

16. A point made by Boxill in "The Morality of Preferential Hiring," 246–47.

17. A recent Doonesbury cartoon illustrates this particularly well. A child returns from summer camp with an armful of engraved cups, ribbons, and trophies. One, he says, was given to him for showing up at camp on the right day, another for remembering his computer password, another for "not missing too many archery practices." His mother says, "My, you must feel very proud of yourself." The boy throws a cup over his shoulder and says, "Yeah, right, Mom." A real-world analogue, involving admissions to a highly prestigious law school, is a case in which numerous Chicana and Chicano students went to the Dean singly and in groups, basically saying, "Tell us we weren't preferentially admitted." Since they would not in fact have been there but for preferential admission policies, the Dean was in a very difficult position.

18. Stephen Carter, for example, in *Reflections of an Affirmative Action Baby* (New York: Basic Books, 1991) expresses concern that the qualifications of black faculty will be undermined by affirmative action. Although she is somewhat vague about just what she is proposing, Gertrude Ezorsky's recommendations for increasing the number of black college professors come dangerously close to treating them as second-class apprentice college teachers. Gertrude Ezorsky, *Racism and Justice: The Case for Affirmative Action* (Ithaca: Cornell University Press, 1991), 42–44.

19. Dorit Bar-On, "Discrimination, Individual Justice, and Preferential Treatment," *Public Affairs Quarterly* 4, 2 (April 1990), 128.

20. I borrow the term "counterfactual meritocracy" from Robert Simon's discussion of Bar-On's argument, "Affirmative Action and the University: Faculty Appointment and Preferential Treatment," in Steven M. Cahn, ed.,

Affirmative Action and the University: A Philosophical Inquiry (Philadelphia: Temple University Press, 1993), 70.

21. I have taken this argument from Simon, "Affirmative Action," 68–69.

22. In fact, I tend to agree with Robert Amdur, who argues that the question of who should pay and why is too important to be postponed until all the other issues have been discussed. So I am loading the case in favor of the compensatory argument by proceeding as I have. Robert Amdur, "Compensatory Justice: The Question of Costs," *Political Theory* 7, 2 (May 1979), 229–44. Reprinted in Steven Cahn, ed., *The Affirmative Action Debate*.

23. See, e.g., Amdur, "Compensatory Justice."

24. See Simon, "Affirmative Action," 318, for an argument to the effect that one who benefits from an unjust social institution need not owe compensation if he has himself suffered from similarly unjust social institutions.

25. For a particularly illuminating discussion of the basis of desert and the way it is connected with theories of justice, see Sandel, *Liberalism and the Limits of Justice*, 82–95.

26. According to the law of "unjust enrichment" the neighbor would have to show that he conferred a benefit on Fullenwider for which he expected compensation and that Fullenwider had either "expressly or implicitly" requested the benefits. *The Guide to American Law: Everyone's Legal Encyclopedia* (St. Paul, Minn.: West, 1985), 210.

27. Thomson, "Preferential Hiring," 384.

28. Eugene Genovese points out numerous ways in which the system of slave labor led to low worker productivity and retarded technological progress. *The Political Economy of Slavery* (New York: Vintage Books, 1967).

29. See Kenneth Stampp, *The Peculiar Institution* (New York: Vintage Books, 1956), 30.

30. Although it could be argued that institutions that are known to have been founded largely on the basis of money from the slave trade (e.g., Brown University) may owe special compensation to the descendants of slaves.

31. *Historical Statistics of the United States* (Washington, D.C.: U.S. Government Printing Office, 1976).

32. *Statistical Abstract of the United States, 1995.*

33. *Statistical Abstract of the United States 1994*, 11.

34. *Statistical Abstract of the United States 1993*, 10.

35. The English have always been exquisitely aware of the nuances of accents and what they indicate about one's social status. Americans are considerably less open about the way a person's accent affects our response to him, but this does not mean that this sort of thing is unimportant.

36. I admit that this observation is based more on impressions than actual scientific studies. Measuring racial, or any other, prejudice is extremely difficult, and much evidence is anecdotal.

37. Consider, for example, the Banneker scholarships at the University of Maryland that were recently judged unconstitutional. They essentially tried to recruit the best black students available by offering them large scholarships, regardless of financial need (so that many middle-class black students who

could have gone elsewhere in terms of their grades came to the University of Maryland because of the generous scholarships offered).

38. This proposal differs from that offered by Lawrence Becker in that the positions would not convert to regular appointments. "Affirmative Action in Faculty Appointments," Steven M. Cahn, ed., *Affirmative Action*, ch. 3. His proposal, it seems to me, would merely postpone the impact on white male candidates.

39. This case would be a very messy one if one really tried to work out the details. Should the land go to the Mexican government? Would the Mexican people living in the conquered territory really be better off had the land remained part of Mexico? What of Mexicans from southern Mexico?

40. *Statistical Abstract of the United States 1993*, immigration statistics p. 11, population statistics p. 18.

41. Boxill, "Preferential Hiring," 249.

42. Uneducated single mothers are, of course, disproportionately poor, but at the other end of the spectrum, women also control large amounts of wealth. They also live longer than men (which is not normally true of oppressed groups). Forty-two percent of those with assets over $600,000 are women (1989 figure from *Statistical Abstract 1995*, Table 755), and over half of all shareholders are female (N.Y. Stock Exchange).

43. Indeed, housing discrimination is arguably one of the most severe sorts of racial discrimination in America at present, and affirmative action does nothing to address this form of discrimination. A valuable discussion of this is found in Douglas Massey and Nancy Denton, *American Apartheid* (Cambridge: Harvard University Press, 1993).

44. I am indebted to Louis Katzner's "Is the Favoring of Women and Blacks in Employment and Educational Opportunities Justified?" in Joel Feinberg and Hyman Gross, eds., *Philosophy of Law* (Encino, California: Dickenson, 1975), for this argument.

45. On this point see Susan Moller Okin, *Justice, Gender and the Family* (New York: Basic Books, 1989).

46. Thomson, "Preferential Hiring," 383–84.

47. Thomson, "Preferential Hiring," 365.

48. *Digest of Education Statistics, 1994* (Washington, D.C.: U.S. Dept. of Education, 1994), 188.

49. *Digest of Education Statistics, 1994*, Table 254.

50. See argument in Chapter 4, section III.

51. See Chapter 5.

52. Thomas Hill, "The Message of Affirmative Action," *Autonomy and Self-Respect* (New York: Cambridge University Press, 1991), 201. Reprinted in Steven Cahn, ed., *The Affirmative Action Debate*.

53. Hill, "Message," p. 209.

54. Hill, "Message," 205.

55. Hill, "Message," 205.

3

Forward-Looking Arguments

A second type of argument commonly offered to justify affirmative action policies is one that, instead of demanding that past wrongs be righted, looks forward to goods obtainable in the future by means of such policies. Such arguments are employed to justify at least tie-breaking in favor of women and people of color, and are usually taken to justify preference in a stronger sense. Women and people of color are, it is thought, able to contribute something important by virtue of their race, sex, or ethnic origin (e.g., they will function as role models for female and minority students, or will increase faculty diversity). Such considerations may legitimately tip the scales in their favor so that they receive a job that would otherwise have gone to a white man.

The forward-looking arguments are frequently combined with some form of the corrective argument. However, they are conceptually distinct, and so it is helpful to analyze them separately. The corrective arguments call into question the fairness of the procedures followed by search committees, the legitimacy of existing professional standards of competence, or both. The forward-looking arguments, by contrast, leave standards of professional competence untouched, but claim that it is appropriate to override these sometimes in order to achieve the sorts of special goods attainable by a racially, ethnically, and sexually diverse faculty.

The forward-looking arguments, therefore, are consequentialist in nature, and to evaluate them we need to clarify the goods sought, to reflect about whether affirmative action for women and people of color will in fact contribute to attaining these goods, and to consider whether there are undesirable consequences likely to result from such policies that would outweigh the goods attained. This, then, will be the task of this chapter.

Very few moral philosophers advocate making moral choices entirely by weighing and balancing consequences (i.e., they do not support unbridled utilitarianism); rather they believe we must impose certain limits upon purely utilitarian reasoning. There are two ways in which this is commonly done.

First, we may want to exclude from our calculations certain types of satisfactions or dissatisfactions on the grounds that they are a function of perverse desires (the classic example of this is the pleasure sadists experience from the suffering of their victims). In the case of appointing faculty members, some things we might wish to exclude would be the dissatisfaction of people who are offended by the presence of women and people of color in high places, or the satisfaction of those who are taking pleasure in acting out (against black people, white men, women, or anyone else) resentments arising from factors in their personal lives (such as economic stress or a painful divorce). The desire to increase tribalization and undermine any sense of communality can also be regarded as a perverse desire (my reasons for saying this will emerge in the course of the argument).

Second, many philosophers have proposed "side-constraints" on legitimate consequentialist reasoning. Consequentialist reasoning, they argue, is legitimate, but only within certain limits. The main side-constraint in the case of preferential affirmative action in faculty appointments is fairness. Even supposing that the goods sought by such policies are in fact attained, and that they are genuinely important goods, such policies still might be unfair so long as their costs fall entirely on one small group of people (untenured white men) rather than being spread in a more equitable manner.

The goods sought by defenders of preferential affirmative action fall into two broad categories: (1) goods that the presence of the beneficiaries of such policies within the university community may be expected to produce for their students and colleagues, and (2) good effects that affirmative action in faculty appointments may be expected to have on persons outside the university. We will consider first the internal goods because most of the external benefits hoped for are dependent on the success of the internal arguments.

I. Goods Internal to the University

The main internal goods thought to be attainable by means of affirmative action in faculty appointments are providing role models and mentors for female and minority students, and the special contribution to the diversity of the university community that female and minority faculty can make. Diversity is a good that benefits the entire community, and not just those students who resemble the faculty member in race, gender, or ethnicity.

Role Models

The Argument

Female and minority students frequently arrive at college with considerable self-doubt. Often they have been socialized to accept limiting stereotypes of themselves, and they may believe that the deck is stacked against them and that they therefore cannot aspire to positions of authority, power, and prestige. This makes them feel alienated and discouraged—something that is exacerbated if they encounter white male faculty who do not take them seriously, or perhaps even manifest overtly racist or sexist attitudes. And even if white male faculty treat them perfectly well, they may still feel a certain sense of alienation in a setting where all their instructors are white men. "Same-kind role models" will help them overcome this, and seeing someone like themselves in a position of authority encourages them to form higher aspirations for themselves and to break out of limiting stereotypes. For this reason it is legitimate when making faculty appointments to accord preference to members of these formerly excluded groups.

Commentary

This argument has at least a prima facie plausibility. Human behavior is largely learned through imitation, and thus if we want students from marginalized groups to develop higher aspirations for themselves, it would seem that the availability of same-kind role models might provide needed encouragement for them. Early role models are likely to have a more important influence on students' aspirations, since their personality has already been largely formed by the time they come to college, but that does not mean that the influence of college teachers is insignificant.[1] The need for role models would naturally be greatest for students who are making life choices unlike those of their family and friends, or for students who believe that they face severe external obstacles to their career advancement on account of their sex, race, or ethnicity. Hence a black student from a professional family would be less in need of a role model than one from a family in which both parents had only a high school education.

But role models can be positive or negative. A positive role model is one who inspires the student to emulate him or her. Someone of one's own race, gender, or ethnic background, however, could also function as a negative role model for those students who find the teacher repellent for any reason. For example, a black professor who celebrates funky ghetto culture could be a negative role model to a middle-class black student from a Southern Baptist background who desires respectability.

Objections to the Argument

(1) The aim sought is ambiguous. Proponents of this argument often fail to specify just what it is the role model is supposed to inspire the student to do. Presumably there will be some positive effect on the student's educational outcome—a lower probability of dropping out of school, better academic performance, or a higher probability of the student going on to obtain further education after the B.A., for example—rather than just making the student feel better. Are they to be regarded simply as role models of success without regard to how that success has been attained? Or are they role models of excellence, and if the latter, are women and people of color supposed to embody different excellences from white men, or the same ones? Are they, perhaps, meant to inspire the students to follow in their footsteps by becoming college teachers themselves? (If so, then this argument presupposes some other argument establishing the desirability of some particular distribution of women and minorities on the faculty—with regard to both their overall share of jobs and their representation within various disciplines.)

(2) There is little or no empirical evidence that same-kind role models improve student performance. One advantage of taking an empirical approach is that the hypothesis to be tested must be clearly stated in order to devise ways of testing it. This requires defenders of the role model argument to specify what good effects they expect will be produced by the availability of same-kind role models more clearly than is usually done. However, at the present time, empirical evidence for the importance of same-kind role models is weak or ambiguous, and research on this question is only just beginning to be done.

In his introduction to a symposium on role models in education, held at Cornell University in 1994,[2] Ronald Ehrenberg expressed concern that "Beliefs often drive public policy, even before they are confirmed as facts," and called for additional research on the extent to which the race, gender, and ethnicity of teachers affect the educational outcomes of their students. The findings presented in the papers delivered at the symposium were only tentative, and contradictory at a few points, but nonetheless some interesting facts emerged.

One paper found no evidence that an increase in the fraction of female faculty in a department was associated with an increase in the proportion of its majors who were female.[3] Role models, thus, seemed to have no effect on the students' choice of major. And a study using data from the National Educational Longitudinal Study of 1988 came up with the conclusion that the match between public high school teachers' race, gender, and ethnicity and those of their students had little association with how much the students learned.[4] On the positive side, another researcher found that the percentage of female faculty at a college was positively associated with the probability that female students would go on to obtain a higher degree. She, however, declined to assert that the higher percentage of female faculty caused the larger proportion of women going on for advanced degrees, since both phenomena might have been caused by a supportive atmosphere for women in the school in question, and called for more research.[5]

Black students who attended historically black colleges and universities (HBCUs) have had numerous black role models, but they generally attain lower test scores (on the entrance exams for law school, for example).[6] This would seem to indicate that same-kind role models, by themselves, do not improve student performance.[7] Evidence about whether attending an HBCU is positively correlated with later career success is inconclusive, and studies have arrived at contradictory results.[8]

(3) The role model argument is self-undermining. Even if we grant for the sake of argument that same-kind role models do have the desirable results claimed for them, the argument that women and people of color should be preferentially appointed so that they can serve as role models for female and minority students is self-undermining on its own terms. If their ability to function as role models for female and minority students was the deciding factor in their appointment (i.e., in the absence of this consideration someone else would have gotten the job) then female and minority faculty cannot function effectively as role models for their students.

To the extent that female and minority students perceive female and minority faculty to have been preferred over better-qualified white men in order to serve as role models for them, they will feel patronized. Any self-doubts they may be suffering from will be increased rather than alleviated, since this sort of policy would confirm their fears that they cannot be expected to compete with white men on their own ground and win. They are also likely to have less respect for female and minority faculty, and their suspicions of them may extend to all female and minority faculty (since students cannot be sure which ones were beneficiaries of this type of preference and which ones were not). A remark made by a black male law student (cited by Anita Allen) illustrates starkly the sort of devaluation of minority faculty that can occur as a result of the perception that they have been appointed especially to serve the needs of minority students. The student said: "I'm not taking any courses from blacks; I want to learn the same thing the white boys are learning."[9]

The paradoxical character of the role model argument affects faculty as well as students. Although women and people of color on the faculty may be happy if female and minority students find them to be inspiring role models, they have good reason not to want their presence on the faculty defended primarily on these grounds. For if white men are appointed for their excellence as teachers and scholars, but black women are appointed as role models for other black women, then this relegates them to a kind of second-class status. As Allen, a black female law professor, puts it, "the role model argument . . . functions as an excuse for employing someone regarded as lacking full merit."[10] A white female philosopher of science of my acquaintance was once told by a search committee that "we are hoping you will be good for our female students." She replied, "I hope to be good for your male students also." She didn't get the job.

(4) What counts as "same kind"? Even if students need same-kind role models, there is no reason to suppose that "same kind" must be defined in terms of race, gender, or ethnic background. People's identities are multifaceted and the components of one's identity that one takes to be most central can vary widely from person to person.

A Catholic woman, for example, might well be far more heartened and inspired by seeing a Catholic of any color, gender, or ethnic background in a position of authority and prestige than she would be by seeing an aggressively secular woman in such a position. In part this could be because she personally regards her religious affiliation as more important to her identity than her sex. Why, after all, must people take their race, sex, or ethnic background to be the most central thing about their identities? To some degree, of course, they may be forced to do this because others do (although one should still resist allowing others to define what is and is not central to one's own identity in this way), but this still does not justify the way the beneficiaries of affirmative action are presently selected. The Catholic woman may also fear that anti-Catholic prejudice might impair her chances of attaining a high place in the academic world,[11] and seeing this successful Catholic may therefore encourage her to aspire to become a professor. Those currently accorded preference are not the only groups who suffer prejudice and discrimination.

(5) One could also attack the role model argument in an even more fundamental way, by arguing that there is no reason to suppose that an effective role model must resemble the student in any salient respect. Who functions as a role model for a person is highly idiosyncratic and unpredictable, and considerations such as personal style, sense of humor, imagination, moral character, analytical ability, and enthusiasm for his or her subject matter are likely to be much more important than race, sex, or ethnic background.

The kind of role model needed also depends on the inner obstacles or fears of a given student. A woman who wants a family, and whose mother warned her that intellectual women become dried-up old maids, will find a female teacher who is feminine, attractive, and happily married to be an appealing role model. Another woman, whose previous female teachers have all seemed drearily conformist and prim to her may be inspired to emulate one who is bold, brassy, and scornful of conventional morality. Thus one woman's positive role model can easily be another's negative role model.

To the extent that the faculty member actively presents himself or herself as a role model for same-kind students, and thus claims to represent something distinctively black, female, Hispanic, Asian, etc., and not simply a teacher and scholar like everyone else, this is likely to increase the intensity of the student's response (positive or negative). Those who understand their identity differently will find such a teacher a negative role model. For example, a black or female role model who embodies a strongly separatist impulse may be unattractive to women or people of color who desire integration.

(6) One negative effect that is specific to the role model argument is its tendency to encourage deceit. For, suppose that a school has appointed a female or minority faculty member and that this person's capacity to function as a role model for female or minority students was the deciding factor in his or her appointment. In such a case, this fact must be concealed if the teacher is to be able to function effectively as a role model. The role model argument, therefore, invites deceit. This in turn undermines the credibility of faculty and administration, poisons the atmosphere generally, and causes people to suspect deceit even when it is not present.[12]

Conclusion

Same-kind role models may be valuable for some students (especially those beset by self-doubt or daunted by what they perceive to be external obstacles to success resulting from the social prejudices against the group of which they are members). But so far there is very little evidence that, as a general rule, having teachers of their own gender, race, or ethnic group has the sort of positive effect on the performance of female and minority students that defenders of the role model argument allege. Indeed, if the arguments presented above are correct, there is no good reason to expect that a teacher will serve as a positive role model simply by virtue of being the same race or gender as the student. In any case, to the extent that female and minority faculty are, or are perceived to be, beneficiaries of preference, this will undermine their value as role models (assuming that their role is to encourage students to believe they can attain excellence, and not merely to demonstrate that a member of their group can obtain a professorship). If someone is given preference in order to serve as a role model, this fact must be concealed; hence the role model argument encourages deceit.

Mentors

A mentor, unlike a role model, does more than motivate the student or provide a kind of template of excellence to be imitated. A professor could be a role model without having any interaction with the student outside the classroom at all. A mentor relationship normally begins in the classroom, but extends beyond it. Mentors provide encouragement and professional guidance, and after graduation they often help the student get into graduate school or find a job (by doing things like writing letters of reference and lining up job interviews through contacts).

The Argument

Mentors are important for all students, especially at the graduate and professional level, and they may be especially important for female and minority students. For such students often lack confidence in their own academic abilities and so a supportive mentor could make a great deal of difference to them. There is some evidence that mentoring may be more important to young women than to young men.[13] Furthermore women and people of color may encounter racism or sexism on the part of white male faculty members, and need a mentor to provide understanding, advice, and support.

Yet women and people of color are likely to have difficulty finding mentors among white male faculty. Teachers tend to identify more strongly with students of their own race, sex, and ethnic group, and to promote the interests of such students more vigorously. Teachers, like parents, are often motivated by a desire to reproduce themselves, to attain a kind of immortality by passing on things they regard as valuable to the next generation. They will naturally be drawn to students who are like themselves when they were young[14] and be inclined to promote the interests of such students more than others. Consequently, appointing more female and minority faculty is necessary in order to make more mentors available for female and minority students and thus enhance their educational and professional prospects.

Commentary and Critique

The term "mentoring" covers such a wide variety of different functions and is so often an informal relationship that it is very hard to investigate it scientifically or to say very much useful about mentoring in general.[15] At one end of the spectrum, mentoring overlaps with the sort of work done by the counseling center—listening to students talk about their problems (some but not all of which are related to coursework or career prospects) and providing advice and encouragement. At the other end there is the sort of mentoring characteristic of graduate programs in which the mentor directs the student's research, sometimes co-authors articles with the mentee, and plays a large role in helping the mentee get a job. Mentoring relationships of a deep sort (ones that go beyond routine things like advising students about courses and plans for further education or future employment) arise spontaneously between two individuals and cannot be simply created at will.

Although mentoring relationships are valuable, they are also fraught with dangers. A mentor may place excessive demands upon a graduate student's time, requiring the student to do the leg work for the mentor's research, or may publish the student's ideas and research under his or her own name, particularly in highly competitive scientific fields. Some professors relish the role of guru and demand slavish conformity to their ideas and intense personal allegiance on the part of their students. Even at the undergraduate level some faculty members encourage the formation of coteries of admiring students who are expected to conform to the outlook and expectations of their mentor and then go out in the world and spread the mentor's ideas. This sort of thing undermines the independence of mind that makes for solid and creative scholarship. Students cannot, however, dispense completely with mentors, since the lack of one places a student at a severe disadvantage professionally.

The question we must address in this section is whether the need of female and minority students for mentors justifies according preference to female and minority candidates for faculty positions.

That same-kind mentors are not necessary is shown by the fact that many women and people of color have been successful in finding and working well with white male mentors. Arguments parallel to those developed above for role models can be constructed to show that there is no reason to suppose that people of different races or genders cannot enter into mentor-mentee relationships. For even if faculty tend to interest themselves more in the well-being of students whom they perceive to be like themselves, there are many ways in which they might be similar other than the race, gender, or ethnic background of the student. For example, one faculty member may be reminded of himself or herself by a student who is very idealistic, while another is particularly inclined to favor someone who is brash and aggressive, and a third may be drawn to be particularly nurturing toward a student who is painfully shy and lacking in confidence. Being from the professor's home town, sharing his or her religious background, or any number of other things may lead a professor to take a special interest in a student.

But even if they have been able to manage to work well with white male mentors, is there, perhaps, reason to believe that having more same-kind mentors for female and minority students will be productive of important goods for such students that could not be attained otherwise?

The short answer, I think, is "no," although tie-breaking (by which I mean "ice-breaking")[16] in favor of women and people of color might under some circumstances be desirable in departments where members of these groups have been almost entirely absent. It is possible that male professors in largely male fields, for example, will have developed a habit of not taking women's minds seriously. But the fact that there are few or no female faculty in a department need not imply that a female student will be unable to find a mentor. And the same is true for minority students. It is necessary to look at whether the department is in fact doing a good job educating its female and minority students—for example, by looking at the quality of their female and minority graduates, and by attending to and fairly evaluating anecdotal evidence that might indicate the presence of racist or sexist attitudes on the part of professors. If there is evidence that female or minority students are having a hard time getting themselves taken seriously intellectually by white male professors, then tie-breaking in favor of female and minority faculty could be warranted. But thinking routinely along the lines suggested by the mentor argument has very real dangers for women and people of color.

The assumption that mentoring will be done by same-kind faculty will cause white male faculty members to conclude that they have no responsibility to mentor women or people of color, since they've appointed special female and minority faculty to do that job. Female and minority students would then be mentored primarily by faculty members who are fairly junior in rank (since women and people of color are disproportionately concentrated at these ranks) and thus kept on a separate track that does not give them access to the most prestigious jobs.

And, if the mentor argument is employed to justify appointing them, female and minority faculty will be expected to assume an unfairly large share of the responsibility for mentoring female and minority students in ways that eat into the time they can devote to their own professional development. Also, as in the case of the role model argument, such professors will feel that they are second class if they are appointed mainly to minister to the needs of minority students while white male teachers are appointed for their teaching and scholarship.

The danger here is especially serious for women. There is some evidence that female faculty tend already to take on a larger share of mentoring students (both male and female) than their male colleagues.[17] This fits with the usual pattern of women tending more toward nurturing roles. The problem is that although women are often good at this sort of role and enjoy doing it, it does hold them back professionally unless they are careful not to let it eat into their research and writing time too much. This sort of pattern may well account for the fact that women tend to be less well represented at the leading research institutions (one gets jobs at such institutions on the basis of one's research and not for one's mentoring abilities). Female faculty should be free to allocate their time as they choose, but the mentoring argument places pressure on them to spend more time doing what they already do more than their share of.

Furthermore, to the degree that women and people of color are beset by professional self-doubt, they will be more likely to feel a need to attach themselves firmly to a mentor and thus become more vulnerable to the possible abuses inherent in the mentor relationship. They might therefore be better advised to cultivate more than one mentor and maintain some distance from all of them. Women, especially, are discouraged from independence of mind by their upbringing as well as by both male and female colleagues and administrators, and they need to be especially careful of mentor relationships for this reason.

In fields where there is intense conflict along racial and gender lines, it is naive to expect that female and black faculty members will naturally take same-kind students under their wings. In such fields (and there seem to be a lot of them these days) both women and people of color are likely to discover that the price of obtaining the favor of a mentor is ideological conformity.

Another danger of encouraging same-kind mentoring is that it feeds tribalization and may lead to a decline in academic standards. The issues are subtle and not easy to resolve. One study found some evidence that white female teachers give higher subjective evaluations to white female students even though those students did not learn more from them than from white male teachers as measured by test scores.[18] On the one hand this might mean that female teachers were better at seeing the latent talent in female students and that over time the students in question would have responded to their teachers' good opinion by putting out more effort and achieving better scores. More research is necessary to determine whether this would happen. But looking for and seeing the good in students with whom one feels some special bond shades over quickly into favoritism, and encouraging same-kind mentoring as a way of promoting the educational and professional advancement of women and minorities would be likely to increase the frequency of this sort of thing.

One might, of course, respond that favoritism is inevitable in any case, so why not help women and people of color get theirs. To do so is to accept the postmodernist argument against academic merit (see Chapter 4, section I), and to make irrelevant most of the arguments concerning affirmative action. One might as well favor one's friends, whether they are defined on gender, racial, ideological, or other grounds.

Finally, emphasizing the role modeling and mentoring functions of faculty can direct too much attention to the psychological needs and career aspirations of students at the expense of their need to actually learn something from the teachers in question. At least some of the functions expected of mentors (nonacademic ones) could be performed by other staff on campus. It is all very well to inspire students to aim for more demanding and fulfilling careers, but if they are not actually acquiring the skills and knowledge necessary for such careers they are only heading for a fall. To the extent that considerations like providing role models and mentors for female and minority students crowd out the usual criteria for selecting faculty—such as expertise in their subject matter and the ability to communicate what they know clearly, to teach students how to write and think clearly, and to inspire them to be more reflective and interested in the life of the mind—students will ultimately be the losers.

Summary

Mentors are certainly of value to students, particularly at the graduate level, although mentor relationships carry with them the potential for some fairly serious abuses. In any case, the necessity for same-kind mentors has not been established. The danger of thinking along the lines suggested by the mentor argument is that it feeds tribalization (especially in disciplines where there is strong ideological conflict along racial and gender lines) and increases the likelihood that women and people of color will be put on a separate track from white men that carries with it a kind of second-class status. The positive value of mentors may be of sufficient importance (especially at the graduate level) in fields or departments where women and people of color have faced serious discrimination in the past and are just beginning to enter, to justify tie-breaking in their favor. But this should be done only if there is genuine evidence that the needs of female and minority students are not being properly served in a given department.

Diversity

Whereas the role model and mentor arguments are cast in terms of the needs of female and minority students only (and thus would not justify appointing minority faculty at an all-white school), the diversity argument claims that greater racial, ethnic, and gender diversity among faculty will introduce intellectual and cultural perspectives that will be beneficial for everyone on campus. It is thus a more general and powerful argument for affirmative action. It is also rather more vague and polymorphous (not to say protean) than the other two, and communication between its defenders and its opponents often seems to be a kind of dialogue of the deaf. Frequently they are working within such different conceptual frameworks that miscommunication is almost inevitable.

Clearing the Ground

Before plunging into the central issues, I will try to clear away some of the fog by stating some propositions about which there appears to be considerable confusion, but which are, I believe, undeniable.

1. Diversity is a mixed good.
   a. Deep differences of outlook between people generate conflict, and this can easily get out of hand unless balanced by a sense of commonality or community. Even narrow forms of ideological diversity generate bitter conflict if developed in a context that discourages working together despite differences.[19]
   b. Not every form of diversity is good. Which kinds are of value is a function of the task to be done.
   c. Diversity will not be educationally valuable unless the diverse people talk to each other and make genuine attempts to understand each other.
2. Including some people excludes others; the pie is not infinite.
3. If you appoint professors on grounds other than traditional standards of professional competence, this will result, over time, in a faculty less qualified by those standards.
4. If you make important benefits dependent on membership in a group(s), this will lead people to identify themselves as members of such group(s), to cooperate with other members of the group to promote their common interests, and to think of themselves as in competition with other groups who also want a share of the benefits in question.
5. If you practice preferential hiring or admissions for a group who are easily identifiable by their appearance, you cast suspicion upon the qualifications of all members of the group.[20]

6. Physical proximity does not automatically generate more harmonious relations between groups. Consider, for example, Catholics and Protestants in Northern Ireland, or black people and Koreans in New York City.

7. People form their opinions about racial and ethnic groups other than their own largely on the basis of their personal experience rather than on the basis of philosophical reasoning or the views presented to them by authority figures.

8. If students graduate from universities unable to write or think clearly, and entirely ignorant of history, this will anger parents, employers, and taxpayers (if the university in question is supported out of state monies). If their education has the effect of making them hostile to their parents' most deeply held values, parents will not be pleased.

9. Parents, employers, and taxpayers can, in the long run, exercise considerable power over universities.

10. If one is serious about resolving social and environmental problems, bashing white men is a bad idea. Many of them are talented and in positions that carry with them sufficient power and influence to do a lot of good.

11. Cultures and their associated social institutions are easier to destroy than to build, and when they collapse it is the most vulnerable members of society who suffer most (e.g., children).

12. Subjecting people to negative stereotyping on the basis of factors over which they have no control harms them and is very likely to cause them to behave in undesirable ways.

13. Despite dramatic claims about the coloring of America, much of the country remains largely white (people of color are largely young and concentrated in big cities), and white people made up 83.9 percent of the population in 1990.[21]

14. If one wants to understand current cultural conflicts, one should not ignore religious diversity.

15. If you attack reason, you cannot use reason to defend yourself against attack. Thus, unless you have a large army at your disposal, doing so is a bad idea.

16. If you talk war, you increase the likelihood of war.

The Value of Diversity for Education: Two Models

Is there reason to believe that preferentially appointing women, black people, Hispanics, Asians, and Native Americans to faculty positions will bring about a sort of diversity that will enhance the educational experience of students and enrich the intellectual and cultural climate on campus? Surely these sorts of goods do not follow automatically from simply increasing the proportion of female and minority faculty. How they are selected and the justifications given for appointing them strongly influence the effects their presence will have (since it affects the way they, as well as their colleagues and students, think about their role on campus). Thus, before proceeding further, it is necessary to step back and reflect about the goods being sought, and what sort of diversity is likely to be useful for attaining them. Although there is currently very little consensus about the purpose of higher education, especially in the humanities, the question of what sort of diversity will be educationally valuable cannot be answered without a brief detour into this heavily mined territory.

A great deal of the miscommunication about diversity stems, I believe, from the fact that people understand the goal of education very differently. What one person regards as a tragic failure of the educational process another may wholeheartedly applaud. The two most important ways of thinking about the role of universities for our purposes are the democratic liberal model and the multicultural model, since both regard diversity as valuable (but for very different reasons). The traditionalist model, often adhered to by religious schools, sees the goal of higher education to be handing on a particular tradition. The "multiversity" model, articulated by Clark Kerr in the 1960s, holds that universities are simply loose aggregates of communities serving the needs of different constituencies in the broader society, without any unifying core purpose at all. Since proponents of these two models are not, for the most part, centrally involved in the dispute over diversity, we shall not go into them here.

(1) The Democratic Liberal Model

On this model, the intellectual purpose of the university is understood to be striking a balance between the discovery of new truths and the handing on of truths already found. In this framework, intellectual diversity plays a positive role in facilitating the search for new truths, since vigorous debate helps expose the deficiencies of proposed theories and can suggest new and more productive lines of thought. Diverse ways of thinking need not be encountered only in the flesh, however, since one can encounter and learn from minds quite different from one's own through the study of history and literature.

If one's goal is the discovery of new truths, then one desirable type of diversity is methodological. Some lines must be drawn, of course; astrology or the reading of tea leaves is unlikely to prove fruitful. And, especially at the graduate level, it may be desirable to concentrate on one methodological approach. Faculty will be able to work together better, and students can choose their graduate school knowing that this is the sort of work done at this school. But it is hard to predict the direction from which new and important discoveries may come, so that some openness to a variety of methodological approaches is always desirable.[22]

The political purpose of higher education on this view is understood to be educating students to become informed and responsible citizens so that America's democratic way of life can be perpetuated. This, they believe, requires handing on some core of shared values, a knowledge of our history as a nation, an appreciation for the uniqueness of the American experiment, and the skills necessary to engage in rational dialogue so that we can deliberate together over what policies we should adopt. It is also necessary to instill a certain civility and willingness to make sacrifices for the common good. In light of the fact that America has always been a nation made up of culturally different groups (and increasingly so in the wake of the massive waves of immigration of the late nineteenth and twentieth centuries), a willingness to try to understand, tolerate, and work with those who are different is also required if we are all to live together peaceably. A culturally and intellectually diverse faculty might be helpful for this purpose.

The type of diversity desirable if we accept this view of the political purpose of the university, then, would be one that broadly reflects the diversity of outlook among Americans. In order to communicate and cooperate with one's fellow citizens, one needs an understanding of the characteristic ways of thinking of groups of which one is not a member, particularly those that are large enough to be politically significant. One of the most important sorts of diversity from this point of view is religious diversity. Most people do not have well worked-out philosophical positions, and their outlook is very much shaped by their religious commitment or lack of it. Thus, for example, since the Christian New Right is an important force politically at the present time, students ought to be given some understanding of how such people think. Appointing articulate and intellectually reputable representatives of the Christian New Right to faculty positions could be of enormous value to students. As things stand now, many academics manifest a phobic attitude toward such people (sometimes called "fundaphobia"). For example, I recently heard them referred to as "fundamentalist yahoos" from the podium of a philosophical association meeting. If this attitude is communicated to students it will discourage them from trying to understand fundamentalists or to search for common ground with them in the ways necessary for living together in a democratic society.

Who contributes to diversity will vary from school to school and department to department, depending on the students and faculty already there, the mission of the school in question, the sorts of careers that graduates typically pursue, etc. A school training students for careers in international business or law or the diplomatic service, for example, would probably find appointing foreign nationals useful. Or a social work program in an area of Texas where there are a lot of very impoverished Mexican Americans might benefit from having some Mexican American faculty. It is not just a case of "one size fits all."

The intellectual and the political purposes of the university on the democratic liberal view, then, are mutually supportive. Rational dialogue is regarded as essential to the discovery of new truths, and also plays an important role in the process of democratic deliberation. The value of diversity, then, lies in its contribution to achieving goods that will benefit everyone, and for this purpose it must be both recognized and to some degree at least contained. If there is too much diversity, dialogue and cooperation are likely to break down, so it must be balanced by some shared values as well. At the very least, people must believe that the search for knowledge is worthwhile and that democratic institutions are of sufficient value to be worth making some sacrifices for.

(2) The Multiculturalist Model

I am using the label "multiculturalist" as an umbrella term, but I realize that multiculturalists do not form a homogeneous group, so I will briefly describe some of the groups that I take to be loosely grouped under this heading. "Weak multiculturalism" is almost entirely uncontroversial; it simply asserts that we can learn things of value from studying other cultures. When I speak of "multiculturalism" this is not what I mean; I refer, rather, to "strong multiculturalism"—a kind of cultural relativism according to which different cultures are both incommensurable and regarded as all equally valuable. It is standardly associated with demands for some sort of proportional representation of minority groups among students or faculty or in the curriculum itself.

"Political correctness" is what happens when strong multiculturalism turns intolerant (as it naturally does toward those who assert their own views to be true—see discussion in Chapter 1) and tries to drive opponents out by shunning, silencing, political machinations, etc. "Cultural leftists" are those who oppose the handing on of traditional Western culture. At the other end of the spectrum are the traditionalists who favor doing so and are considered to be on the right. (This contrasts with the classical political spectrum in which leftists believe in trying to attain a more egalitarian distribution of wealth and power, while the right endorses a more hierarchical view of society.)

"Postmodernists" are often allied with strong multiculturalists. A rough approximation of their views is that all forms of structure are oppressive, because they violate the "diversity" that represents the true nature of things (and more importantly of people).[23] For that reason, they pursue a policy of "decentering" institutions and cultures, and of promoting the outlook of the "marginalized" (or in practice, selected examples of the marginalized). Deconstruction is one intellectual technique used by postmodernists, in order to discredit authoritative "texts" such as the *Dialogues* of Plato and the American Constitution. Postmodernists cannot, however, coherently argue for their view that diversity represents the true nature of things, for talk of the nature of things, and especially of human nature, is in their view itself oppressive.

No doubt some of those who defend affirmative action for women and people of color in order to increase faculty diversity think in terms of the democratic liberal model, but a great many of those who most strongly support such policies do not think in these terms. Rather they have their own distinctive vision of the sort of academy they aspire to create, which I am calling the "multiculturalist model."

Such people are united by their concern for the way in which minorities have been and still are oppressed. But they also share the view that difference or diversity is something good in itself—to be celebrated rather than integrated into a higher unity of any sort, and this is the reason why I am grouping them together for our purposes here. In part their celebration of diversity results from the fact that many of the groups in question have their roots in the rejection of what they took to be false claims to universality on the part of the leadership of the New Left.[24] However, they went further, under the influence of Michel Foucault, denying the possibility of any sort of commonality at all, and accepting a way of thinking about truth that ultimately had its roots in Friedrich Nietzsche. On this view, there is no over-arching truth in relation to which anyone's claims to truth could be checked and corrected. All there is, is a struggle of wills in which each person strives to impose his or her vision of reality on others, and in this battle any claim to know the truth is merely an illegitimate attempt to assert hegemony over others by asserting one's own vision and marginalizing or repressing theirs.

In place of the pursuit of truth, they take the intellectual purpose of education to be a kind of liberation of the student from the hegemony of the dominant discourse. Those marginalized by that discourse should be given voice and empowered. Students must be opened up to new ways of thinking and experiencing the world; they must learn not to assert that their way of life is better than others. Relativism, thus, shapes their pedagogy and functions as a kind of established religion.

Needless to say, this vision of the intellectual purpose of education has ramifications for one's understanding of its political purpose. The political purpose is sometimes seen as mobilizing students on behalf of the marginalized. But often the university itself is taken to be the main locus of political struggle, and subversion of the hegemonic discourse plays the role that revolution played for Marxists. Or perhaps the ideal is closer to Mao Tse-tung's "continuing revolution," since setting up a new center or hegemonic discourse is taken to be either impossible or undesirable.

Thus, on the multiculturalist model, the intellectual and the political purposes of education are mutually supportive, just as they are on the democratic liberal model. Common to both are the celebration of diversity, but there are two sides to this program.[25] It involves an affirmation of the equal value of all cultures, but also an attempt to actively undermine all claims to truth or commonality by constantly setting the margins against the center (or any position that tries to set itself up as a center). For this latter purpose, the sort of diversity that would be especially valuable would be the introduction of those viewpoints that most deeply challenge and unsettle conventional ways of thinking. Since ways of understanding sexuality, sex roles, and the family are particularly central to any culture, views that run radically counter to traditional ways of thinking about these will be particularly useful (as Foucault well knew).

From the point of view of the democratic liberal model, the effect of universities performing successfully the sort of intellectual purpose envisioned on this model would be largely a negative one. Since multiculturalists subvert or deconstruct any center or sense of shared common humanity, they undermine the foundation for something that democratic liberals regard as essential to the functioning of a democratic society—namely, a core of shared values, a conception of human nature that grounds people's claims to possess rights, and a sense of commonality in the name of which people can be asked to make sacrifices. The sort of rational dialogue that was so central to the democratic liberal model is also not encouraged on the multiculturalist model, since, on this model, intellectual life is just politics all the way down— a struggle to attain the power to define the dominant discourse according to one's own vision—with no truth to act as an external check.

Problems with the Multiculturalist Diversity Argument

I intend to argue that trying to increase faculty diversity by preferential appointment of women and people of color is unlikely to have the sorts of good results hoped for if it is conceived and implemented according to the multiculturalist model. Specifically, it is unlikely to encourage dialogue among those with differing outlooks, to lead to more tolerant or flexible attitudes on the part of students, or to prepare them well to participate in the broader global community. Nor is there any meaningful sense in which affirmative action along these lines makes universities more democratic. My argument is not primarily an empirical one,[26] but has to do with structural features of the multiculturalist diversity argument that tend to increase tribalization and decrease dialogue (which is not to say that affirmative action is the only or even the most important source of these problems).

Diversity as understood on the democratic liberal model, by contrast, if pursued intelligently, is likely to improve the educational experience of students and enrich the intellectual climate on campus. Most academics are, I believe, sympathetic to the democratic liberal model, and genuinely hope that the bitter factionalism that seems to be on the rise in the academy is merely temporary. Unfortunately, given the way affirmative action programs are currently justified and implemented, they are likely to exacerbate rather than alleviate these problems. The moral is "don't buy just anything that has the word 'diversity' on the label."[27]

One frequently hears complaints that higher education has become too politicized and that the multiculturalists are to blame for this fact. Most of those making this sort of argument tend explicitly or implicitly to contrast our current situation with some previous golden age in which universities were peopled with scholars engaged in a purely disinterested search for the truth. Opponents, then, have a ready retort— namely, pointing out that there never was such a golden age.[28] Perhaps, however, the problem is that the multiculturalists are not political enough, or that they are political in the wrong way.[29]

My criticisms of the multiculturalist defense of preferential affirmative action will be organized under the following seven headings: (1) the rhetoric of representation; (2) the pitfalls of symbolic politics; (3) problems with the selection of beneficiaries; (4) divisive effects of giving preference; (5) harm to beneficiaries; (6) effects on students; (7) the dark side of the Rainbow Coalition.

(1) The Rhetoric of Representation
Despite the fact that they embrace a Nietzschean view of truth and politics, the multiculturalists still see their ideal as consistent with, and even conducive to, democracy. At first blush, this is puzzling. Nietzsche, after all, was no democrat. And if, as proponents of the democratic liberal model believe, a functioning democracy requires shared values and a sense of commonality, then an educational program that undermines these will put a serious strain on democratic institutions. Furthermore, the view that those with political power are the ones who define the dominant discourse blurs any distinction

between truth and politics and reduces everything to naked power relations. This, in turn, leaves no room for the sort of rational dialogue that prevents democratic communities from disintegrating into the tyranny of whatever groups are able to command the instruments of state power.

How, then, can the multiculturalist vision of the university claim to be a democratic one? The key move is adopting the rhetoric, if not the substance, of representative democracy (given the deep commitment of Americans to representative democracy, this is a brilliant move rhetorically). Doing this provides a rationale for affirmative action, and has profound implications for their understanding of "diversity."

The argument goes something like this: Until very recently white (heterosexual) men have controlled the academy, and therefore their perspective has been almost entirely dominant. We need to appoint more women, people of color, and members of other marginalized groups (the disabled or homosexuals for example) to faculty positions, so that they will be able to speak for or "represent" the perspectives and interests of these groups. Universities, thus, are like a sort of model United Nations. The crucial question, however, is on what grounds female or minority faculty can legitimately claim to "represent" the perspectives or interests of the groups to which they belong.

Simply being a member of a group does not automatically entitle one to represent it. To represent a group means to speak for it, to stand in for it, or to function as an advocate for its interests. But how do some people come to represent others? A lawyer represents a client because he or she is paid by the client. A senator is elected by the voters in a given area, and can be voted out if he or she fails to do what the voters want. But there is no mechanism for ensuring accountability in the case of a college professor who is appointed to increase the representation of women or people of color. Indeed, there seems to be no reason why professors should be thought to represent anyone but themselves.

Women, black people, Hispanics, Asians, and Native Americans are internally divided on a number of issues, and since those who have attained the level of education necessary to be in the running for a professorship are almost always among the elite within each group (on this point see the Rodriguez essay reprinted in this volume), they are unlikely to hold views representative of the group as a whole. For example, the way in which academic women articulate the perspective of women differs radically from the way most American women think.[30] For example, a 1996 poll indicated that more women, when faced with two equally attractive candidates, one of whom is pro-life and one of whom is pro-choice, would support the pro-life candidate (45 percent versus 42 percent). For nonwhite women the figures were 54 percent pro-life to 31 percent pro-choice.[31] On what grounds, then, can professors claim to represent the perspective or interests of the marginalized groups to which they belong?

One possible answer is along the lines of Vladimir Lenin's theory of the vanguard party. Marginalized groups are frequently inarticulate and confused about their own interests, and therefore those with superior insight must sometimes step in and represent their true interests. Lenin, however, believed that the party had privileged insight into the laws of history in virtue of which it could discern the true interests of the workers even though workers' perception of their own interests was distorted by false consciousness. This sort of move is made fairly frequently by those who claim to speak for women. But multiculturalists cannot consistently take the Leninist position. For one thing, since they do not believe there is such a thing as truth, at least not of the sort in which Marxists believed, they cannot claim privileged access to truths that ordinary people do not know in order to justify their conception of someone's interests when it conflicts with the person's own understanding of his or her interests.

And if we set aside metaphysics, and look at the problem on a merely political level, their position is no more satisfactory. Claiming to represent some group in the absence of any mechanism by means of which one is made accountable to them, or even any regular two-way communication with them, is likely to make them very angry. And while Lenin had real political and military power behind him, multiculturalists do not.

The most troubling thing about the situation is their indifference to the actual beliefs and desires of those whose views are purportedly being represented. This is not just an oversight, because this sort of investigation would bring to the surface deep inconsistencies in their position.

Multiculturalists want to overthrow the dominant or hegemonic discourse and give voice to the marginalized, and at the same time want to be democratic and egalitarian. But the dominant culture, almost by definition, is the one accepted by most people, so going against it pits one against the majority. If there were a coherent new majority in the name of which multiculturalists could speak, then they could still claim to be democratic. But the current list of protected groups is not a genuine, functioning political alliance, and it is made to look like a majority only by throwing in all women. If one began actually to talk to the members of the groups in question about their beliefs and their conception of their own interests, the whole thing would fall apart. Hence that is the last thing multiculturalists want to do, for if they are forced to abandon their claim to be democratic, they would have no basis for their moral authority.

There is one final difficulty for the view that the proper role of preferentially appointed female and minority faculty is to represent the perspectives or interests of the group to which they belong. It embodies an inappropriately authoritarian conception of the role of the teacher. Multiculturalists appear to have embraced a very top-down model for both the intellectual life and politics. And this position follows naturally from a conflation of truth and politics; if reasoning is impossible between those with conflicting views, then conflicts can be resolved only by force. But if one understands the role of the teacher in terms of helping students learn to intelligently think out their own positions rather than in terms of the teacher imposing his or her vision of reality on them, then one should avoid using the language of "representation" with its political connotations.

(2) The Pitfalls of Symbolic Politics

There is also a nonpolitical sense of "representation" that may be involved in the multiculturalist argument for affirmative action. Perhaps female and minority faculty represent other members of their groups by virtue of resemblances they have to them, as a woman is chosen to play Lady Macbeth or a black man to play Othello. In this case the representation is dramatic or symbolic. Just as President Bill Clinton sought to appoint a cabinet that "looks like America," so, likewise, universities may intend to appoint more women and people of color to faculty positions as a way of making a symbolic statement about the importance of inclusiveness and the value of diversity.

But to view according preference to female and minority candidates for faculty positions as a kind of morality play intended to communicate our commitment to inclusiveness and diversity is really no more appropriate than thinking of it as setting up a model United Nations. For one thing the inclusiveness is highly selective, since including some necessarily excludes others. Thus this symbolic statement conveys exclusion as well as inclusion. Furthermore, faculty are appointed in order to do a particular job—namely, educating students and doing research—and when normal professional standards are overridden in order to engage in expressive politics, this is likely to interfere with the university's ability to do its own proper job well.

This is not to deny that symbols are important in politics. They are. And there are some political positions that have a predominantly symbolic function—the vice-presidency in America, the monarchy in Britain. Nonetheless, to appoint professors on primarily symbolic grounds is to convey the wrong *symbolic* message—namely, that the intellectual and educational functions of the academy are not really all that important, that the academy is a vestigial institution without any proper purpose of its own, and for that reason available for whatever social agenda some politically active group might want to impose.

(3) Problems with the Selection of Beneficiaries

There is no reason to suppose that appointing members of the currently preferred groups will produce a sort of intellectual and cultural diversity that will be valuable educationally. The categories usually accorded preference on diversity grounds were not, after all, selected on intellectual or cultural grounds, but were handed to universities by the political processes we traced in Chapter 1.

The politics of which statistics get collected and which ones do not is a fascinating study.[32] Some governments do not collect racial statistics at all—Mexico, France, and Canada, for example. The French, disturbed by the behavior of the Vichy government who supplied racial data to the Nazis, insist that everyone is equally a citizen regardless of race. The Puerto Ricans do not collect racial statistics largely because so many citizens are of mixed racial ancestry. The categories into which the U.S. population is divided by those governmental agencies that collect statistics were in large part chosen (in the 1970s) to facilitate the administration of various federal programs, especially those designed to help groups in need of special assistance.[33]

The currently used categories are not cast in stone; black people, Hispanics, Asians and Pacific Islanders, and Native Americans do not form what Aristotle called "natural kinds."[34] It is very easy to look at a group of which one is not a member and see more similarity among its members than is actually present (the "all the Chinese look alike" fallacy). For example, the category "Hispanic" includes an incredibly heterogeneous array of different groups divided by skin color, class, education, and culture, who frequently can't stand each other (some of whom might be better classified as Native Americans as a result of having Indian ancestry). Thus, for example, a Puerto Rican is very unlikely to be satisfied with the appointment of a Cuban to represent the "Hispanic" perspective. Once we get beyond the cardboard images of Native Americans (found, for example, in the movie *Pocahontas*), we discover that the indigenous American peoples include a staggeringly large range of very different sorts of cultures. And not only is each group internally diverse, but other deep and important differences cut across the categories used in affirmative action programs. A rural black Southerner will be more culturally similar to his or her white neighbors than to a black person from a ghetto in Detroit. Cambodian boat people will have more in common with a Haitian refugee than with a third-generation Japanese American businessman.

Women are even more culturally diverse than any of the other groups since they are more or less evenly distributed in all classes and cultural groups. To the extent that there is any such thing as a distinctive women's culture handed on from mother to daughter it is not likely to be relevant to their qualifications for college teaching positions.[35] There are, however, significant biological differences between men and women, and if it were true that these affect how men and women think, then it would provide a good reason for supposing that appointing women will automatically add genuine diversity to the university community. But the biological-difference rationale for claiming that women will add diversity is unpopular, especially among multiculturalists. In the case of racial differences, such a view would be very difficult to distinguish from out-and-out racism. And although male-female biological differences are sufficiently large that they might be expected to have some effect on the way men and women think, very little is known about how they do or might affect it.

There are other types of diversity more likely to be educationally valuable than those now used. Academia has its own distinctive subculture, so if we want to diversify university faculties, this could sometimes be accomplished by adding members of groups not marginalized in the broader society (such as political conservatives). Another important sort of difference is regional difference. Midwestern culture differs considerably from that prevalent on the coasts, and Southern culture is, to most Northerners, an unexplored continent.

Religious difference cuts deeper than other sorts of diversity, since cultures characteristically form around a religious nucleus. Members of the same religious community share certain fundamental assumptions about the nature of human beings and the world that have far-reaching implications for all areas of their lives and affect the way believers approach a wide range of different academic disciplines. Those whose religious beliefs are important to them are likely to find contemporary disputes about cultural diversity frustrating because no one seems to be acknowledging their concerns at all. It is as though there is an elephant in the middle of the room (namely, religious difference) that everyone is tiptoeing around but not mentioning. Having at least some general idea of how people of various religious faiths understand the world would be valuable to students, and a faculty who reflected the religious composition of the broader society could be helpful for this purpose.

There are also methodological and theoretical differences within each discipline that have direct bearing on what students learn and how. These also are likely to be more productive of intellectually fruitful dialogue than skin color, reproductive organs, or having a Spanish surname.

(4) Divisive Effects of Preference

Awarding members of some groups preference over others by overriding the usual standards of judging professional competence to favor them for jobs will encourage members of the favored groups to band together to defend their common interests. Groups not so favored will be angered by their perception that this is unfair. Even tie-breaking affirmative action can cause resentment,[36] but actual preference is certain to do so. I am not claiming that this necessarily implies we should never give this sort of preference for any reason at any time, but merely that if we do, we should realize that it is very likely to encourage tribalization and increase intergroup strife—especially when desirable jobs in a given field are very hard to come by (as they are in academia).

Cultural or intellectual diversity might function as a reason for preference on the democratic liberal model, but only in cases where a candidate has an intellectual or cultural perspective that there is some reason to believe would be educationally beneficial in a given school or department at a given time, and in this sort of case their special perspective could count as a legitimate job-related qualification. In some cases their uniquely valuable perspective might be connected to their sex or race, but there is no reason to expect that this will be the case generally.

(5) Harm to Beneficiaries

Besides the fact already noted that giving preference to groups who are visibly different from other faculty members will tend to undermine the status of all members of these groups, preferential appointment of women and people of color has other adverse consequences for the beneficiaries. Many people will take preferential policies as evidence that women and people of color are unable to make it on their own because they just don't have what it takes. And if preferentially appointed faculty are, in fact, visibly less qualified than their white male colleagues, this will reinforce whatever negative racial and sexual stereotypes their students and colleagues may have.

When coupled with the rhetoric of representation, preferential appointment of women and people of color subjects them to strong pressures to conform to what someone else considers to be the perspective of women, or of black people, etc. A black man who resists the picture of black people as victims, and who searches out and teaches his students about black people who have been highly successful in various ways (entrepreneurs, doctors, inventors, respected landowners, community members, etc.) and about positive images of blackness and black people in religion and art, may well have to face considerable opposition from other black people. Likewise, a woman who opposes permissive abortion laws (even if she does so on the grounds that she believes them to be to the disadvantage of women) is unlikely to be welcomed with open arms by her sisters.

A recent article in the *Chronicle of Higher Education* notes that the new faculty cohort (those appointed in the 1970s and 1980s) is only 43 percent native-born white men, but that the new faculty are "doing the same damn thing as the old people"—namely, 70 percent of them are relying on lecturing—and that this "raises a lot of alarm bells."[37] But why should anyone suppose that women or people of color would lecture less than white men? This sort of treatment denies them the right accorded to white men to be themselves and make up their own minds about substantive and pedagogical issues,[38] and is particularly alienating since people are assigned to the groups in question on the basis of attributes over which they have no control, such as sex, race, or national origin. If a candidate's contribution to diversity were judged in terms of what he or she had done, or in terms of some freely chosen attribute, then according them preference for this would not rob them of their moral agency and autonomy in the same way.

(6) Bad Effects on Students

There is also reason to believe that preferentially appointing women and people of color in order to enhance diversity on campus will actually lessen dialogue on campus. For one thing, the fact that preferentially appointed professors are not in any sort of regular two-way communication with those whose perspective they are to represent means that there is less room for them to enter into dialogue with their colleagues. The official positions of each group become reified because there is no way to go back and check with the constituency being represented to allow them to change their minds.[39] A lawyer can go back to his or her client and suggest that perhaps it would be in the client's interests to modify his or her demands or to settle out of court. But since professors cannot do this, they can only continue to express the views they take to be those of their group (discovering exactly how the official view of a given group gets defined would be fascinating from a sociological point of view), and this results more in preaching than in dialogue. Hence what emerges is an elite group with an artificially homogenized "culture" that is not rooted in the community they present themselves as representing.

Lack of dialogue among faculty is educationally very damaging to students. If their teachers work within totally different conceptual frameworks and make no attempt to respond to positions other than their own, students tend to become hopelessly confused, give up even trying to develop coherent beliefs of their own, and retreat into just giving each professor what he or she wants. They will write feminist papers for feminist professors, conservative papers for conservative professors, and then go out and conform just as readily to whatever demands their employers make on them with scarcely a thought to what they really believe and why.

(7) The Dark Side of the Rainbow Coalition

The Rainbow Coalition is defined almost entirely by exclusion; its members are *not* white (heterosexual) men. It would seem in principle at least that they could just think of themselves as offering new and valuable perspectives that had been previously overlooked by the dominant culture—perspectives they hope will complement and enrich the existing intellectual life of the college community—without necessarily being hostile toward white men. Unfortunately this has not happened.

In part this results when preferential affirmative action is practiced, because in order to morally justify a policy that appears to be on the face of it unfair, there is a need to show that those who are harmed by the policy are not entirely innocent. They have profited unfairly from injustices in the past, they have behaved (or are behaving) in oppressive ways, deep in their hearts they harbor racist and sexist attitudes, their characteristic ways of thinking and acting are evil (aggressive, dominating, hierarchical, violent, competitive, objectifying), and so, after all, they deserve to be passed over for faculty appointments. To the extent that what the Rainbow Coalition groups share is the experience of marginalization, it is white (heterosexual) men who have marginalized them, and if one ups the ante and moves from marginalization (which could, it would seem, be inadvertent) to victimization, then white (heterosexual) men are cast in an even worse light. And directing one's hostilities toward a common enemy is a well-known way of maintaining group solidarity.

And there is something even deeper and more disturbing going on, often very close to the surface.[40] One of the distinctive things about postmodern culture is its rejection of "the Father." Although many people have, of course, had bad experiences with their fathers, the "Father" in question is more of a mythic figure. Some religious writers take the "Father" to be God. One plausible hypothesis in Freudian terms is that hostility toward the Father is really resentment of the "reality principle" which it is the traditional duty of fathers to enforce. To this should be added a broader hostility toward our cultural tradition for its invocation of what Rudyard Kipling called "the gods of the copybook headings" and the supposedly oppressive behavior they have been used to legitimate. As one representative of the cultural left put it, "perhaps the noblest task of the popular historian is to make us ashamed of our forefathers."[41]

All these different strands come together to generate hostility toward white men of a sort that has very little to do with the particular individuals who suffer its effects. Those most severely damaged by preferential affirmative action (white men forced out of the profession) never get their foot in the door at all, but all white men feel the effects of these attitudes to some extent. The situation is worsened considerably if faculty or students in special programs such as Women's Studies or Black Studies express racial and sexual hostility toward white men, or if special "diversity" consultants come on campus and subject people to humiliating treatment simply because they are white men.[42]

Being subjected to negative racial and sexual stereotypes is likely to cause white heterosexual men to become excessively placating (until the worm turns and rage takes over) or else to internalize the negative stereotypes and act on them.[43] These patterns do not make for harmonious and healthy relationships among colleagues.

Concluding Questions on Diversity

(1) What sorts of diversity are valuable? In practice no one advocates limitless diversity. Appointing defenders of adult-child sex or virulent racists (of any color) might well increase diversity, but no one (I hope) proposes granting them preference. On what grounds should the beneficiaries of affirmative action be selected? Multiculturalists have failed to provide any sort of principled way of determining which groups ought to be selected as beneficiaries of affirmative action. They usually defend their choice of beneficiaries by relying on the notions of "marginalization" and "victimization."

If the intellectual purpose of education is liberating students from the sway of the dominant (or hegemonic) discourse and according more of a voice to the marginalized, then selection should be made on the basis of marginalization in the broader society. But who is marginalized and how do we determine this?

There are a number of ways people can be marginalized, but the ones that seem most salient in the thinking of the multiculturalists are (1) the relative scarcity of persons of a given group in visible positions of power and wealth in the broader society (black people, for example), or (2) their holding beliefs or engaging in practices that are rejected, condemned, or regarded with distaste by most people (e.g., homosexuals).

Criteria (1) and (2) need not go together, however. A group may not have attained to a proportional share of positions of power merely because its members are disproportionately recent immigrants, poor, young, uneducated, or because many of its members prefer to stay home with their children. But they may, for all that, hold highly conventional beliefs. Homosexuals engage in practices condemned by many, but they are not disproportionately poor[44] and many of them are highly educated, articulate, and influential politically.

A related way of defending one's choice of the beneficiaries of affirmative action is by pointing to the fact that all the groups have suffered oppression or victimization. Therefore they have special insights into our culture that others lack, and can supply a uniquely valuable perspective on campus. There are, however, some serious difficulties with justifying one's selection of the groups deserving preference in terms of their victim status. First, not all members of the groups currently accorded preference have been victimized, and lots of other people have been victimized just as badly or worse. Second, there is no special reason to think that being victimized gives people superior insight. Third, having a permanent stake in defining oneself as a victim is degrading to people.[45] Fourth, lumping types of victimization together in this way tends to trivialize real oppression. People in all walks of life no doubt suffer their own inner agonies, but to treat the suffering of a middle-class college woman who feels oppressed by pressure to please men as on a par with that of a recent Mexican American immigrant who lives in a drug- and crime-infested barrio does not seem right.

Perhaps a persuasive justification on grounds of diversity for the list of currently favored groups can be provided, but I have so far been unable to discover one.[46] At this point, then, political considerations and the desire to promote the careers of people who think in the way they do necessarily take over.

(2) How valuable is diversity anyway? Suppose you are opening a factory to produce widgets (e.g., milking machines). Suppose that you preferentially hire members of some ethnic groups with less experience and training for jobs on the grounds that these groups have been underrepresented in the dairy industry. Since they are recent immigrants and their English is poor, they have trouble communicating with their supervisors and each other. You then go out and hire some animal rights advocates (followers of Tom Regan) who believe that milking cows is exploitative (and who consequently throw shoes into the machinery when no one is looking), some Hindus who regard cows as sacred, and some aggressive supporters of agribusiness ideology who believe only in the profit motive and consequently seek to increase the yield of milk by any means possible regardless of discomfort to the cows. Clearly this is not a recipe for putting together a particularly harmonious and productive work team. (The analogy is not perfect for education, but often the educational goals of different faculty members are as unlike as the goals of the Hindus, agribusiness representatives, and followers of Tom Regan in the parable.)

Internal Arguments: Summary

Those who justify affirmative action by appealing to the three internal goods discussed so far—role models, mentors, and diversity—have some laudable aims. They seek to make universities more inclusive, to encourage female and minority students and make them feel welcome, and to broaden the range of intellectual and cultural perspectives available to students. These goods are widely accepted as valuable both by those who think in terms of the democratic liberal model and by multiculturalists.

However, if the arguments developed above are sound, then trying to attain these goods by awarding *preference* to women and people of color for faculty jobs, and justifying this policy along the lines suggested by the multiculturalist model, is not the right way to proceed.

If role models and mentors for female and minority students are obtained by means of preferential rather than merely procedural affirmative action, this will undermine their status in the eyes of students and colleagues and impair their ability to serve as role models. Those appointed will be in danger of being marginalized themselves within the university community and taking their female and minority students along with them into a kind of second-class enclave. And the expectation that female and minority students will be mentored mainly by same-kind faculty increases the likelihood of a separate track system that places such students at a competitive disadvantage when they graduate.

Preferential appointment of women and people of color in order to increase diversity seems on the face of it more promising and less divisive because diversity should benefit everyone. But, as has been argued above, the way such policies have been justified and put into effect has tended to increase tribalization, to decrease dialogue, and generally to cause harm to those who were supposed to benefit from it. At this point, however, it is important to realize that one person's unwanted side effect may be something ardently desired by another. Those adhering (implicitly or explicitly) to a democratic liberal model of education are troubled by the escalation of tribalization, but for the more extreme multiculturalists (those most influenced by postmodernist philosophy), the phenomenon described by their opponents as "tribalization" is something they celebrate—in fact it is the very point of the whole exercise.

One source of the problem, thus, is the lack of consensus about the purpose of humanities education. Throwing together people who are very different in values and culture has always been a recipe for intergroup conflict, particularly if it is done in a way that makes some members of the community feel they have been unjustly treated. Diversity is most manageable and fruitful when it is a type of diversity that we have some reason to believe will contribute to fruitful dialogue (and this must go deeper than sex or skin color), and when it is balanced by a shared commitment to something higher—such as a political cause, a religious tradition, the love of literature, or the search for truth. Conflict is to be expected when diversity is introduced at a time when any sense of commonality is under attack, and thus it is not surprising that intergroup conflict in universities is on the increase.

II. External Goods

Beyond Fantasy Politics

What goes on in universities clearly does have an effect on the broader society. In order to see clearly what it is, however, it is necessary to break free of the sort of fantasy politics that has become common in academia. Decentering or deconstructing the dominant (or hegemonic) discourse in classrooms or scholarly journals should not be confused with bringing about a revolution. To do so is to fall into the error of the Left Hegelians who believed that since the real and the rational were the same, it was sufficient to show that an institution was irrational in order to abolish it in practice. This way of thinking is idealistic in that they believed that thought determines reality.

Instead of trying to actually change society in ways that will alleviate human misery, the academic left has become increasingly ingrown and caught up in battles whose stakes are largely symbolic and often of interest only to the intellectual elite, thus leaving the real centers of power in society largely untouched. The battle over inclusive language is a case in point. The underlying assumption is that if we make people talk in the right way this will change their hearts and actions in some deep way.[47]

The Influence of Universities

Although their power to reshape culture is limited, universities are in a position to exercise a unique sort of influence on the broader society. A very large percentage of the population passes through them (in 1994, 61.9 percent of those who had graduated from high school in the preceding twelve months were enrolled in college),[48] and they play a central role in the transmission of culture from one generation to the next. There are two main ways in which their influence is felt by those outside the university: (1) the example they set for other institutions (as a kind of "city on a hill"), and (2) the students who graduate from them and go out to become tomorrow's citizens and leaders.

The City on a Hill

One way of thinking about the role of universities is the idea that universities ought to serve as a kind of "city on a hill." This idea has deep roots in the American psyche, since Americans have so often thought of their country as a kind of "city on a hill." John Winthrop wrote: "For we must consider that we shall be as a City upon a hill. The eyes of all people are upon us."[49] Essentially this is the role model argument writ large. The university, thus understood, can serve as a kind of model or paradigm for how people of different races, cultures, and convictions can learn from each other and coexist in peace and mutual respect. This way of thinking about the role of universities is not merely fantasy politics because it involves a sort of praxis; faculty and students must participate in a certain way of life together.

A related argument is that universities can serve as a kind of beacon of hope to the disadvantaged. The city on the hill will inspire other institutions to follow its example, and therefore those who are oppressed can hope that they will not be left out forever, but will ultimately attain their place in the sun also. It is hoped that this will keep them from despairing of the possibility of success, and encourage them to stay in school and work hard.

The "city on a hill" argument provides support for affirmative action only if such policies in fact contribute to there being places where people of different races, cultures, and convictions learn from each other and coexist in peace and mutual respect. This external argument, then, is entirely dependent on the success of the internal arguments.

The difficulty with the beacon of hope argument is that the most severely disadvantaged are unlikely to be much helped by preferential appointment of women and people of color to the professorate. Although ghetto residents may aspire to become successful, they are unlikely to think of success in terms of being college teachers, and will not know much about faculty appointment policies in any case. Even if they did know that some individual who has the same skin color or ethnic background as they do has attained a prestigious position, this does nothing at all to actually improve their life prospects. Its value, if it has one, is entirely symbolic, and in the absence of serious efforts to do something of more concrete value to them, the symbol will probably not have much power to inspire them.

Moreover, if, in the wake of affirmative action policies, racial and ethnic tensions worsen, and universities become war zones, then those outside the university will not be drawn to imitate them. (One could, of course, take the position that we should "do justice though the heavens fall" and that this is the example universities should set, but at this point we are no longer dealing with a consequentialist argument.) And if they fail as cities on the hill, this will also impair their ability to function as beacons of hope to the disadvantaged.

Likewise, preferential appointment of women and people of color for teaching positions, far from inspiring citizens to build a more just society, is likely to exacerbate one other dangerous social trend—namely, the crisis of legitimacy affecting all public institutions.[50] More and more people are coming to believe that the government is not genuinely representative of them, that elites are running the country, playing elaborate bureaucratic shell games to hide what they are doing, and employing high-sounding rhetoric to put things over on them, while holding them and their concerns in contempt.[51] Preferential faculty appointment policies are very likely to add fuel to this particular fire.

Since the vast majority of Americans oppose preferential treatment based on race, gender, or ethnic background, engaging in it is to them a sign that universities (state schools, especially), like other public institutions, are being run by people who are wholly unresponsive to their preferences and moral convictions. This might not be bad necessarily, since there are reasons why universities sometimes need to be insulated from having to pander to the preferences (or even the moral convictions) of voters. But the situation is more complicated in this case.

Insofar as multiculturalists claim to be democratizing the university but don't listen to the concerns of members of the (marginalized) groups whose interests they claim to represent, they are setting an example for the broader society that confirms the widespread perception that people in elite positions are engaging in a spurious pretense of being democratic, while being indifferent to them and their concerns. Students who do not have any realistic hopes of becoming members of the elite themselves are especially likely to be angered by this. And those who do think of themselves as members of the elite will acquire a perverse model for elite behavior. In short, we have the precise opposite of the kind of city on a hill a reasonable citizen might desire.

Effects on College Graduates

The other main way in which universities have an impact on the broader society is through their graduates. What will students take with them when they leave college, and what impact, if any, will preferential appointment of women and people of color for faculty positions have on this?

Preferential affirmative action policies usually appeal for justification to the multiculturalist model (since most of the other justifications tend to have demeaning implications for the beneficiaries).[52] And if, as a result, students receive an education along the lines envisioned by this model, this is unlikely to have good consequences for the broader society—either those hoped for by proponents of that model themselves, or ones that are desirable on other grounds.

Judged by relatively traditional criteria, an education along the lines envisioned by the multiculturalist model may in fact fit students to do more harm than good. The habits of thought that they acquire are likely to stay with them longer than the specific views they are taught. If they do not learn to engage in respectful and intelligent dialogue with those who disagree with them while they are in college (but rather adopt a purely tribalistic stance and employ ad hominem arguments against all opponents), they probably won't learn to do so at all, and this will be a major loss for society. It will contribute to the general loss of civility and seriously jeopardize the survival of democratic institutions.

If universities do not get students critically engaged with the Western tradition so that they can learn from the past—building on the good and reforming the bad—then there is no other institution that can step in and fill the gap. Cultural traditions are easier to destroy than to build, and a new culture cannot be produced just by willing it. Students will emerge from college without an in-depth knowledge of *any* culture—something that will impoverish and narrow their lives. And without some knowledge of history and culture (their own and those of at least some other societies), they will not have enough of a sense of the world within which they live to function effectively as citizens.

These objections against people who regard our cultural tradition as corrupt and do not want to see it handed on are not distinctively conservative. In fact Karl Marx would agree wholeheartedly with them, for not only would he be critical of contemporary cultural radicals for redefining the ground of political struggle in an excessively idealistic direction, he would also be quite horrified by their rejection of the Western cultural tradition. Marx was concerned with the democratization of culture, in the sense that he wanted the proletariat to be freed from oppressive and alienating kinds of labor that stunted their human potential and to be able to share in the riches of their cultural tradition. He believed passionately that they should be able to read Shakespeare and Aeschylus, to go to art museums, and to listen to Beethoven.[53]

Apart from exposure to their cultural tradition, students also need the critical thinking skills that will enable them to intelligently evaluate the various claims made on their time, money, and moral energies, both as individuals and as citizens. They also need to acquire the ability to speak and write clear and grammatical English. Not all multiculturalists believe that teaching students logic and grammar is an illegitimate imposition of white heterosexual male hegemony, although some clearly do.[54] But to the extent that such people have influence in the curriculum, or that other sorts of pedagogical goals are allowed to crowd out teaching students basic writing and thinking skills, this neglect will handicap students the rest of their lives. It is also likely to bring down the wrath of outside forces on the universities as more and more employers discover that they can no longer presume that job candidates with B.A.s are able to write and think clearly. American universities have long enjoyed more independence from the government than those in most other countries, but they may soon lose this independence if things continue as they are going.

Defenders of the multiculturalist model hope that their students will become more open-minded, flexible, tolerant of difference, and accepting of people whose way of life is unlike their own. This sort of education will prepare them to be citizens in an increasingly multiracial and multicultural America, and to participate more effectively in the global economy. These students, they hope, will go out and transform society by converting others to these sorts of attitudes—particularly insofar as they are able to attain power in those institutions that confer legitimacy such as the media and education.

The power of professors to significantly affect the values and attitudes of their students, however, is rather limited. Ideas acquired in the classroom are likely to be a thin veneer over well-entrenched ways of thinking derived from their families and previous experiences, and one that they will shed quickly when they marry and settle down. Students tend to regard required humanities courses as less important than those in their major, and think very much in terms of preparing for their future careers. Moreover, there are features of the multiculturalist program that actually tend to be counterproductive—to achieve results quite the opposite of those intended, such as making students less flexible and tolerant, and producing "anti-evangelists" (students who go out and tell the world how terrible their college experience was).[55]

Strong multiculturalists influenced by postmodernism are the ones most responsible for the counterproductive effects in question. Teachers who take the attitude that it is their job to liberate students from the culture they were raised in and to expose them to a variety of perspectives deeply alien to their own while forbidding them to make any moral or intellectual judgments about the relative merits of different ways of life are likely to generate considerable anger and resistance in their students. This is especially true if they try in direct and aggressive ways to effect a deep personal transformation in their students (something which students naturally find invasive). People who feel that their whole way of life is under attack are likely to become more, rather than less, rigid, defensively tribalistic, and hostile to those they perceive as different or alien to them. This will generate a sort of ripple effect in the broader society. Many people presently feel that their entire way of life is under attack, and what they hear about what is going on in universities is likely to feed their fears, increase their tendency to become rigid and strident, and thus make social peace harder to attain.

The Redistributive Argument

For some people the desire to create a more just society is the most important reason for supporting affirmative action. Like affirmative action policies in such fields as the construction industry, fire departments, or banks, affirmative action in faculty appointments has a redistributive effect. By awarding professorships to members of previously disadvantaged groups it contributes to a more equitable distribution of relatively prestigious and well-paying jobs. The redistributive effect of preferential appointment of women and people of color for college teaching jobs, however, is fairly small. The number of college professors is not large enough to have a major impact on the distribution of wealth in our society, teaching jobs characteristically do not pay all that well relative to the other professions, and since such jobs necessarily go to the most educated members of the groups in question, those who are most severely disadvantaged economically will not be benefited.

It may be objected that although the redistributive effect of preferential appointment for college teachers is small, preferential affirmative action is morally required in order to bring about a more equitable distribution of wealth, power, and prestige in our society, and there is no reason why universities should be exempt from this general requirement (even if it does have some educationally undesirable consequences). To resolve the issue at this general level, however, goes beyond the purpose of this chapter, which has been to show that the consequences of such policies being followed for faculty appointments are more bad than good. Some criticisms of the model of justice underlying the more general form of the redistributive argument will be offered in Chapter 5.

Possible Bad Effects of Discontinuing Affirmative Action

We must also consider the bad consequences that might follow from discontinuing a well-entrenched policy of affirmative action. Those disadvantaged people who had begun to hope that they might ultimately attain a more equitable share of society's good things might become disheartened by the abandonment of affirmative action policies and stop trying to better themselves. And, given how deeply entrenched such policies are, the sort of structural changes involved in eliminating them might themselves be destabilizing and produce serious conflicts.

The negative effects of discontinuing affirmative action policies are difficult to foresee, although not for that reason necessarily negligible. If we confine ourselves to the appointment of college teachers, however, the effects are unlikely to be terribly large. It is hard to tell just how much the most severely disadvantaged know or care about faculty hiring policies, or even affirmative action generally, since such policies benefit better-off members of the disadvantaged groups in any case. Discontinuing preferential admissions to college and professional schools might be more likely to discourage such people, although how much impact even that would have is open to question.

As for the argument that affirmative action has become too well entrenched to change without causing conflict and dislocation, it does seem that if a policy is in fact having bad consequences, the fact that it is entrenched is not a reason for keeping it. Inflexibility is not a virtue, and there is no reason to despair of finding other ways of resolving the problems that affirmative action was intended to remedy.

III. Conclusion

Preferential appointment of women and people of color for faculty positions has a natural affinity with the multiculturalist model of education. If such policies are already in place (for whatever reasons), they encourage people to develop new justifications for them; theories can generate practices, but practices already in place also generate justifications. The multiculturalist defense for affirmative action is particularly popular because it emphasizes positive qualities possessed by the beneficiaries themselves. But when accompanied by a multiculturalist rationale, affirmative action is particularly pernicious in its effects, since it accentuates tribalization and thus results in increased social conflict. And the democratic liberal model, as I have argued above, fails to support the sort of preferential affirmative action defended and practiced in the contemporary academy.

Certainly it is possible that if justified by some rationale other than multiculturalism, preferential policies aimed at improving the position of racial and ethnic minorities might succeed in decreasing racism and prejudice in the long run. But the opposite seems to be happening, and other countries that have adopted preferential policies of these sorts have likewise experienced increased conflict along racial and ethnic lines.[56] Hence the burden of proof is on those who claim that the long-term effect will be one of lessening racism. Perhaps if they can point to a successful program of this sort in some other country or period of history, we might be able to learn something about how to avoid the sorts of problems we are currently experiencing.

Until we are given good reason to believe that the long-run effects will be better than those being experienced in the present, it seems altogether appropriate that universities should concentrate on doing their own proper job well, and only engage in symbolic politics or efforts to attain greater redistributive justice to the extent that these do not get in the way of their primary task.

In short, the forward-looking arguments for preferential affirmative action largely fail. And the same is true, as we saw in Chapter 2, of backward-looking arguments. But both these families of arguments take existing academic standards and appointment procedures to be legitimate, and argue only that they should be overridden in some cases. The natural recourse of the defender of affirmative action, therefore, is to argue that existing appointment procedures or standards of professional competence are systematically biased against women and people of color, and that some form of corrective affirmative action is therefore necessary in order to get the best candidate. If this sort of argument can be made out, the state of the question would be changed in fundamental ways. The corrective argument is therefore our next concern.

Notes

1. Although I must confess to some skepticism about the importance of teachers as role models. I have, for years, asked my sophomore ethics classes to write a short essay describing a person they admire and would like to imitate, and I could count on the fingers of one hand the number of times a teacher has been selected.

2. The papers from the symposium are published as "Role Models in Education," *Industrial and Labor Relations Review* 48, 3 (April 1995), 482–579.

3. Brandice Canes and Harvey Rosen, "Following in Her Footsteps? Faculty Gender Composition and Women's Choice of Majors," *Industrial and Labor Relations Review* 48, 3 (April 1995), 486.

4. Ronald G. Ehrenberg, Daniel D. Goldhaber, and Dominic C. Brewer, "Do Teachers' Race, Gender, and Ethnicity Matter? Evidence from the National Educational Longitudinal Study of 1988," *Industrial and Labor Relations Review* 48, 3 (April 1995), 547.

5. Donna Rothstein, "Do Female Faculty Influence Female Students' Educational and Labor Market Attainments?" *Industrial and Labor Relations Review* 48, 3 (April 1995), 515.

6. Anita Allen alludes to their lower test scores in "The Role Model Argument and Faculty Diversity," *Philosophical Forum* 24, 103 (Fall-Spring 1992–93), 276. Reprinted in Steven Cahn, ed., *The Affirmative Action Debate* (New York: Routledge, 1995).

7. Test scores, however, are not the only measure of academic success. Graduates of HBCUs may, for example, have a lower dropout rate in graduate school than those who attended predominantly white schools, or may be more successful in their careers. Whether HBCUs offer special educational advantages for their students (and if so what the advantages are) is controversial. For a sophisticated analysis of the issues involved, see Ronald Ehrenberg, ed., *Choices and Consequences: Contemporary Policy Issues in Education* (Ithaca: ILR Press, 1994), ch. 4.

8. See Jill Constantine, "The Effect of Attending Historically Black Colleges and Universities on Future Wages of Black Students," *Industrial and Labor Relations Review* 48, 3 (April 1995), 531–47, and Ronald Ehrenberg and Donna S. Rothstein, "Do Historically Black Institutions of Higher Education Confer Unique Advantages on Black Students? An Initial Analysis," in Ehrenberg, *Choices and Consequences*, 89–139. There is some evidence at least that even though their test scores are lower, graduates of HBCUs have a lower dropout rate in college and in graduate school, but the sample involved is small and more research is needed (data supplied for the field of physics by Roman Czuijko, American Institute of Physics).

9. Allen, "Role Model Argument," 277.

10. Allen, "Role Model Argument," 273.

11. This sort of anti-Catholic prejudice is of course more prevalent in certain parts of the country and in certain disciplines than it is in others, but the same is true of all prejudices.

12. The problem that the role model argument invites deceit could be obviated if one could successfully show that the appointment process itself and/or the criteria used by search committees are unfair and contain unnoticed biases against women and people of color. In this case, the person appointed as a role model would not really be less qualified but only wrongly perceived to be so. This argument (the "corrective argument") will be evaluated in chapter 4.

13. R. Halcomb, "Mentors and the Successful Woman," *Across the Board* 26 (1980), 13–18. Ann Preston's work also confirms the importance of mentors for women in the sciences, although she has not yet found evidence that women need female mentors. She is at the University of New York at Stony Brook, and has work in progress on this question.

14. I am indebted to a conversation with Nina Cappolino for this insight. She finds this sort of thing to be an obstacle to female students in her own field (classics).

15. There is some literature on mentoring in academia, but much of it is anecdotal in character, involves small samples or surveys with low response rates, or is heavily ideological in character. References to some work in the area can be found in the essays by Kathleen Day Hulbert and by Gary A. Olson and Evelyn Ashton-Jones in Sara Munson Deats and Lagretta Tallent Lenker, eds., *Gender and Academe: Feminist Pedagogy and Politics* (Lanham, Md.:

Rowman & Littlefield, 1994). See also M. L. Hall and W. R. Allen, "Race Consciousness and Achievement: Two Issues in the Study of Black Graduate/Professional Studies," *Integrated Education* 20, January/April 1982, 56–61. Some difficulties that, to my mind, vitiate much of the research done in this area are that they often rely exclusively on reports by students and do not employ white or male control groups.

16. See discussion of different sorts of remedies in Chapter 5.

17. One study, for example, found that at a large research-oriented institution, 7 percent of the faculty were women, but they acted as mentors to 21 percent of the male students and 37 percent of the female students. Cited by Kathleen Hulbert, "Gender Patterns in Faculty-Student Mentoring Relationships" in Sara Munson Deats and Lagretta Tallent Lenker, eds., *Gender and Academe*, ch. 18

18. See Ehrenberg, Goldhaber, and Brewer, "Do Teachers' Race, Gender, and Ethnicity Matter?"

19. Consider, for example, the bitter differences between various sorts of Protestants and Marxists.

20. Preferentially admitting black students, therefore, has different effects than giving preference to the children of alumni or to veterans. This has nothing to do with whether one sort of preference is more fair than the other, but is merely a function of the fact that the beneficiaries are easily identifiable by sight in one case but not in the other.

21. Looking at projected figures for 2050 (which are of course very speculative) America will still be 72.3 percent white. These projections, however, assume no procreation across racial and ethnic lines, but the number of births of mixed-race babies rose at a rate 26 times as fast as that of any other racially defined group, and our present ways of categorizing people may well be superseded by others by 2050. Todd Gitlin, *The Twilight of Common Dreams* (New York: Metropolitan Books, 1995), 110–13.

22. A psychology department that appoints only behaviorists is depriving its students of exposure to other legitimate traditions of thought within their discipline. And the same is true if an economics department appoints only followers of Milton Friedman, or a philosophy department appoints only Thomists or only Phenomenologists.

23. Foucault, for example, says that "What is found at the historical beginning of things is not the inviolable identity of their origin; it is the dissension of other things. It is disparity." From "Nietzsche, Genealogy, History," in Michel Foucault, *Language, Counter-Memory, Practice: Selected Essays and Interviews by Michel Foucault*, Donald F. Bouchard, ed., trans. Donald Bouchard and Sherry Simon (Ithaca: Cornell University Press, 1977), 139–64.

24. As expressed, for example, in the slogan "unity in our love of man," which was used as late as 1970.

25. On the connection between these see the argument in Chapter 1.

26. Considerable anecdotal evidence to support my conclusions can be found, however, in any number of recent books. For example, Lynne Cheney's *Telling the Truth* (New York: Simon and Schuster, 1995) and Richard Bernstein's *The Dictatorship of Virtue* (New York: Knopf, 1994).

27. I also believe that the traditionalist model has an important place in the current intellectual climate. Diversity among as well as within universities can be very valuable. Many schools are too small to represent a large variety of points of view, and students should be able to choose (within some limits such as schools inculcating racial hatred) to obtain an education within a particular tradition if they want to (consider, e.g., Brandeis or Notre Dame).

28. The McCarthy era is an example of politics impinging on education from without. Another example might be the way Thomas Jefferson set up the University of Virginia in order to teach his own political views.

29. In fact, I think that both these accusations are correct, as will emerge in the course of this chapter.

30. For empirical data confirming this fact, see, e.g., Elizabeth Fox-Genovese, *Feminism Is Not the Story of My Life* (New York: Doubleday, 1996).

31. Eighty-five percent of women aged 30 to 49 supported mandatory parental consent or notification for abortions involving minors. Polls conducted by the polling company in Washington, D.C., (202) 667–6577.

32. For example, the reason why the census does not collect data on religious affiliation is because Jews (particularly older ones) have strongly opposed doing so.

33. Directive 15, issued in May 1977, introduced the present breakdown and required government agencies to collect and publish data on at least these groups.

34. Aristotle's favorite examples of natural kinds were the various species of animals and plants.

35. Historically and cross-culturally much of women's distinctive lore and rituals have centered around fertility, rites of initiation connected with the onset of menstruation, herbal medicine, midwifery, the care of infants, and (probably) ways of tiptoeing around the male ego and getting what they want (I haven't seen hard data on this one). Although there are a few places in the curriculum where such lore might be of value (such as women's health care), such places are rare, and there is no special reason to assume that most contemporary American women will be knowledgeable about such subjects.

36. This is especially true, of course, when layoffs are in question.

37. *Chronicle of Higher Education* (Feb. 2, 1996), A18.

38. Anita Allen, for example, complains that she finds it a burden to feel she must always be perfectly black and perfectly female. "The Role Model Argument," 274.

39. I owe this point to Phil Devine.

40. For example, a colleague of mine once told me that the purpose of a proposed critical studies program was "to kill the father."

41. Dennis Porter, quoted in Lawrence James, *The Rise and Fall of the British Empire* (New York: St. Martin's Press, 1994), 602.

42. I hope her accounts are not typical of the behavior of those leading "diversity training workshops," but some of the tactics described by Lynne Cheney in *Telling the Truth*, ch. 2, are quite disturbing.

43. These patterns are ones that develop in anyone subjected to negative racial or sexual stereotyping. Black people and women have also manifested these sorts of patterns, as is well known.

44. It has been claimed that they have higher incomes than heterosexuals, but a study by Lee Badgett of the University of Maryland published in *The Advocate*, Oct. 4, 1994, disputes this claim. To my knowledge no one claims that homosexuals have generally lower incomes than heterosexuals.

45. For example, I am reliably informed of several cases involving the media in which enormous pressure was put on people to downplay or deny facts about prominent black people that conflicted with the image of black people as victims. The motivation to present black people as victims was on several occasions so strong that it led people to actually falsify evidence.

46. I am not alone in this judgment. One of the more philosophically sophisticated multiculturalists, Will Kymlika, in *Multicultural Citizenship* (Oxford: Clarendon Press, 1995), 144–46, admits that the proliferation of "oppressed groups" is a real danger (on one estimate, that proposed by Iris Young, 80 percent of the U.S. population would count as oppressed), and that the problem of which groups should be represented has not been resolved satisfactorily to date.

47. Experience does not seem to bear this out. Men who assiduously use inclusive language quite often treat women worse than men who do not. Latin does not distinguish male and female singular genitive pronouns but Rome was brutally patriarchal for all that.

48. *Digest of Education Statistics 1995* (Washington, D.C.: U.S. Government Printing Office, 1995), Table 178.

49. Robert Winthrop, ed., *Life and Letters of John Winthrop* (Boston: Ticknor and Fields, 1867), II, 18–19. John Winthrop was a seventeenth-century governor of Massachusetts Bay colony.

50. Only 20 percent of Americans believe they can trust the government in Washington to do what is right most of the time. Three-fourths say that they are dissatisfied with the way the political process is working, and a similar percentage believe that government is run for the sake of a few special interests. Poll data in Michael J. Sandel, *Democracy's Discontent* (Cambridge: Harvard University Press, 1996), 353 n. 1.

51. Rush Limbaugh articulates this sort of view in a crude but rhetorically effective way.

52. The compensatory argument emphasizes how damaged they have been by their victimization, and the corrective argument often comes across as a demand for bending the standards in favor of certain groups.

53. Writers sympathetic to the New Left, like Christopher Lasch and Todd Gitlin, have also criticized academic leftists on this ground.

54. Although it seems that this position would be the most consistent one for a multiculturalist to take. An example of someone who holds this view is Andrea Nye, *Words of Power* (New York: Routledge, 1990).

55. A good example of the anti-evangelist phenomenon is Sacks, in David Sacks and Peter Thiel, *The Diversity Myth: "Multiculturalism" and the Politics of Intolerance at Stanford* (Oakland, Calif.: Independent Institute, 1995).

56. See, e.g., Thomas Sowell, *Preferential Policies: An International Perspective* (New York: W. Morrow, 1990), p. 15.

4

Corrective Arguments

Many defenders of affirmative action justify it as a remedy for presently existing prejudice and discrimination rather than as a compensation for past wrongs and harms, or as a way of attaining desirable goals in the future. Bias against women and minorities, it is argued, has crept into the appointment process, and therefore measures must be undertaken to counteract it. The corrective argument has a pivotal role in the overall case for affirmative action because all defenders of affirmative action propose some change in the way faculty are currently being appointed. If they thought that leaving our present appointment procedures to operate without interference would result in women and minorities being appointed in the desired proportions, then the right thing to do would be to sit back and wait.

The corrective argument, if sound, holds out the hope that we can achieve the desired numerical results without appointing a candidate who is in fact less qualified. Those who favor preferential treatment of women and minorities in faculty appointments on the basis of compensatory or forward-looking considerations therefore usually include a corrective component in their arguments, since most are reluctant to advocate appointing a less qualified person. For not only would doing so evoke opposition from students and from taxpayers at state schools (who would feel shortchanged by such policies), and from white men (who will complain that they are being unjustly treated), but it would also brand the beneficiaries of such policies as second-rate and cast suspicion on the accomplishments of women and people of color who would have succeeded without affirmative action. But if it can be shown that the appointment procedures currently in place are biased against women and minorities, then adopting corrective measures, even quotas, need not have these undesirable implications. They correct bias rather than introducing it. As James Rachels (reprinted in this volume) succinctly puts it, "the quota does not introduce a new element of prejudice. It merely cancels one out."

The corrective argument is difficult to evaluate philosophically, since it is not easily laid out in a structured way with premises and conclusion clearly identified. It consists, rather, of a number of rather loosely connected considerations that are taken to indicate the existence of bias in faculty appointment procedures, together with recommendations for correcting the problem. When one tries to map out the argument, it becomes apparent that those making the corrective argument have different reasons for believing that bias is at work, are motivated by different sorts of concerns, and often do not share the same philosophical presuppositions. Sometimes the same person may appeal to more than one variant of the argument, but it will be most helpful, I think, to set out and evaluate each one in its pure form.

I begin with what I take to be the weakest argument for corrective affirmative action and work up to the strongest, asking for each one what is the central concern or motivation of its proponents, evaluating the evidence they provide for the existence of bias on the part of university search committees, and finally asking for each one how we could determine when bias has been eliminated. Answering this last question is important not only practically (for in the absence of an answer, preferential policies would become never-ending) but also theoretically because it helps bring underlying assumptions out into the open. In the conclusion, I highlight some of the central features common to all or most versions of the corrective argument.

I. The Postmodernist Argument

Postmodernists believe that the standards of excellence employed by search committees are necessarily biased against women and minorities simply because they have been formulated by white men. Their critique is based not on empirical evidence about specific ways in which the criteria for evaluating excellence contain bias, but on a broader philosophical theory concerning the possibility of attaining or even approaching objectivity or truth. Postmodernists regard the "objective" standards devised by white men within the various academic disciplines as a sham—as merely a way of exerting hegemony over women and people of color. Difference is something that cannot be bridged; there is no common human nature that can ground claims to rationality, truth, or objectivity. White men cannot understand the experience of those who are different from themselves, and they necessarily set up professional standards that reflect their own experience and perpetuate their dominance.

Reasoning about these standards is impossible; beneath the mask of rationality and objectivity lie only their own passions and will-to-power. Their "standards" must therefore be replaced by criteria—if need be, quotas—that give women and people of color their proper share of academic positions. Thus Stanley Fish, for example, argues that notions like "fairness" or "merit" are necessarily defined by those in power in accord with their own interests and perspectives,[1] and he defends affirmative action on the grounds that "the playing field is already tilted in favor of those by whom and for whom it was constructed in the first place . . . and the resistance to altering it by the mechanisms of affirmative action is in fact a determination to make sure that the present imbalances are continued as long as possible."[2]

Integral to the postmodernist approach is something called "the hermeneutics of suspicion." This is a method of interpretation based on suspicion of the person whose ideas are being interpreted. (More precisely, this suspicion applies to texts rather than persons, but I shall ignore this complication here.) The person's own account of his or her motivation is discounted in favor of an interpretation that attributes to him or her some sort of discreditable motive. For postmodernists influenced by Marxism it is rationalization of one's own class interests, for Freudians the motives are largely sexual, and for Nietzscheans the driving force in all human social life is the will-to-power (it is the Nietzschean version that is currently most influential). When looking at appointment decisions through the suspicious eyes of the postmodernist, we simply presume bias and regard claims by white male search committee members that they are applying objective standards as mystifications designed to cover up their attempts to assert hegemony over women and people of color.

The hermeneutics of suspicion, then, is at work whenever bias is presumed rather than shown. It runs through the corrective argument in most of its forms. For this argument does not merely demand that search committees that practice racial or sexual discrimination should be ordered to stop and be subject to legal penalties if they do not. Rather, it approaches those making decisions about faculty appointments with a presumption that they cannot be trusted to make decisions on proper professional grounds, either because they are themselves corrupted by prejudice or because the standards, having been formulated by white men, necessarily reflect their biases and perpetuate their dominance. People who are not themselves full-fledged postmodernists often employ this sort of hermeneutics of suspicion to strengthen their case for imposing corrective measures on recalcitrant departments, and it is always important to attempt to discern in each case the basis on which the presumption of bias rests.

Postmodernism is entwined in complex ways with a deepening sense of malaise and loss of confidence in the Western tradition that has become especially evident in humanities education, and it raises deep philosophical problems that require serious and careful treatment of a sort that goes well beyond the limits of this book. Fortunately, however, this sort of treatment is unnecessary for our purposes. For even if we were to concede (as I do not) that they are correct, their argument undercuts itself in several ways, and provides no reason whatsoever for supporting affirmative action for women and people of color.

First, the postmodernist cannot provide reasons why those who have no personal stake in advancing the careers of women and minorities ought to favor affirmative action for these groups. They do not and cannot invoke justice or fairness in the way others who complain of bias in faculty appointment procedures do, since fairness and justice, on their view, are mere mystifications just as much as white men's "objective" standards are. No cure is possible; bias is inescapable. Those who hold this sort of position would, no doubt, prefer a situation in which more academic positions were awarded to those they regard as their allies, but they have undercut any shared principles by means of which they might persuade others that such a situation would be better than the one we now have. Hence, all that remains is political struggle, and there is no reason to promote the interests of women and minorities unless they are your friends. White men may quite legitimately prefer to promote the interests of other white men, or indeed of anyone they like for any reason.

Second, the hermeneutics of suspicion is a game any number can play and therefore it is a weapon that turns back upon the one who employs it. Advocates of affirmative action may be suspected of having their professional judgments distorted by, for example, a desire to promote their own academic careers and those of their friends. Women who employ it against white men may find it directed against them by other women. Harriet Baber, for example, expresses concern that feminist philosophy is a refuge for women who are unable to compete with men on their own ground, and as such in the end undermines academic feminism.[3] If one adopts Baber's view, then, any form of corrective affirmative action that undertakes to change the standards of academic performance to favor women doing less rigorous work than men is simply an attempt to promote the interests of some women at the expense of others. The hermeneutics of suspicion is equally available to those holding traditional or conservative views. For example, Phillip Johnson, a spokesman for the religious right, has argued that contempt for traditional religion pervades conventional forms of science, education, and law,[4] and that this bias corrupts the professional judgment of those working in these fields.

Furthermore, there is no principled way to limit the application of the hermeneutics of suspicion to criteria employed by search committees. It can also be extended to the criteria by which we determine that there is a problem requiring attention and to the associated background conceptions of social justice—whether "gut" or philosophically articulated—in terms of which we debate questions such as discrimination and affirmative action. Mary Anne Warren, for example, takes a "just" society to be one that is fully egalitarian, and one feature of such a society would be that "no one could assume that women, any more than men, ought to be supported by their spouses."[5] Is she not, perhaps, behind a smoke screen of talk about justice, simply trying to promote the interests of career women over those of women who prefer the traditional roles of homemaker and mother? Even the assumption that racial or sex-based discrimination requires a federal remedy can be understood, once the genie of suspicion has been let out of the bottle, as a mask for the will-to-power of groups that get their social position through access to the federal bureaucracy including the courts, and hence have a vested interest in increasing the power of the federal government.

In the context of a Marxist theory of society, or some other theory that claims to have discovered important truths about human nature and history, such suspicions can be contained. We can limit our suspicion to those writers who have an emotional or financial investment in a social and economic system to which we object on independent grounds. But the generalized hermeneutics of suspicion that has entered the intellectual world with the decline of Marxism contains no resources for doing so other than outright partisanship. And when all else is called into question, the illusion that numbers are somehow solid and objective cannot be maintained. No warrant can be given for selecting one set of numbers rather than another. Therefore postmodernism does not support quotas aimed at promoting proportional representation of women and minorities.

Postmodernists, then, although they do allege that bias is operative in decisions about faculty appointments, ultimately believe that bias of one sort or another is inevitable. If we accept their diagnosis of the problem, it is an incurable one, and all that remains is a political struggle in which whoever comes out on top gets to make the rules.

Not only does postmodernism fail to provide support for affirmative action policies in universities, but embracing it is likely to have particularly disastrous consequences for educational institutions. No doubt ulterior motives of all sorts are at work in the affirmative action debate, as elsewhere in politics, but a generalized hermeneutics of suspicion embitters all sides and makes rational discussion of affirmative action, or of anything else for that matter, impossible. If universities are to be places where rational dialogue is possible among colleagues and students, we must take one another's judgments, and the arguments supporting them, at face value, until we are provided with persuasive reasons for regarding them as fraudulent. Search committees, like everyone else, should be regarded as innocent until proven guilty.

II. Bias Embedded Within the Traditional Disciplines

Postmodernists are not the only people who believe that the traditional academic disciplines and their associated standards of excellence have been developed by white men along lines that marginalize the concerns, perspectives, or ways of thinking characteristic (for whatever reasons) of women and people of color, and that this may make it harder for such people to flourish in academia.[6] Some people who do not share the postmodernists' rejection of the possibility of reasoning about these issues have made similar claims. So long as the previously neglected perspectives are not viewed as radically incommensurable with those of white men, this type of critique can avoid falling into the nihilism characteristic of the postmodernists, for whom all there is to intellectual life is a battle of wills-to-power. If difference can be, to some extent at least, bridged, then it will be possible to reform and enrich the disciplines by bringing in the perspectives of women and people of color in such a way that the disciplines will be more hospitable to members of these groups.

I will examine this version of the corrective argument as it has been developed by women, since they have articulated the argument in most detail. They argue that the traditional standards of professional competence are rigged against women because the disciplines themselves are androcentric (i.e., they reflect men's concerns and characteristic ways of thinking).[7] We must, therefore, examine the reasons given for this claim.

Establishing the Existence of Bias

Selective Invocation of Postmodernism

Not all those alleging androcentric bias are motivated by the same concerns, or at least not to the same degree. Nor do they all share the same philosophical assumptions. Often what is going on is a kind of selective invocation of postmodernism in order to discredit established standards of professional competence when the central concern of those making the argument is to show that the imposition of numerical target percentages for appointing women and minorities (something they may wish to do for any number of reasons) will not result in passing over better-qualified candidates. When no attempt is made to show how the disciplines and their associated standards of excellence are androcentric, and no alternative set of standards is offered, this is usually an indication that we are dealing with selective postmodernism. Postmodernism might appear to support their argument because it supplies an easy route to the claim that the disciplines are androcentric (because founded and largely developed by men).

Postmodernism, however, cannot be arbitrarily limited to undermining the *traditional* standards for what counts as professionally competent work in the various disciplines, since if one accepts postmodernism it follows that bias is inescapable. If the only alternative to androcentric bias is gynocentric bias, then no reason can be given why men should not choose to perpetuate the androcentric structure of their disciplines. In fact, the possibility of men and women working together in one discipline at all becomes highly problematic on postmodernist assumptions (indeed the very concept of "a discipline" is undermined). And those taking this sort of position are vulnerable to all the other criticisms leveled at postmodernism in the preceding section.

Statistics

Selective postmodernism might be supplemented with a statistical argument. It might be argued that the scarcity of women in some disciplines is itself evidence of androcentric bias. This assumes that in the absence of bias, women would be proportionally represented in all disciplines. But this is a highly speculative assumption, and arguments against it are offered below in section III.

Attempts to Pinpoint Androcentric Bias

Some of those making this sort of argument, however, do try to specify ways in which the traditional academic disciplines marginalize the concerns, interests, and ways of thinking characteristic of women, and to make suggestions for correcting this sort of bias. Arguments have been offered to this effect along several different lines.

One way that bias against women is sometimes shown is by pointing out that men often do not take feminist methodology seriously intellectually. Leslie Francis, for example, argues that "Whole fields of research may be downgraded because of improper discrimination against a field of inquiry, as when feminist approaches are viewed as problematic."[8] Feminism, thus, is taken to represent the perspective of women, and the cure for androcentric bias on this view would appear to be reshaping the disciplines in accordance with feminist methodology, or at least according feminist thought a larger place in the curriculum.

Francis does not provide any definition of what she takes feminist methodology to involve, but the most prevalent version of it in academia requires one to take gender as one's central organizing concept, and pay special attention to power relationships between the sexes, and to the ways in which gender has been socially constructed to produce and sustain male hegemony over women. Since they take as their goal empowering women and removing obstacles to their attaining positions of power, prestige, and wealth, they encourage women to break free of traditional sex roles and to cultivate the qualities that make for success in the public realm. I shall refer to this view as "Feminism" with a capital F.[9]

There are serious reasons, however, to refrain from identifying Feminism in this sense with the perspective of women, and discrimination against it with bias against women, at least if one is genuinely concerned to enrich the disciplines by bringing in the perspective of previously marginalized groups (in this case women) and not just to achieve certain numerical results. (The majority of courses employing Feminist methodology are taught by women, so that offering more courses in this area entails more jobs for women.) Academic Feminism does not represent the perspective of the majority of women in America.[10] And academic men who are critical of it are not necessarily biased against women. They *may* be acting out of a knee-jerk hostility toward uppity women. But a person (male or female) could have serious reservations about Feminist scholarship in some particular field without having any bias against women as such, and resistance to appointing women may sometimes flow from opposition to Feminism, rather than vice versa (negative attitudes toward women leading one to oppose Feminism).[11] Indeed, I would not be surprised if much of what is commonly taken to be bias against women in academia (at least in some disciplines) is motivated by people's perceptions or misperceptions of feminism.

But more importantly for our purposes in this section, academic women themselves are strongly divided on the question of whether there is androcentric bias in the traditional disciplines and, if so, how it should be corrected, although the differences between these women are obscured by the fact that they all call themselves "feminists." A significant number of academic women totally reject the idea that traditional academic disciplines and their associated standards of excellence need to be reformed in order to reflect the concerns, perspectives, or ways of thinking characteristic of women, and insist that women can and should do the same sort of work men do and be judged by the same standards. They do not think, for example, that there is or should be such a thing as feminist epistemology.[12] These women are frequently resentful of other women who want to revise the standards in the direction of what sounds to them like mere woolly-headedness.[13] They are often (but not always) feminists in a political sense, but do not believe that the content of their professional work reflects any sort of special feminine or feminist perspective.

Another group of academic women agree with the Feminists that women have a distinctive point of view that has been marginalized by mainstream (or "malestream") thought in the traditional academic disciplines, but provide a very different characterization of the distinctive perspective of women (which they sometimes describe as the "feminine voice"). These women wish to reaffirm the value of virtues traditionally associated with women (by contrast with Feminists who regard traditional feminine virtues as bad because they open women up to being exploited). The perspective of women, according to the feminine voice theorists, is largely a function of the experiences they share, in part as a result of the roles they have traditionally played in our society (e.g., as nurturers of small children).[14] But, unlike Feminists, some of the feminine voice theorists would also allow a role for biological differences in shaping women's distinctive perspective.

Advocates of the feminine voice in the academy see themselves as broadening and enriching their disciplines by counteracting the overly "masculine voice" way in which they had been defined, and affirming the value of women and their characteristic ways of thinking. This sort of work can only be done from within each discipline. It cannot be generated at will because someone thinks it would be a good idea, and there is no reason to suppose that every discipline will benefit to an equal degree from these sorts of reforms. A few examples of how feminine voice theorists have attempted to counteract androcentric bias within their disciplines may be helpful.

Carol Gilligan, for example, saw herself as correcting the masculine bias in the work of Lawrence Kohlberg.[15] Kohlberg, she argued, had defined the stages of moral development in a way that took characteristically masculine ways of thinking about moral decision making as normative, and he consequently found girls to be less developed in their ethical reasoning than boys of the same age. Gilligan argued that Kohlberg's emphasis on justice, hierarchy, moral principles, and impartiality was characteristic of the "masculine voice," and that those guided by the "feminine voice" in moral reasoning (also called "the ethics of care") approach ethical decisions differently. The care perspective emphasizes our interdependence and our responsibility to

care for others. It enjoins us to preserve the complex web of relationships in which we find ourselves, and to resolve conflicts by seeking
consensus rather than by the imposition of authority or by violence.

If one takes the justice tradition and the care perspective, then, to be
complementary and equally important to moral reasoning, then what
Gilligan did was to argue for a new and broader understanding of the
psychology of moral development. The difference between the two perspectives is, on her view, a matter of emphasis, since boys and girls are
both able to use the language of the care perspective as well as that of
the justice tradition. There is a difference, but it is not an unbridgeable
one as it is on the postmodernist view.

A parallel development in ethical theory is the recent trend toward
the study of special obligations (ethical obligations we owe to some
persons—such as family, friends, and neighbors—but not to everyone)
rather than moral theories such as Utilitarianism and Kantianism that
focus on obligations we owe to all persons equally and that emphasize
impartiality as a virtue.[16] If Gilligan is right about the way men and
women characteristically think about moral choices, then the renewed
interest in special obligations in ethics (also called "particularism") is
a healthy antidote to the overly "masculine voice" approach that had
previously reigned in ethical theory. Particularism can also be seen as
a manifestation of the feminine voice because women, for a variety of
reasons, have historically devoted much of their energy to their roles
within families and neighborhoods (rather than politics on a broader
scale) and thus are more likely than men to be interested in particular
relationships.

History is a particularly valuable field to look at for our purposes,
since all three types of academic women have done work in this area.
Those who do not think there is anything distinctively feminine or
Feminist about their work have done work that is presumably like that
done by men on whatever topics interested them (consider, for example, Barbara Tuchman's *The Guns of August*).

Feminists have examined history using gender as their central organizing category, focusing on the ways in which women have been kept
subordinate to men. They tend to view the family as a primary locus of
oppression, to be critical of traditional religions, and to search for
Feminist foremothers who broke free of traditional female roles. They
have become increasingly hostile to the universalistic and objective
pretensions of traditional scholarship,[17] seeing it as a mask for pre-
serving male hegemony, and favor an approach that is admittedly per-
spectival and politically committed.[18] This approach has become
dominant in Women's Studies programs, which exist in a somewhat
ambiguous relationship with the broader discipline of history, and

these women claim that women's history can only be legitimately written from a Feminist standpoint.

Historians sympathetic to the feminine voice approach have been more inclined to do social history than political history, and, like Feminists, they accord importance to gender and to analyzing marriage and family life. However, they generally look more favorably on women's contributions in the communal, religious, and familial spheres than Feminists do. Feminine voice theorists need not see themselves as having a distinctively feminine cognitive style. Female historians doing work on the history of marriage and family in the Middle Ages, for example, may not see themselves as employing a methodology differing from that employed by male historians (like men they try to cross-check their sources, avoid reading back modern categories of thought into other periods of time, etc.) or claim that this sort of research is something only women can do. But some female historians in the feminine voice tradition do think of themselves as having a distinctively feminine cognitive style—one that involves empathy, and seeing globally and contextually. One female historian, for example, describes her attitude toward the past as "maternal" and speaks of "wanting to bring people to life again as a mother would want to bear children."[19] The feminine voice approach to history, therefore, can affect the topics studied, the attitude with which one approaches women's lives in other periods, and one's cognitive style.

In light, then, of the fact that academic women are divided about whether there is androcentric bias embedded in the traditional disciplines, and that those who allege such bias have such deeply different understandings of what it involves, the claim that the traditional disciplines are pervaded by androcentric bias cannot be successfully established. A discipline or subspecialty that one woman experiences as alienating, another woman may take to like a duck to water, and thus reforms that make a discipline more hospitable to some women will make it less hospitable to others.

The underlying problem with the androcentrism argument is that the groups of women who employ it are inspired by inconsistent social philosophies. The feminine voice approach tends in a broadly communitarian direction, and its values and concerns are largely those of the familial sphere rather than those that pervade the public arena, since women, for whatever reason, have been more influential in the familial and communal spheres and whatever distinctively feminine culture women have developed has been shaped by this. They are thus critical of the competitiveness and individualism that pervade the male-dominated world of business and politics.

Feminists, by contrast, value autonomy very highly, and are concerned to empower women by moving more of them into positions of influence in the public realm. They tend to take the individualism and competitiveness characteristic of business and politics as a given, and encourage women to cultivate the sorts of virtues that make for success in the public sphere. They are hostile toward those espousing the "feminine voice," fearing that it may lead to women being confined again to traditional roles as nurturers and caregivers, and thus allow their exploitation to continue unabated.[20] Those committed to the "feminine voice," for their part, criticize Feminists for working too much within a competitive, masculine, hierarchical model, in which power and control are taken to be central.[21]

Even though the differences between the Feminists and the different voice feminists are often papered over by rhetoric about contextualism and connectedness, any attempt to correct for "androcentric bias" in practice would quickly disclose the fact that they pull in opposite directions.

Failure of the Androcentric Bias Argument to Justify Affirmative Action

The argument that women must be preferentially appointed to faculty positions in order to correct for androcentric bias in the traditional disciplines fails because the three groups of academic women hold positions that are irreconcilable, and thus the crucial term "androcentric" is incoherent or ambiguous.

If one were to embrace the position of one of the three groups of women, it would still be impossible to justify affirmative action for women as a corrective for androcentric bias because simply getting *a woman* guarantees nothing whatever about whether she will help counteract androcentric bias (however you define this). If you want a greater representation for the "feminine voice," for example, appointing a woman who thinks like Judith Jarvis Thomson will be no help. Women, then, tend to advocate affirmative action only for those women who share their ideological perspective, and often accuse those they find uncongenial of not being "real women."[22] But this is unacceptable; it is simply pushing the interests of one group of women at the expense of the others.[23]

Furthermore, just as women may be interested in traditionally masculine areas of research (such as military history) men as well as women may be attracted to the new areas of research opened up by female scholars, and some of them do excellent work in these areas.[24] Hence the connection between appointing more target group members and enriching the disciplines becomes even more tenuous.

Perhaps if one took seriously the possibility that women might think in importantly different ways from men as a result of biological differences between them, it could be argued that there is a close connection between appointing *a woman* and enriching the discipline by introducing a different perspective. But such an assumption is highly speculative, and very few feminists adopt it.[25] None of the parties to the affirmative action debate, to my knowledge, take this position.

The Grain of Truth

Despite its failure to justify affirmative action for women across the board, there is something of value in this version of the corrective argument. When bias is successfully pointed out (and not just presumed as it is by postmodernists), real growth in understanding can occur within a discipline, as the examples given above show. Female scholars have done groundbreaking work in some areas, and it is certainly possible that their distinctive experiences as women have sometimes contributed to their ability to raise new questions and think about problems in a different way.

But one cannot assume that appointing more women will automatically stimulate creativity in every discipline; the distinctive experience of being a woman is more likely to affect the way one approaches sociology than the way one approaches chemistry, for example. There is no general recipe for creativity and we cannot know from what direction new insights will come. No doubt very different things will be required in different disciplines; one size does not fit all.

Simply enforcing nondiscrimination laws and maintaining traditional standards of open-mindedness would, I believe, be enough to ensure that women and people of color are able to make their contributions to the various disciplines.

III. Argument Based on Underrepresentation

Another concern that has led some people to propose corrective affirmative action is the desire to further the cause of social justice for women and minorities. As Dorit Bar-On puts it:

> I shall assume, first, that the present distribution of positions of power, wealth, prestige and authority—a distribution under which those positions are for the most part concentrated in the hands of white men, to the exclusion especially of blacks and women—is an *unjust* (and hence undesirable) distribution.[26]

The underrepresentation of women and minorities on university faculties, then, is simply one case of a more general problem—i.e., the
unjust distribution of positions of power, wealth, prestige, and authority—and proponents of this type of argument would consider the problem resolved only when proportional representation was attained in
college teaching and all other desirable jobs.

Exactly how underrepresentation of women and minorities on university faculty provides evidence of bias on the part of *search committees* is seldom spelled out clearly, but there is a widespread sense that
this state of affairs is either unjust in itself or indicative of the presence
of injustice and that steps therefore have to be taken to correct it, and
these intuitions play an important part in fueling demands for changes
in appointment procedures. In order to clarify the issues, let us for a
moment suppose that we are anthropologists from an alien culture
attempting to understand why the proportion of women and people of
color among college teachers is smaller than their proportion in the
population.

The current distribution of women and minorities is unjust or
indicative of injustice only if there is reason to expect that in the
absence of discrimination and injustice women and minorities would
be proportionally represented among the professorate (relative to their
proportion in the population as a whole). Some deep issues in social
philosophy lurk beneath the surface here. They will be touched on in
Chapter 5, but briefly put, the question at issue is whether we think of
society as a collection of unconnected individuals competing for positions of wealth, power, and prestige (the atomistic picture), or whether
we think of it as being made up of a number of overlapping communities or traditions—regional, ethnic, familial, religious, and so on. On
the latter assumption, we would expect to find human social reality to
be "clumpy" rather than homogenized (as would be the case on the former assumption).

Anthropologists are, of course, attuned to the ways in which cultures
and subcultures shape people's preferences, and so our hypothetical
alien anthropologist would try to determine whether culturally shaped
preferences might explain the distribution of the target groups among
the professorate. Both past and present preferences must be considered of course, since due to the tenure system, the *current* composition
of faculties is the result of numerous appointment and tenure decisions over a period of thirty to forty years, and the preferences of the
groups may have changed.

To the extent that black people, Hispanics, Asians, and Native
Americans form at least partially self-contained communities, members of one community will value different sorts of character traits,

encourage the acquisition of different skills, and have different ideas about what sorts of jobs carry the most prestige.[27] In one culture, scientists might be particularly respected, while in another being a media personality might be viewed as the height of success. The respect accorded Torah scholars in traditional Jewish culture, for example, may predispose those brought up in this culture toward careers as scholars or lawyers. Cultures that are highly verbal might be expected to produce more teachers than others. In addition, of course, as some members of a community go into a particular field, others aspire to go into it also since they already know something about it from their friends and relatives and have contacts in the field.

So even if equal percentages of the members of all racial and ethnic groups might desire some sort of prestigious job, there is no reason to suppose that all of them would regard the same jobs as prestigious. Or to put the point more bluntly, not everyone would regard being a professor as especially prestigious. And there are special reasons why college teaching might be less attractive than other professions to those who are trying to struggle out of poverty. Because of its low salaries relative to the amount of training required, college teaching has long tended to attract people brought up in relatively secure financial conditions, plus a few other individuals who feel a strong calling to the intellectual life. Certainly there are some prestigious research institutions where professors make excellent salaries, and in business and technical fields professors can often make good money consulting and exercise some power in the larger society, but the salary of the average academic has not kept pace with salaries in other professions. In addition, the social status of professors (particularly in the humanities) has declined from what it was in the 1950s and 1960s. And if one also takes into account the widespread loss of a sense of purpose among academics (again, particularly in the humanities) and the resulting demoralization among faculty, as well as academia's reputation for nasty politics, ambitious young members of minority groups might quite reasonably prefer careers in law, politics, industry, or the media.[28]

The preferences of the racial and ethnic groups in question are not the only reason for their underrepresentation among the professorate. The absence of large numbers of Hispanics might also be partly accounted for by the fact that so many of them are recent immigrants whose English is poor, and by the fact that they are disproportionately young.[29] Also, to the extent that injustice or bias are operative, there is good reason to suppose that they are operative elsewhere in our society. The deteriorating condition of inner-city schools is a major culprit here. And many minority students are so deeply scarred by poverty and sometimes racism that they have dropped out of school long before attaining the qualifications necessary to even apply to professional school. Although this is tragic, it does nothing to establish that there is prejudice against them at the university level, and to correct appointment procedures in order to compensate for bias when none is present is simply to introduce bias.

Women, unlike racial and ethnic groups, do not form an even partially self-contained community, but are evenly distributed throughout society. Nonetheless, their preferences are to some degree shaped by cultural conceptions of masculinity and femininity and expectations about women's role in the family and society, and these will have a significant impact on whether they choose academic careers, and what disciplines they tend to go into within the academy. The precise shape these culturally determined expectations take, however, varies markedly according to social class, ethnic group, and religious affiliation. In some subcultures (and until recently in most of them), being seriously intellectual is thought to be inconsistent with being feminine and that by itself might be enough to deter young women from aspiring to become professors. (The same type of explanation probably accounts for the striking absence of men from working-class backgrounds in college teaching. In their culture, being intellectual or interested in high culture is regarded as effeminate.)

The expectation that women will take a larger role in childrearing and homemaking than men has also been (and continues to be) very widespread, and this has often led them to avoid highly competitive and demanding careers and to choose jobs that can be more easily arranged around their family responsibilities. No doubt these sorts of traditional sex-role expectations are open to criticism, and they have been changing in recent years, but that does not affect the question at issue, namely whether underrepresentation of women among the professorate or in certain fields is evidence of discrimination against them on the part of universities. To the extent that their own preferences explain their underrepresentation, there is no reason to blame universities for it. Some may argue that it is inherently unjust that women have been socially conditioned into different sex-role expectations than men, but we ought to beware of paternalistically telling people how to arrange their personal lives.

Another possible explanation is the fact that women differ biologically from men in a way that black people or Asians do not differ from white people (e.g., in bodily structure, reproductive role, glandular and perhaps brain function). Whether and how biological differences between the sexes might explain differences in their choice of professions or disciplines within academia is not a question that can be answered on the basis of our present scientific knowledge, but the possibility cannot be ruled out. In fact, there are any number of possible reasons (including, no doubt, ones we haven't thought of yet) why women might have different preferences from men.

This point is conceded by Warren, who defends quotas governing new appointments as a form of corrective affirmative action. She says:

> It is possible that in a fully egalitarian society women would still tend to avoid certain academic fields and to prefer others, much as they do now, or even that they would fail to (attempt to) enter the academic profession as a whole in much greater numbers than at present.[30]

The preferences of the groups in question, then, may well account for their distribution among the professorate. Furthermore, the preferences of some groups (especially women who are flocking into academia, and entering fields where they were previously largely absent) have changed massively in the past thirty years, and the tenure system slows down the impact of changed supply conditions. Therefore, simply finding a lot of all-male departments in certain fields does not establish that discrimination has occurred against women if, at the time most of the current faculty members were tenured, there were few or no women with Ph.D.s in that field (and the same applies to racial and ethnic minorities). Past discrimination and discrimination located elsewhere in society (such as secondary schools) could also account for the scarcity of certain groups even in the absence of any bias at all at the university level. Hence, persuasive evidence of bias on the part of search committees must be sought elsewhere.

In the next section we turn to consider a more persuasive type of argument for corrective affirmative action—namely, that which focuses on the qualified applicant pool rather than the population as a whole, and on recent appointments rather than overall faculty composition.

IV. Identifying Bias in Recent Appointment Patterns

In trying to discover whether faculty appointment procedures are currently biased against women and minorities, the most relevant data would seem to be recent appointment patterns. These can be examined either (1) nationwide by discipline or (2) more locally at specific schools or in particular departments.

The preceding argument was frankly one concerning justice in the distribution of lucrative and prestigious jobs (in this case college teaching jobs), and the standard of justice accepted by proponents of the argument was a statistical one. In the argument about whether bias is at work in the current appointment procedures of universities, two very different sorts of considerations intersect. On the one hand, there is distributive justice—are women and people of color getting jobs in proportion to their proportion in the qualified applicant pool? (This is a limited version of the previous argument.) On the other hand, there is the question of whether qualifications of women and people of color are being systematically misperceived in such a way that better qualified women are passed over for less qualified men (taking what count as qualifications as unproblematic).

On a discipline by discipline level, there are different sorts of measures we might look at in order to determine whether women and people of color are suffering discrimination in the job market. Unfortunately, some of the statistics that would be most relevant are not being collected in a systematic way. Ideally, we need information about the proportion of women and minorities among those with Ph.D.s in the field actively seeking full-time work who are currently unemployed, working only part-time, or teaching in jobs with no hope of permanence compared with the proportion of white men in this situation.

There are several types of statistics currently being collected which are of some use, although none of them provide quite what we need, and even this sort of rudimentary data is not available in many fields.[31] First, placement rates for new Ph.D.s would be useful and some professional associations collect such data. Have women and minorities now coming out of graduate school attained parity with white men when it comes to finding jobs? Data on the types of jobs they are attaining (e.g., tenure track or nontenure track) would be helpful if it were available. Second, one could begin with the pool of candidates who have submitted vitas at the placement centers at the annual meetings of the various professional associations, and try to determine what proportion of the female or minority candidates among them have been successful in getting jobs and what sorts of jobs they have obtained, comparing this with comparable data for white male candidates. This has the advantage of including not only new Ph.D.s but also those who have been squeezed out by adverse tenure decisions or who are struggling along on part-time employment or one-year-only positions trying to stay in the field, as well as people who have been unemployed for a while, or who are trying to return to teaching from some other sort of employment. But this is still not quite the right measure for our purposes; it will be overinclusive in that some candidates already have tenured or tenure-track jobs but are trying to move on to better ones, and many of those who put in their vitas at such placement centers are only very minimally qualified. Comparative unemployment rates for women, people of color, and white men within the various disciplines would also be useful, but are seldom readily available.

What data I have been able to locate indicate that women and people of color are not suffering serious discrimination in the job market, and indeed there is evidence that they are doing better than white men in several disciplines. In history and physics, for example, their placement success is the same as that of white men. In law and political science they are doing slightly better.[32] Generally speaking, to the extent that women are currently experiencing discrimination in academia, it is far more likely to involve pay, tenure, or promotion.[33]

It could, of course, be argued that the gains are due to affirmative action, and that if such policies were discontinued, things would go back to the way they were in the 1950s and 1960s. This assumption, however, seems very speculative. Enforcement of antidiscrimination laws might well be enough to ensure the continued success of women and people of color. And even if preferences for these groups were required at one time, they might no longer be necessary.

It is possible, of course, that serious and persistent bias of a sort that requires correction is at work in the appointment practices of certain departments or schools even if the overall placement success rate of women and people of color is as good as or better than that of white men. But this bias must be established on a case by case basis, rather than presumed.

For example, suppose a dean or provost observes a given department over time, and notes that although it makes numerous appointments, it never or almost never appoints any women, even though there is a reasonable proportion of them in this field seeking work (i.e., in the "qualified applicant pool"). The administrator begins to suspect that some sort of prejudice is at work causing better qualified female candidates to be passed over for less qualified men, and therefore decides to institute corrective measures in order to be sure that the school is getting the best faculty possible. I call this sort of reason for affirmative action the "frustrated administrator argument."

It is possible that statistical imbalances of this sort might be the result of benign causes, including pure chance if the sample is too small to be statistically significant, so the frustrated administrator needs to sift through the evidence to try to ascertain the cause before undertaking corrective action. Being on the spot and often having known the committee members for many years, he or she may already have anecdotal evidence about their attitudes. But in the absence of clear anecdotal evidence indicating serious prejudice on the part of committee members, the accusation of bias is standardly grounded on the statistics themselves, strengthened by an appeal to the prevalence of racism or sexism in society generally, intended to generate a presumption that search committee members have such prejudices (either conscious or unconscious).

Statistics alone cannot establish bias, although they may suggest it (I am not speaking here of the legal requirements for a disparate impact case, which may be weaker than what I set out here). Statistics, however, are essential to this argument, for if women and minorities were being appointed in numbers roughly proportional to their presence in the qualified applicant pool, our administrator would not become suspicious in the first place. In presenting the statistical argument, I draw on James Rachels's argument, since his is, I think, the clearest presentation of it (although he also appeals to other considerations).

Suppose the administrator notices that a philosophy department has vacancies almost every year, but that women are almost never appointed to fill them (they have only one female member), even though there are lots of females in the field looking for work. The search committee sometimes lists the top woman candidate first on their list, but when she has predictably been snapped up by a more prestigious school (your school is "good but not one of the most prestigious"), no women in the second tier are considered. As Rachels puts it, you wonder if, perhaps, philosophical talent is "distributed in a funny way: While the very best women are equal to the very best men, at the next level down the men suddenly dominate. But that seems unlikely." The administrator therefore concludes that prejudice, conscious or otherwise, is corrupting their judgments of merit, and therefore it will be necessary to intervene in established appointment procedures if the school is to get the candidate who is in fact best qualified.

In order to create a presumption of bias on the part of the search committee, however, the case needs to be sharpened up considerably. For one thing, most departments make appointments infrequently, so it is not easy to get a sample large enough to be statistically significant.

The notion of the "qualified applicant pool" also needs to be refined. People often compare the track record of the department in question with the proportions of women and people of color among candidates actively seeking full-time work in the discipline. This is far too approximate. Women and people of color are not evenly distributed among subspecialties in the various disciplines, and since departments normally seek candidates with particular areas of expertise, this fact needs to be taken into account for each search. If, for example, a department is seeking someone with a specialty in philosophy of cognitive science and only 5 percent of those with this specialty are women, then the fact that women make up 25 percent of those seeking full-time work teaching philosophy is irrelevant.

If we define the qualified applicant pool as the number of actual applications received by a school, this is not quite right either. First, some applicants are not in fact qualified. Many do not have the subspecialty the department is seeking, and people who are very marginally qualified often send vitas to nearly every school with an opening. Second, the pool of available qualified candidates may be larger than the set of applications submitted. For if an advertisement makes it clear that the department is strongly motivated to appoint a woman or a minority member, qualified and available white men may fail to apply. And, finally, just because a department receives an application from someone does not mean that he or she is in fact available. In these times of tight academic markets, candidates frequently send out very large numbers of applications (one hundred is not at all uncommon) and a school may be at or near the bottom of this candidate's list, and this fact artificially inflates one's applicant pool. To the extent that women still try to locate themselves close to their husband's place of work rather than vice versa, this would mean that a school in an isolated area would expect to get more turndowns from female candidates than males. Candidates with particularly good credentials have more bargaining power in the market, and although they may apply just as widely as others (as a safety net), they are unlikely to be driven to take a job at a school near the bottom of their list.

The bargaining position of the school in question is another factor that must be taken into account when examining the appointment pattern of a given department in order to assess whether bias is at work. This becomes important in a market where other schools are simultaneously trying to increase their female and minority faculty. Even a school in, say, the eightieth percentile of attractiveness to candidates[34] may have difficulty getting women and people of color who are not inferior to available white male candidates. Suppose women are 25 percent of the applicant pool (this is currently the proportion of women among new Ph.D.s in philosophy) so there are 75 men and 25 women. More attractive schools will have skimmed off, say, the top third or more from an already smaller group of female candidates. If the top ten men and the top ten women have already found jobs, more of the high-ranking men will remain available even if talent is distributed identically in men and women. Thus white men who are still available will be better qualified than available women and people of color (since there are far fewer people of color in academia, the argument developed here applies even more strongly to them), and the department in question might quite reasonably conclude that since there is a run on female and minority candidates this year, they can probably do better by appointing a white man. Being organized enough to act very quickly before other schools have made their decisions will help here, but won't completely eliminate the difficulty.

Statistics thus provide prima facie evidence of bias only in a rather narrow range of cases, once we have also considered subspecialties and the school's bargaining power, and ruled out the possibility that random variation might explain them (if our sample is too small).

In light of the difficulty of establishing bias on statistical grounds alone, proponents of the corrective argument usually try to strengthen their case by appeal to the pervasiveness of racism and sexism in our society generally. They do not simply assert that these exist in our culture—something few would deny, although a lot of analytical work needs to be done to sharpen what is meant by these terms. They take racism and sexism to be so deeply engrained in our culture that virtually no one can claim to be free of them. Rachels, for example, after discussing the racial prejudice of the Alabama State Police, points out that university people are likely to think they are superior—that others may be guilty of bias but they are not. "But of course it is almost always a mistake to think oneself an exception to tendencies that are well-nigh universal among human beings. Few of us are saints." And a 1995 article in *The Nation* announces that "Denial of racism is much like the denials that accompany addiction to alcohol, drugs or gambling."[35]

No doubt defenders of the corrective argument appeal to the pervasiveness of racism (and sexism) in this way partly for rhetorical reasons; they do not want to sound as though they are pointing a finger at their colleagues and singling them out as particularly guilty of these prejudices,[36] and pointing to the prevalence of such attitudes in society generally softens what might otherwise sound like a personal attack. Nonetheless, this appeal to the deep-seated and all-pervasive nature of racism and sexism plays an important role in the argument for corrective affirmative action.

For if racism and sexism are very widespread, appointment procedures that appear to be fair and reasonable can function to perpetuate discrimination. Even search committee members who are well-intentioned and not themselves racists or sexists might unwittingly employ criteria that in fact work against female and minority candidates without being relevant to their ability to do the job. Discriminating against candidates with gaps in their vitas, for example, is not on its face a sexist practice. But it will work against women more often than against men, since under present arrangements women are generally expected to assume more responsibility for child care than men.[37] To the extent that we are able to identify those criteria that bear more heavily on women without being relevant to their ability to perform the job, however, the problem could be resolved fairly easily. Search committees could scrutinize the criteria they are employing carefully and eliminate any that are likely to have this sort of effect.

But if search committee members have negative stereotypes of women or people of color, or feelings of hostility towards them, then these prejudices can infect the appointment process in ways that can be difficult to pinpoint. Reliance on personal contacts (the old boy network) is not an overtly discriminatory practice, but it nonetheless disproportionately excludes women and people of color if they are, as a result of the prejudices of the members of the network, less able to tap into these networks.[38] Similarly, people can follow "fair" procedures but subvert their purpose. Departments may interview female or minority candidates but accord them only cursory interviews or question them in a more hostile manner than they do white male candidates.[39] I know of a case where a department under affirmative action pressure interviewed a large number of women but behaved in an insulting manner toward them during the interviews in order to ensure that none of them would accept the position if offered to them. And there are doubtless countless other subtle ways in which the prejudices of search committee members could insinuate themselves into the appointment process, since academics are likely to be sophisticated enough to conceal their prejudices effectively.

The most important purpose of the appeal to the pervasiveness of racism and sexism is to shift the burden of proof to search committee members by generating a presumption that their judgments are corrupted by these particular prejudices. The claim is not merely that lots and lots of people have these sorts of negative attitudes toward women and people of color, so that in all probability some given group of people will turn out, upon examination, to have them also. For the presumption of racism and sexism is, according to Rachels, strong enough to override their (to all appearances sincere) denials that they have these sorts of attitudes and to justify attributing unconscious prejudices to them.

Insofar as such prejudices are presumed rather than shown to be present, we are dealing with another form of the "hermeneutics of suspicion," and must inquire what this presumption rests upon. Unlike the postmodernist version of the hermeneutics of suspicion, this one does not rest upon a metaphysics of difference, or a belief that the will-to-power is what is most ontologically basic about people. It is not so much that white men are irreducibly different from women and people of color and so cannot understand them, but rather that they have negative feelings toward them or negative stereotypes of them that distort their perceptions of the qualifications of members of these groups. Nor do those alleging the near universality of sexism and racism reject notions of truth and objectivity in the sort of wholesale way the postmodernists do, for they believe that sexism and racism are irrational and get in the way of a correct perception of the qualifications of candidates.

Such prejudices appear to have an almost metaphysical character, being engrained in what we are, like the sort of taint or stain on the soul that results from Original Sin. And, like Original Sin, they have important epistemological implications, warping our cognitive abilities, although this warping is confined to one's perceptions of the qualifications of women and people of color, rather than producing a more global cognitive distortion.[40]

But why focus on racial and sexual prejudice in particular once we opened the door to this sort of vague, miasmatic guilt? None of us can be sure that his or her heart is wholly pure, but is it not rather arbitrary and ad hoc to limit the ways in which the corruption of our hearts can distort our perceptions of the qualifications of candidates to sexual and racial bias? Age discrimination is at least as important, as is religious bias (especially against people with conservative religious views). Moreover, someone who feels intellectually burned out is very likely to perceive the impressive publications of a candidate through the distorting lens of envy, rationalizing this as a commitment to "teaching excellence." Or someone who is particularly power hungry will often discount the credentials of a candidate perceived as having a strong and independent personality, rationalizing this as concern that the candidate would not be a good "team player." These two particular forms of cognitive distortion on the part of search committees have probably resulted in passing over better-qualified candidates at least as often as racism or sexism.

Furthermore the *unconscious* character of the prejudices in question creates serious difficulties, since such prejudices, if they exist, will be both impossible to measure and incurable. If they are unconscious, we cannot try to rationally persuade those afflicted by them, so force of some sort must be employed. Thus administrators or federal officials must intervene in the appointment process in order to counterbalance them. But why should we suppose that *they* can stand outside or above this all-pervasive taint in order to determine which candidate is in fact best qualified? It seems entirely arbitrary to suppose that faculty but not administrators, Southerners but not Northerners, white people but not black people, and men but not women will be affected by unconscious prejudices. And if no one has a special, privileged bias-free perspective, how can we tell when we have adequately counteracted the prejudices without introducing an opposite bias?

This leads into the main problem not only for Rachels's argument but for the corrective argument generally—how are we to determine when bias has been eliminated? The answer for Rachels, at least, appears to be that bias has been eliminated when women and people of color are appointed proportionally to their numbers in the qualified applicant pool. It is statistical imbalances that alert us to the existence of bias, and statistical proportionality that assures us that the problem has been resolved.

The problem being corrected for is bias or prejudice that causes better-qualified female or minority candidates to be passed over, but the way of telling that it has been corrected is numerical. And there is no very clear connection between these, especially when quotas are employed. For example, suppose that a proportional quota governing new appointments is imposed on the department described by Rachels. Departments do not like being subject to outside constraints in making appointments, so they are likely to want to fill their quota quickly. Those pushing for the appointment of more women and people of color will also be motivated to press for getting it filled quickly, since it is uncertain how long affirmative action policies will be in place. Suppose that the best candidate this year is in fact a man, but they appoint a woman, and the same thing happens next year. Four years later, the best candidate is a woman, but having filled their quota they go back to their old ways and appoint a man. The numbers look better, but bias has not been corrected, and the department has not got the best candidates.

V. Conclusion

Corrective affirmative action, then, appears to be justified only in a fairly narrow range of cases. It should be undertaken on a department by department basis by administrators who have serious reason to suppose that bias or prejudice against women or people of color is at work in appointment decisions. Administrators should carefully weigh all the evidence, taking into consideration appointment patterns over a period of time, the bargaining power of their school, the size and composition of the qualified applicant pool, and finally anecdotal evidence bearing on whether search committee members take women or people of color seriously intellectually. (The issue of what sorts of remedies are appropriate and why will be discussed in the next chapter.)

When attempts are made to extend corrective affirmative action beyond this sort of case by case application, statistics are made to carry more weight than they can bear and the hermeneutics of suspicion comes increasingly into play. As we saw in section III, statistical underrepresentation is not necessarily evidence of discriminatory appointment procedures, and even if we confine ourselves to new appointments (see section IV), statistical evidence needs to be scrutinized far more carefully than is usually done by those alleging bias. Postmodernists, of course, do not rely on statistics to establish bias.

But then, on their premises, bias is inevitable anyway, and although they tend to support quotas for women and people of color, their argument gives no support to such policies (and indeed undermines the very possibility of rational dialogue about this or any other issue).

Those who allege bias in the traditional disciplines themselves have an argument that does not rely on statistics (or at least not heavily) to establish the existence of bias. This argument, however, runs into the difficulty that it fails to provide any way to determine when bias has been corrected. All other variants of the corrective argument fall back on statistics in order to determine when the problem of bias or discrimination has been corrected, and this fact inclines those making this sort of argument to favor quotas. But getting the numbers to come out right, however "right" is defined, is only very tenuously connected with correcting the sort of bias in appointment procedures complained of.

Even if it were true that in the absence of injustice women and people of color would be proportionally represented in all professions and disciplines, simply creating a simulacrum of justice by producing the numerical distribution of the various groups that would obtain under conditions of justice is not to produce justice. A healthy person might have rosy cheeks, but producing rosy cheeks by putting on rouge does nothing to produce health.

When corrective affirmative action is extended beyond specific cases, it has the unfortunate effect of institutionalizing the hermeneutics of suspicion, since some version of this is required to entitle us to presume bias without showing it to be present. Whether this suspicion takes a postmodernist form, or the form more characteristic of liberal social theory—namely, the all-pervasive taint of racism and sexism—it has destructive effects. Given that academics are trained to be self-critical already, they are likely to be thrown into paralysis by this sort of systematic undermining of their professional judgment and to surrender to bureaucratic number crunchers who move in to fill the vacuum. Vague allegations that all the disciplines and their associated criteria of professional competence are infected by androcentric or other bias are also likely to cause faculty to lose confidence in the value of what they are doing without offering any positive suggestions for improvement, and this loss of confidence will lead to demoralization.

Attempts to enrich the disciplines by bringing in the perspectives of previously marginalized people can sometimes be very valuable, but there is no reason to suppose that proportional representation of these groups is either necessary or sufficient for this purpose. To be sure, if there were *no* women or people of color within a certain discipline, one might well wonder whether an important perspective might have been neglected. But one such person with a powerfully creative mind does more to represent a new point of view than any number chosen to fill a quota or represent an ideological position. Simple nondiscrimination, combined with the openness to new perspectives traditional among academics, suffices to make reform of the disciplines possible if that is required. It remains only to do the necessary intellectual work.

The most fundamental flaw in the corrective argument is that there is no effective criterion for deciding when bias has been removed and fairness achieved. In practice, advocates of the corrective argument fall back on the arbitrary demand that groups be represented in the academy (and in its component disciplines) in proportion to their numbers in the larger society. It seems obvious to many writers that women and people of color ought to be proportionally represented in this way. But the arguments developed earlier in this book have called this assumption into question. In Chapter 2 I argued that proportional representation of these groups is not a requirement of compensatory justice. In Chapter 3 I argued that neither the role model argument nor the diversity argument supports the demand for proportional representation. In this chapter I have argued that distributive justice does not require this sort of proportional representation. Finally, I have argued that (1) if a given department persistently fails to appoint women and people of color in proportion to their numbers in the qualified applicant pool, this may indicate that bias against them is at work, but only under certain narrowly circumscribed conditions; and (2) nonetheless, their being appointed in the proper proportion does not necessarily indicate that fairness has been attained or that the department in question has succeeded in appointing the best-qualified candidates.

Why, then, does the goal of proportional representation seem obviously right to so many people? Some very deep questions of social philosophy are involved here, and my discussion in the next chapter will attempt to clarify the reasons for people's conflicting intuitions on this issue.

Notes

1. Stanley Fish, *There's No Such Thing as Free Speech and It's a Good Thing Too* (New York: Oxford University Press, 1994) 20.

2. Fish, *Free Speech*, 62–63.

3. Harriet Baber, "The Market for Feminist Epistemology," *Monist* 77, 4 (October 1994), 403–23.

4. See Phillip Johnson's *Reason in the Balance* (Downers Grove, Ill.: InterVarsity Press, 1995). See also his *Darwin on Trial* (Washington, D.C.: Regnery Gateway, 1991) and Johnson et al., *Evolution as Dogma* (Dallas, Tex.: Haughton, 1990). A more moderate version of the same argument is George M.

Marsden, *The Soul of the American University* (New York: Oxford University Press, 1994).

5. Mary Anne Warren, "Secondary Sexism and Quota Hiring," *Philosophy & Public Affairs* 6, 3 (1977), 248–49.

6. Considerable overlap exists between this variant of the corrective argument and the forward-looking argument based on the need for diversity. What distinguishes the corrective argument is its focus on the need to revise the criteria of professional excellence employed by search committees.

7. A similar argument could be constructed for black people. See, e.g., *The Afrocentric Idea* (Philadelphia: Temple University Press, 1987) by Molefi Asante. But black people have tended to be more reluctant than women to make this type of argument, perhaps because the suggestion that they think in different ways from white people could be seized upon by racists as an indication of black inferiority.

8. Leslie Pickering Francis, "In Defense of Affirmative Action," in Steven M. Cahn, ed., *Affirmative Action and the University: A Philosophical Inquiry* (Philadelphia: Temple University Press, 1993), 21.

9. I use the term "Feminism" to refer to this particular group without prejudice to the right of the other two groups of women to call themselves feminists. I do so because they tend to claim exclusive title to the term "feminist."

10. This point has been made often, most recently in Elizabeth Fox-Genovese, *Feminism Is Not the Story of My Life* (New York: Doubleday, 1996).

11. For example, there is some evidence at least that the department discussed in section IV who insulted female candidates were acting out of a desire not to be forced to appoint a Feminist rather than any hostility to women as such. (I do not, of course, mean to suggest that this excuses their behavior.)

12. On the question of feminist epistemology, see the debate between Naomi Scheman and Louise Anthony at the APA meeting in Boston in 1993, and Susan Haack, advisory editor, *Feminist Epistemology: For and Against*, *Monist* 77, 4 (October 1994).

13. See, e.g., Harriet Baber, "The Market for Feminist Epistemology," *Monist* 77, 4 (October 1994). The parallel case for black people is made by Stephen Carter, who says that he is particularly delighted by people who like his work before they know that he is black, and his sense of relief that it is really the work itself they like and not "the-unexpected-quality-of-the-work-given-the-naturally-inferior-intellects-of-those-with-darker-skins." *Reflections of an Affirmative Action Baby* (New York: Basic Books, 1991), 61.

14. On this point, see Sara Ruddick's *Maternal Thinking* (New York: Ballantine, 1989).

15. Carol Gilligan, *In a Different Voice: Psychological Theory and Women's Development* (Cambridge: Harvard University Press, 1982).

16. See, e.g., Christina Sommers, "Filial Morality," and Annette Baier, "Hume, the Women's Moral Theorist?" in Eva Kittay and Diana Meyers, eds., *Women and Moral Theory* (Totowa, N.J.: Rowman & Littlefield, 1987).

17. For a valuable discussion of the anti-universalist thrust of Feminist women's history, see Peter Novick, *That Noble Dream* (Cambridge: Cambridge

University Press, 1988), 491–510. (His discussion of black history is equally valuable.)

18. For a thoughtful critical discussion of the Women's Studies community see Daphne Patai and Noretta Koertge, *Professing Feminism: Cautionary Tales from the Strange World of Women's Studies* (New York: Basic Books, 1994). They are particularly critical of the separatist stance taken by so many Women's Studies programs, and the deleterious effects of their overly close links with political activism.

19. Natalie Zemon cited in Novick, *That Noble Dream*, 495.

20. See, e.g., Susan Faludi, *Backlash* (New York: Crown, 1991), and Sandra Bartky, *Femininity and Domination* (New York: Routledge, 1990), especially the chapter on "Feeding Egos and Tending Wounds." See also Joan Tronto, *Moral Boundaries and the Ethics of Care* (New York: Routledge, 1993), and Rosemarie Tong's book on *Feminine and Feminist Ethics* (Belmont, Calif.: Wadsworth, 1993).

21. For an excellent critique of this way of thinking about power, see Jean Elshtain's *Power Trips and Other Journeys* (Madison: University of Wisconsin Press, 1990).

22. For example, Naomi Wolf accused Jeane Kirkpatrick of having a voice "uninflected by the experiences of the female body." "Are Opinions Male? The Barriers That Shut Women Up," *New Republic* (Nov. 29, 1993), 22.

23. Laverne Shelton, for example, includes in the favored class of "newtraditionals" only *most* women. "An Ecological Concept of Diversity," in Steven M. Cahn, ed., *Affirmative Action and the University*, 248.

24. Consider, e.g., social historian Peter Laslett's book *The World We Have Lost* (London: Methuen, 1965).

25. Some radical lesbian separatists hold that women are inherently superior to men. See, e.g., Sally Miller Gearhart, "The Future If There Is One Is Female," in Pam McAllister, *Reweaving the Web of Life* (Philadelphia: New Society, 1982), and Mary Daly, *Gyn/ecology: The Metaethics of Radical Feminism* (Boston: Beacon Press, 1978).

26. Dorit Bar-On, "Discrimination, Individual Justice and Preferential Treatment," *Public Affairs Quarterly* 4, 2 (April 1990), 111 (emphasis in original).

27. Perhaps instead of conceptualizing society as a pyramid with one top, we should think of it as a group of hills with many different peaks; people may choose different paths to wealth, power, and prestige.

28. And, in fact, far more black students enroll in professional schools (especially law) than enroll in Ph.D. programs; in 1992–93 2,284 received law degrees [table 266], 3,966 received M.B.A.s [table 261], 900 received M.D.s compared with 1,352 Ph.D.s [table 262]. *Digest of Educational Statistics, 1995.*

29. For example, 32 percent of Mexican Americans are under 15, and 83 percent under 45, compared with 22 percent and 67.6 percent for the general population. *Statistical Abstract of the United States 1995*, Tables 10 and 53.

30. Warren, "Secondary Sexism," 255.

31. Lawyers, not surprisingly, keep good statistics. Philosophers, so far at least, do not, and there is considerable variation in record keeping among professional organizations.

32. Information obtained from the professional organizations for each discipline.

33. Mariam Chamberlain (Project Director of Task Force on Women in Higher Education), ed., *Women in Academe* (New York: Russell Sage Foundation, 1988), 178.

34. I am assuming for the sake of argument that such a thing as "bargaining power" can be roughly quantified. Such ranking can be, at best, extremely approximate, since the very features that attract one candidate to a school will repel others. Some things at least are attractive to all of them, such as high pay, intelligent students, and colleagues with whom one can establish friendly collegial relationships. Being not too far from some sort of cultural center and having time to do research, support for travel, etc., are also likely to attract almost everyone. But many other features might attract one and repel others, for example, size, degree of community among faculty or between faculty and students, religious orientation or lack of it, or being in the South or the North, East, or West.

35. Roger Wilkins, "Racism Has Its Privileges," *The Nation* (Mar. 27, 1995), 412.

36. I owe this idea to Steven Cahn, who suggested it to me in conversation.

37. Warren makes this point in "Secondary Sexism."

38. My own experience does not bear out the claim that women are less able to tap into such networks. For example, at a recent convention, I was approached by a male friend on behalf of a student of his who was seeking a job in my husband's department. A classic case of the old boy network, but both the contact person and the candidate were female. Furthermore, the student in question was my husband's first choice for the position, but he was outvoted by his department, with several of the strongest opponents of the candidate being women.

39. Leslie Francis makes this point in "A Defense of Affirmative Action," 26–30.

40. Believers in Original Sin hold varying interpretations of how extensive its cognitive effects are. Extreme Calvinists hold it to be so far-reaching in its effects that they are in danger of undercutting the possibility of appealing to reason in support of Christian faith, whereas Catholics in the Thomist tradition hold a more moderate position, allowing an important role for reason in theological reflection.

5

Conclusion

As shown above, the general arguments for affirmative action in faculty appointments largely fail. The compensatory argument is subject to a number of objections. It involves an unfair distribution of burdens and benefits, and in two ways. First, the choice of groups to be benefited is arbitrary; the argument works best for black people and Native Americans, and breaks down for women, Hispanics, and Asians (for different reasons). Second, even in the strongest case (black people), it benefits those who have been least harmed and places the burden of compensation on those who are not in a position to have reaped the benefits of earlier injustice. Furthermore, the underlying tort law model breaks down when applied to wrongs that span many generations. It runs aground because it requires counterfactual knowledge of a sort that is unattainable, and this makes it unsuited to function as a guide to public policy.

The forward-looking arguments also break down. The role model argument is empirically unsubstantiated and self-undermining, and reliance on it has undesirable consequences for the intended beneficiaries. The mentor argument encounters some of the same difficulties as the role model argument, although it may sometimes justify tie-breaking affirmative action[1] under special circumstances. Diversity, I have argued, will be educationally valuable when understood and introduced in ways consistent with the democratic liberal model of education, but will be damaging to all concerned when understood and justified in terms of the multiculturalist model.

The corrective argument comes in several different forms. The postmodernist version cuts the ground out from under itself. The claim that bias is embedded in the structure of the various disciplines themselves cannot be simply asserted to be true a priori of all disciplines, but it can be made out successfully in some cases. This, however, does not automatically justify according women and people of color preference unless

153

it can be persuasively argued that all and only members of these groups will be able to correct for the biases in question.[2] The lack of representation of women and people of color proportionate to their numbers in the population as a whole provides no evidence of discrimination or bias against them in the appointment process. If they are underrepresented among recent appointments relative to their proportion in the qualified applicant pool, this fact *may* be evidence of discrimination, but only under certain narrowly circumscribed conditions.

The failure of the arguments that would justify affirmative action as a routine policy, however, does not mean that there are no circumstances at all under which it might be justified. I thus begin by discussing when affirmative action might be justified and what sort would be appropriate.

Next I discuss how we might move beyond the current impasse on this controversial issue. The continuing intransigence of those on both sides in the academy suggests that more is necessary than just the arguments provided above. Its defenders seem to cling to affirmative action with increasing zeal the more the arguments that support it are shown to be weak. Its opponents frequently take the attitude that all we need to do is beat back the barbarians and return to business as usual. But this is not just a debate in which the audience votes at the end and a winner is declared. We need to look more deeply at what is really going on—to step back and think about the problem in a broader context and see if it is possible to shift the ground of the debate in ways that will acknowledge the legitimate concerns of both sides and bring them closer together. This will involve two things: paring away some of the other issues that have become entangled with affirmative action, and bringing into question some assumptions shared by people on both sides.

Finally, I will conclude with a discussion of the proper role of the university, and make some suggestions about how to reconceptualize the social and political situation out of which affirmative action has arisen.

I. Remedies

First, we ought to continue to enforce antidiscrimination laws. There is a certain amount of preference already built into them, even though they are, on their face, neutral in that they forbid *all* discrimination on the basis of race, sex, or national origin. For, given the intentions of those who framed the laws and the political context within which they are enforced, it will be easier for members of protected groups to obtain relief, and thus employers, who are naturally highly averse to lawsuits, are likely to be more careful in their dealings with members of such groups. But for present purposes we may take such laws as uncontroversial.

Second, procedural affirmative action may be justified when there is reason to suspect that discrimination against women or people of color is currently at work in a particular department. Since it is present discrimination that is relevant, it is recent appointments that should be scrutinized, and to determine whether one's suspicions are well grounded it is necessary to consider the evidence carefully along the lines indicated in Chapter 4, section IV. If there appears to be discrimination, then it may be necessary for someone to sit down with the search committee and discuss the procedures and the criteria they are employing. This sort of oversight of search committees should, however, be limited to cases of suspected discrimination because it involves administrative intrusion into an area that has traditionally been a faculty prerogative. Territory once lost is difficult to regain and future administrators might use such powers in undesirable ways.

Distinguishing procedural from preferential affirmative action, however, is not always easy. As long as those who are investigating a particular department's appointment procedures do not actually override the considered professional judgment of the hiring committee, but rather try to persuade them rationally to revise their procedures or criteria by showing that they contain undetected bias against women or people of color, then we are still in the realm of procedural affirmative action. When pressure is put on them to appoint a candidate who, in the department's considered judgment, is not the best qualified, then we are dealing with preferential affirmative action. But rational persuasion shades off gradually into strong-arming. Pointing out that penalizing candidates for gaps in their vitas disadvantages women is clearly procedural, and demanding that the search committee give female and minority candidates extra points to counteract their own unconscious bias against members of these groups has crossed over the line into preferential. But given the inequality in the power relationship and the complexity of the issues involved in trying to persuade the search committee that they are systematically overlooking certain excellences characteristic of female and minority candidates, the possibilities for emotional manipulation are legion, and procedural affirmative action tends to drift toward preferential affirmative action—another reason why procedural affirmative action should be used sparingly.

In light of the arguments presented in this book, there is no reason to pursue proportional representation of women and people of color either on the faculty as a whole[3] or in particular departments. Its absence is not necessarily indicative of injustice or discrimination of any sort,[4] and a situation in which such proportional representation obtains is not necessarily preferable to one in which it does not.[5]

Quotas and set-asides are (rightly) illegal, and "flexible goals" are equally questionable theoretically since they specify the proportions of women and people of color that the department must aim at. They differ only in allowing a bit more time to attain the goal, and given that departments are likely to want to attain their goal quickly in order to get outside pressures off their backs, and defenders of affirmative action are also likely to want to move quickly in light of the current uncertainty about the future of affirmative action policies, the practical effects will be similar. Any outcome-forcing remedy is very likely to result in the appointment of a less qualified person (unless your school is in an especially strong bargaining position), since other schools are simultaneously trying to increase their female and minority faculty. And putting pressure on search committee members to bend their standards in order to arrive at the right numerical outcome (unless reasons have been given to show that the standards are genuinely in need of revision) is likely to be demoralizing and corruptive of professional standards.

The difficult question is whether it might be legitimate to engage in some sort of affirmative action that is stronger than merely procedural affirmative action but weaker than quotas or goals aiming at proportional representation of some sort—such as "tie-breaking," a "one-time-only mandate," or "ice-breaking" affirmative action. There does seem to be room for some such thing, but one must be careful in delineating just what should be allowed.

Such measures should be undertaken only in cases where there are few or no women or people of color in a given department, and where there is both statistical and anecdotal evidence of discrimination or bias against members of these groups on the part of department members. In assessing the statistical evidence one should examine recent appointments, taking into account the qualified applicant pool, including the subspecialties involved in each search as well as the bargaining position of the school in question. If there does seem to be genuine bias present that proves resistant to merely procedural affirmative action, then some sort of "ice-breaking" may be in order (calling it "tie-breaking" is misleading, since academic appointments involve incommensurables).

The problem is in determining how much preference should be accorded to female and minority candidates. Since the purpose of this sort of affirmative action is to break down negative stereotypes of women and people of color on the part of their colleagues, and to provide mentors for same-kind students, it would be counterproductive (as well as unfair to students) to require them to dip into the bottom half of their applicant pool. For if the new faculty member was perceived to be markedly less qualified than the rest of the department, this would only confirm their negative stereotypes. On the other hand, if the department sends up three names to the administration with a woman or person of color in third place, passing over the top two candidates might not be unreasonable. It is difficult to be precise about just where the line should be drawn; there is no easy formula for doing this sort of thing, and it should be done only where there is a serious problem and other remedies have failed.

The chief justification for affirmative action, then, is corrective. It may be objected, at this point, that I am thinking too much in terms of administrators putting affirmative action pressures on recalcitrant search committees and overlooking the fact that many search committees themselves desire to engage in affirmative action. In fact, I do believe that pressure to engage in affirmative action very often originates from trustees and administrators rather than faculty.[6] But certainly members of a search committee may be sincerely concerned about social justice and wish to see more women and people of color in the professions. They may be disturbed by the scarcity of women and people of color in their disciplines and want to give an edge to female and minority candidates as a way of opening up the discipline to more members of groups that have traditionally been absent from them. Shouldn't this sort of voluntary affirmative action be permissible (both legally and morally)?

The answer to this question is not simple. Search committees, legally, are acting as administrators *pro hac vice*. In state universities, therefore, they are agents of the state and consequently cannot treat individuals differently for purposes of employment on the basis of their race, sex, or ethnic origin. Private universities, however, are in a somewhat different position. They have their own distinctive educational missions, and there seems to be no a priori reason why some schools might not be entitled to grant some degree of preference in faculty appointments to women, black people, or members of certain religious or ethnic groups, so long as their educational mission is clearly stated, and its relation to their faculty appointment policies is made public.[7] One problem with the three types of general arguments for affirmative action examined in this book is that they require identical appointment policies of all universities, and thus do not allow for diversity between educational institutions.

There are, of course, limits to the range of permissible educational missions, but just where to draw the line is a difficult question that I will not attempt to answer here. In any case, the burden of proof is on the institution to justify its faculty appointment policies in terms of its particular educational mission. Dartmouth College, for example, was founded in part to educate Native Americans and therefore might argue that according preference to Native Americans for faculty positions helps fulfill its distinctive educational mission. One important reason why affirmative action has been so deleterious to white men in academia is because legal and social pressures have combined to cause almost all schools simultaneously to favor women and people of color.

II. Getting Around the Impasse

The circumstances under which affirmative action might be justified are, if my arguments so far are correct, quite narrowly circumscribed. This does not necessarily imply, however, that all is well or will be well if only we discontinue affirmative action. Both universities and the broader society are now beset by very serious problems involving race and gender, and universities are in a good position to do something about many of them. We are failing to do so effectively largely because we misconceive the nature of the problems we are facing in ways that make affirmative action look like a solution to them when it is not.

In part, of course, people are clinging to affirmative action because it seems to be the only game in town. It may not be working very well, but perhaps it will do at least some good, and that would be better than nothing.[8] This way of thinking, however, betrays a serious lack of will and imagination to find better alternatives. What is called for is flexibility and creative thought—not holding on like grim death and going down with the ship.

But there are conceptual reasons why it is very difficult to get clear about this issue. First, people are displacing their concerns about other problems onto affirmative action. This results in muddy thinking and hiding the ball (sometimes even from oneself) in such a way that people adopt affirmative action policies in order to pursue goals different from those stated, or expect them to resolve problems that they are ill-adapted to address. Second, people on both sides are limited in their ability to reconceptualize the issues by their acceptance of a faulty social paradigm.

The Politics of Displacement

We should begin by separating affirmative action from other issues that have wrongly become entangled with it, and addressing those issues directly. Some of the problems facing us as a nation come to the fore in the political process, while others are swept under the rug, or at least are not articulated in the public forum in a way that is responsive to the felt needs of those most affected by them. Sometimes this sort of thing happens because any attempt to resolve certain issues would come up against opposition from large blocs of voters or well-organized interest groups, and thus politicians are motivated to ignore such issues. Sometimes it results from historical accidents that have linked certain issues in people's minds in a way that constrains political dialogue. There are also concerns stemming from things, such as religion, that are usually kept out of the public square, and whose public ramifications we fail to confront honestly. Feelings associated with such issues, therefore, get displaced onto other issues such as affirmative action.

Economic Factors

The growing gap between rich and poor and the economic squeeze on the middle class are extremely important issues that need to be addressed thoughtfully. The belief that a large and prosperous middle class is conducive to social stability is one that many political philosophers have espoused, going back as far as Aristotle. One of the earliest arguments against allowing a large gap between rich and poor is found in *Politics*, Book IV, Chapter 11, where Aristotle argues that "a city ought to be composed, as far as possible, of equals and similars; and these are generally of the middle class" (1295b25–26), because this state of affairs is most conducive to friendship among the citizens. He also says that where the middle class is large "there are least likely to be factions and dissensions" (1296a7–9) and that a state in which the middle class is large will be well administered.

Affirmative action has diverted attention and energy away from directly confronting these vexing questions about the erosion of the middle class. Both supporters and opponents of affirmative action are at fault here. Many supporters of affirmative action think of it mainly as a way of helping the poor. Many of those most opposed to affirmative action for women and people of color are (not surprisingly) white men who are hurting economically. Whether their difficulties are the result of affirmative action or whether they are victims of downsizing or structural shifts in the economy, they are likely to blame affirmative action and to oppose it strongly. Given that the pie is no longer growing at the rate it used to, increased ethnic and racial tensions naturally result.

A Marxist would see affirmative action as a way of weakening working-class solidarity by buying off a few of the most talented workers and setting racial and ethnic groups against each other. A dyed-in-the-wool cynic would say that people of color are being set up to be scapegoats for the anger of white workers who are suffering economically. One need not be either a Marxist or a cynic, however, to recognize that battles over affirmative action sometimes crowd out serious thought about how to deal with growing social inequality. But a strategy that accords a central place to affirmative action as a way of dealing with the increasing gap between rich and poor suffers from two fatal defects. (1) It confuses race and class, and this renders invisible the white poor (who outnumber the black poor by two and one-half to one). (2) It benefits those members of the protected groups who are already better off (the polarization of income among both black people and women has increased during the years affirmative action has been practiced).

Social Issues

Another important issue that has become entangled with affirmative action is the changing role of women and its impact on family structure and the rearing of children. Affirmative action for women is connected with this issue in two ways.

(1) The analogy between racism and sexism. Affirmative action policies reflect and reinforce ways of thinking that make it very hard even to discuss the special difficulties women face in combining work with motherhood and other family responsibilities. The problem lies in thinking of women's problems as the result of "sexism" (understood by analogy with racism). Although this way of thinking may seem natural to us, the analogy is by no means an obvious one; feminists in other countries do not tend to be obsessed about race as Americans are, and they think about women's problems in different sorts of terms. The invention of the term "sexism" is largely the result of historical accident. The current wave of American feminism originated in the sixties, and the shape it took was deeply influenced by the black civil rights movement.[9] Similarities between the difficulties facing women and those facing black people were emphasized, and the women's movement at its inception drew on the moral capital of the civil rights movement—as, for example, when women were added in an amendment to a bill concerned with job discrimination against black people (Title VII).

Thinking about women's problems as caused by "sexism" has the result that problems facing women that have no analogue in the case of black people are neglected, shoehorned awkwardly into the category of "sexism," or denied. The biological and reproductive differences between men and women have no analogue in the racial case. And although black people were often confined by law or custom to limited social roles, these were not systematically connected with family structure and childrearing practices in the way traditional social roles of men and women have been. Thus those of women's problems that are directly connected with biological or reproductive differences or with their traditional role in the family have no analogue in the case of black people and have tended to get swept under the rug. Moreover, the distinctive character of antiblack prejudice is obscured by the analogy with "sexism." The feeling that one may be tainted by physical contact with the other, for example, and the accompanying horror of miscegenation, have no analogue in the case of women; apart from a few pathological cases, men do not regard women this way. And as more and more "isms" are spawned, each modeled on racism (such as "heterosexism," "ablism," and so on), the unique character of racial prejudice is progressively lost from view.

(2) Proportional representation and changing sex roles. As racial policies began to take proportional representation rather than color blindness as their goal, feminists, following out the logic of the sexism/racism analogy, did the same. But unlike protecting women against discrimination in employment, promotion, or pay, attaining proportional representation of women in all occupations and at all levels would require major changes in family structure. Women are "underrepresented" in certain sorts of jobs for a variety of reasons. Discrimination is only one reason; their preferences for certain sorts of work and their family commitments are also important explanatory factors.

The trend toward seeking proportional representation in employment of women, therefore, has occasioned yet another sort of displacement. Many people support affirmative action for women as a way to liberate women from traditional roles so that they can have fulfilling careers of the same sort men have. Others oppose such policies because they are apprehensive about the impact such policies may have on the family and on children. And women who prefer traditional sex roles, particularly mothers of small children who want to stay home with them, are likely to oppose job preferences for women because such policies might endanger their husband's job.[10] Given the relative flexibility of teaching schedules, these issues are less important for college faculty than for people in other occupations, but even faculty do not have unlimited time and energy.

Whether or not massive changes in family structure are something we ought to encourage, the issue is one we need to confront directly. Very few people believe that women ought to be prevented from pursuing whatever career they choose, or denied equal pay for equal work when they do work outside the home (even Rush Limbaugh and Pat Robertson favor equal pay for equal work). As soon as we try to go beyond these sorts of uncontroversial beliefs, however, there is very little agreement, and people's feelings about the issues surrounding sex roles, family structure, and childrearing are both intense and ambivalent. But this state of affairs is all the more reason why we need to make some collective decisions about the direction we want to go, and if we do decide we want to continue with policies that encourage the entry of more and more women into the full-time workforce, we need to give thought to how we can provide for the needs of children. There are all sorts of ways of making it easier for working parents to be able to give their children the time and attention they would like, and we could get useful ideas from looking at the workplace policies developed by other industrialized countries.[11] But the one thing we should not do is continue to evade the issue or adopt policies without reflecting about their implications.

Debates over affirmative action for women, then, are often a mask for conflicts over sex roles within the family, and disentangling the issues would make it easier to resolve them. It is difficult to reason clearly about sex-related issues, but we ought at least not to pretend that justice in employment of itself requires a revolution in our sexual, reproductive, and family lives.

Displaced Religious Motivations

A number of public policy decisions touch upon issues that have important religious ramifications. Yet the rhetoric surrounding the affirmative action debate is especially pervaded by themes that carry heavy religious connotations—guilt, atonement, the quest for purity of heart, and the longing for a perfectly just society. While the desire to make up for past injustice, to free ourselves from racist and sexist attitudes, or to set up a more just society is not itself inherently religious, the zeal with which these goals are pursued and the thirst for perfection often manifested by proponents of affirmative action bespeak at least some admixture of displaced religious motivations. (This is not surprising since such motivations were very influential in the civil rights movement of the sixties.)

The compensatory argument wrestles with a sense of collective guilt hanging over the white community as a result of the evils of slavery and subsequent racial prejudice and discrimination. Black people are owed a kind of moral debt, and white people are consequently placed in the uncomfortable position of constantly struggling to establish their innocence in the face of an undercurrent of imputed racial guilt.[12] In this context, affirmative action is easily seized upon as a way of achieving white innocence. It expresses repentance for past wrongs, it involves a sacrifice (albeit an involuntary one) on the part of the rejected white job candidate,[13] and it includes an attempt at reparation in that it tries to make the black person whole from his or her injuries. The tort law model, however, breaks down when applied to wrongs spanning many generations. The debt owed black people cannot be calculated (for reasons argued in Chapter 2) and thus becomes for practical purposes limitless, so that the guilt can never finally be assuaged.

In the religious context, of course, it is God Who grants absolution, and the penance performed by the penitent is merely a symbolic expression of sorrow for sin and desire to turn away from it. It is recognized to be beyond the power of human beings to undo the "temporal effects of sin" and restore things to the way they would have been had the sin not occurred. (Even Karl Marx, for all his ambitious aspirations, did not expect to be able to root out all present effects of past injustice.) But when politics taps into these deep levels of the human psyche, and one group holds (or claims to hold) the power of absolution over another, this state of affairs is unhealthy and harms members of both groups.

The corrective argument in some of its versions touches upon a related theme—the quest for purity of heart. John Rawls, in the last sentence of his *Theory of Justice*, appeals to this idea at the level of decisions about the fundamental principles of social life: "Purity of heart, if one could attain it, would be to see clearly and act with grace and self-command from this point of view."[14] Defenders of affirmative action also ask us to root prejudice out of our hearts—a goal which, however, they take to be unattainable. As Jeremiah said, "the heart is deceitful above all things, and desperately corrupt; who can understand it?" (Jeremiah 17:9). Racism and sexism infect us at ever deeper levels, and constitute a sort of miasmatic taint from which we can never be sure we are free. Consequently search committees must be constantly scrutinizing themselves and trying to compensate for their unconscious biases against women and people of color.

There are two difficulties with permitting the quest for purity of heart to motivate public policy in this way. Since purity of heart is taken to be unattainable, policies undertaken to counteract our deep-seated prejudices will be both unsuccessful and never-ending. And, more importantly, proponents of the corrective argument appeal to the corruption of the human heart in a highly selective way. Those religious traditions that emphasize the twistiness and deceitfulness of the heart (e.g., Judaism and Christianity) do not limit this corruption to the hearts of white people, or, worse yet, to those of white *men*. No doubt the powerful are in a position to commit different sorts of sins than the powerless, but absolute purity of heart is just as unattainable for the slave as it is for the master.

I am not arguing that religious motivations have no place in politics. People's conceptions of social justice are often deeply influenced by their religion, and their motivations deeply rooted in the same soil— consider, for example, the antislavery movement or the speeches of the Reverend Martin Luther King Jr.—and it is oppressive and alienating to forbid people to vote or act politically on the basis of their most deeply held convictions, as some would have us do.[15] The difficulty in the affirmative action case is that these religious motivations appear in a fragmentary and distorted form and that their quasi-religious character is unrecognized, which makes them dangerous in a way that overtly religious motivations are not.

Another way in which affirmative action takes on a religious (or perhaps magical) character is its use of rituals and symbols. The rainbow is selected as a symbol, the same formulaic list of marginalized groups is intoned, and the same prejudices are ritually inveighed against (racism, sexism, and sometimes also homophobia, classism, ablism, and so on). Preferential appointment for members of marginalized groups is also frequently justified on the basis of a comprehensive worldview in which Diversity plays a role analogous to that played by God—it reveals to us somehow what is real at the deepest level.

The practice of affirmative action is often explicitly defended as a symbolic expression of our commitment to inclusiveness and diversity. Symbols are important in politics as well as religion, and the line between religious and political symbolism is not always easy to draw. But if one gets too caught up in the symbolic aspect of affirmative action, it becomes very difficult to evaluate such policies in instrumental rational terms. We get locked into making the same symbolic gesture again and again, even when the consequences appear to be quite the opposite of those intended.

Moreover, while affirmative action does carry with it a certain symbolic meaning, the meaning of the symbol is not merely a function of our intentions, since preferential appointment of faculty has consequences—for rejected white male candidates, for students and the sort of education they will receive, for the sort of collegiality or lack of it that will prevail on campus, and for the broader society—and these necessarily affect the symbolic meaning it conveys. (The imaginary garden has real toads in it.)[16]

Our symbols can also convey untoward implications by themselves. One might undertake affirmative action as a way of communicating a welcoming attitude toward everyone regardless of race or sex, but communicate the opposite in practice. Routinely sending all job candidates an affirmative action form to fill out as soon as their application is received communicates the important symbolic message that their race, ethnic group, and sex are among the most significant things about them and will be important to those evaluating their credentials. This message will divide the affirmative action community: some genuinely desire inclusiveness, and will regard it as a regrettable side-effect, whereas others will celebrate the racial and gender divisiveness it implies.

In addition to the sort of expressive or dramatic symbolism discussed above, there is also a quasi-magical reliance on getting the numbers to come out right. Since defenders of affirmative action believe (wrongly) that in a perfectly just society women and people of color would necessarily be proportionally represented in each profession at every level, simply getting the numbers to come out right is thought to somehow effect what it symbolizes, and bring about a just society. But this way of proceeding does nothing to bring about actual development of the black community, or of other disadvantaged people. There is no shortcut that will enable us to bypass the hard work and sacrifices (on the part of everyone—not just black people or white people) that will be necessary to improve the life prospects of the disadvantaged.

Politicians, daunted by the confusing and apparently unmanageable nature of the postmodern economy and discouraged by the persistent failure of our attempts to change social reality for the better, have understandably tended to fall back on making symbolic gestures as a way of rallying support. But the symbol too easily comes to replace what it signifies. I am reminded of the case cited by Søren Kierkegaard in which a man sees a sign in a shop window "SUITS PRESSED HERE" and goes in to have his suit pressed, only to discover that it is a store that sells signs.

Finally, to the extent that symbols remain necessary in politics, affirmative action policies are making the wrong symbolic statement in that they are divisive, encourage obsession with race, concentrate the costs unfairly on a few people, and fail to help the worst off. A symbol that would be less divisive would be a focus on children as the future of America.[17] Richard Rodriguez, for example, in a recent symposium on affirmative action in *Dissent*,[18] attributes the failure of affirmative action to help poor blacks to its concentration on a few elite institutions and calls instead for the president to declare next year "The Year of the First Grade," and to sink large amounts of resources into helping poor children in the first years of school where so many get lost. If a decision were made to dismantle the burgeoning affirmative action bureaucracy this would free up enormous amounts of money that could be used to fund this sort of program.

Children are a group with no political voice, but if we want to help the worst off, then the earlier we start the more effective our efforts will be. Since poor white children would be helped along with poor black children, relying on the symbol of children as the future of our country could unify people in a way affirmative action cannot.

Defects in the Prevailing Social Paradigm

Proponents of affirmative action tend to conceive of society in an erroneous way, and this fact has shaped the way such policies are designed and justified. Opponents of such policies have usually not called these ways of thinking into question either, and thus fight their opponents on shared ground.

The Atomistic View of Society

Much contemporary social philosophy is pervaded by a view of society as a collection of essentially unconnected individuals. This view finds expression in Rawls's *Theory of Justice*, for example, in three ways. (1) Thinking about social justice in terms of distributive justice directs our attention to things that can be distributed to and possessed by individuals. (2) When we go behind the veil of ignorance we are expected to leave behind our communal affiliations and with them our conception of the good life. (3) The basic goods recognized by the theory include wealth and income but not friendship.[19] In his later writings, Rawls backs down in part from this sort of atomism and maintains that his theory is "political not metaphysical." Nonetheless, he continues to assume that our society at least is best understood in these terms.

This sort of social atomism enters into the affirmative action debate in a number of ways. Opponents of such policies have emphasized the fact that it is individuals who possess rights and not groups. Individuals, they believe, should be accorded equal opportunity and rewarded according to their deserts.

On the face of it, supporters of affirmative action appear to have a more social view of the human person—one that recognizes the degree to which human beings are shaped by the families and communities they grow up in. For example, they emphasize ways in which the black community in America still bears scars from slavery and racism, and they point out that Asians and Hispanics are shaped by cultures that differ in important ways from WASP culture.

But when they assume that in the absence of injustice members of all different racial and ethnic groups would be proportionally represented in every profession at every level, they have succumbed to an even more extreme form of social atomism than their opponents. For it is in large part *because* people's personalities and aspirations in life are so deeply influenced by their families and by the distinctive culture of the communities they grow up in that members of various racial and ethnic groups do not distribute themselves randomly throughout society. This is not to say that prejudice is nonexistent—only that there is no reason to suppose that it is the most important explanation for the fact that human society is clumpy rather than homogenized in texture. To will a society in which men and women and members of all racial and ethnic groups are distributed in this sort of way is to will either a society so anomic as to be scarcely recognizable as a society at all or else one in which the government exercises an extraordinary degree of power over people's career choices and employers' hiring decisions.

The obsession with statistics on the part of proponents of affirmative action also manifests a conception of the human person that is both atomistic and curiously abstract. To the extent that proportional representation is taken to be essential to social justice, individual members of the various groups must be treated as fungible. It is rather like a recipe in which one must add two cups of flour, one cup of sugar, three tablespoons of oil, etc., or like an aesthetically pleasing mosaic produced by rearranging black, brown, yellow, white, and red particles. All that makes one woman or one black person different from another (including both unchosen attributes such as one's family and class background, and things one has freely chosen such as one's convictions or one's commitment to a marriage partner) drops out.

Society as a Race

Not only do the parties to the affirmative action debate tend to envision people as disconnected atoms, they also think of each individual as competing against the others in a race to attain positions of wealth and power. The image of society as a race was first articulated clearly by Thomas Hobbes, who said that "There is no other goal, nor other garland, but being foremost."[20] Although not many people embrace this model wholeheartedly, it has continued to exert a deep influence on Western political theory. This way of thinking has been deeply embedded in affirmative action policies from the start, when President Lyndon Johnson gave his famous speech comparing black people with shackled runners. But there are deep problems with viewing society as a race.

First, even if we accept the race metaphor, it is misleading to think of the race as one between individuals, especially when affirmative action for women is at issue. Many women are in long-term, stable relationships with men in which their assets are held in common, and couples ought to be allowed to allocate breadwinning and homemaking tasks between themselves in whatever way they desire. Ensuring that women are not discriminated against in hiring, pay, or promotion is entirely appropriate, but giving them preference makes life harder for couples who want the husband to be the main breadwinner and the wife to do more of the homemaking and childrearing. If he is unable to get full-time work and she has to become the chief breadwinner, the statistics may look better, but both will be less happy than they would have been without affirmative action.[21] Giving part-time professors the proper fraction of full-time pay and benefits or offering "mommy track" jobs (which could be taken by either parent but not both) would be very helpful to academic couples with children.

Second, the race metaphor does not accurately reflect the way most people think because the goals of the race are defined in ways that exclude things people value, such as relaxation, aesthetic pleasure, friendship, time with their families, the opportunity to hand on their values to their children, or a community to live in where someone will pick you up if you collapse in the street. They will consequently be willing sometimes to accept a job that pays less or is less prestigious in exchange for such benefits as less stress, congenial co-workers, flexible work hours, protection against compulsory overtime or forced relocation to another state, or other intangible benefits. Not everyone is equally enamoured with the bitch goddess success.

Third, encouraging people to think of society as a race has a number of undesirable consequences.

1. It leaves no room for a concept of the common good.
2. It encourages people to become obsessed with social status—constantly looking behind them to see if others are overtaking them, and ahead to see if they are gaining on their competitors. Their self-esteem becomes dependent upon their status, and those who get left behind blame themselves or resent those who are successful or both.
3. It leads people to overvalue social mobility. Social mobility is a mixed good and not a cure-all for our social problems. First, moving a few black people up into the professional classes does nothing for those left behind. Second, social mobility (either up or down) can be destabilizing because, so far as social position is concerned, for one person to move up another person has to move down. Third, social mobility, upward or downward, leads to the breakdown of friendships, and weakens familial and communal ties. I am not advocating the elimination of social mobility, since allowing talented individuals to rise to the top ensures that jobs will be done by those best qualified to perform them well. But efficiency is not the only good.
4. Viewing social life as a *single* race has a debilitating effect on those in the middle or at the bottom. As Christopher Lasch has

argued, the vitality of a democracy is dependent on the cultivation of virtue and competence at all levels of society.[22] Thinking of society as one big race and promoting a few of the most talented into the professional elite classes, Lasch argues, does nothing toward achieving this goal, and in fact tends to undermine it. Nonprestigious jobs and those who perform them are devalued.

It is elitist to suppose that only top-paying and high-prestige professional jobs (lawyers, doctors, top business executives, etc.) can be fulfilling. If one takes human diversity seriously, it would seem obvious that people will find different sorts of work fulfilling, and that a skilled builder or a parent caring for his or her children can attain as much job satisfaction as a doctor. (It is not true that inside each man, woman, and child, there is a yuppie lawyer struggling to get out.)

Fourth, not everyone can be upwardly mobile; to think otherwise is to succumb to the logic of Lake Wobegon where "all the children are above average." There is only so much room at the top, and large numbers of people are not even in the race to start with. Children cannot hold their own in the race. Nor can people who are retired on fixed incomes, the disabled, or ghetto residents who lack even the minimal qualifications to compete successfully for jobs.

Jobs as Plums

An atomistic conception of society, coupled with a tendency to view social life as a race, naturally leads to thinking of jobs primarily as sources of income and self-esteem to the person who is appointed. This way of thinking is pernicious. A teaching job, for example, provides a person with an opportunity to have a role in shaping the next generation and preparing them well for the demands they will face.

The Rhetoric of Rights and the Litigious Society

A one-sided focus on individual rights (to the neglect of responsibilities) and an overemphasis on litigation as a way of resolving disputes is one of the characteristic vices of American society.[23] The civil rights movement and the policies that evolved out of it, such as affirmative action, have been cast very much in this mold, relying heavily on regulatory legislation and litigation as ways of improving the condition of black people (and later also women, and other people of color). Universities undertook affirmative action programs largely under threats of litigation in the 1970s, and still struggle to thread their way between the Scylla of a primary discrimination suit and the Charybdis of a reverse discrimination suit.

Reliance on litigation or the threat of litigation as an engine for social change has drawbacks, however. Viewing society as composed of plaintiffs in search of a defendant with deep pockets tends to generate conflict (and is fundamentally flawed besides). Another drawback of this strategy is that courts need to have a workable instrument for measuring compliance with the law, and consequently tend to fall back on simple measures like racial body counts.[24] Stephen Halpern puts the point this way:

> The litigation process itself seems to alter how we define problems and what we do about them. It redirects the focus of reform and saps energy and attention from other initiatives. It seduces us—too often producing illusory and largely symbolic gains.[25]

In his recent book on Title VI of the Civil Rights Act of 1964, Halpern argues that Americans since the sixties have lapsed into a focus on legal rights and litigation as a way of combating racial inequality in education because of a failure of the political will to actually *do* something to ameliorate the complex problems besetting black Americans, and that this approach has proved both very costly and largely ineffective. A similar point can, I think, be made about faculty appointments; the racial and sexual body count approach that reliance on litigation brings in its train is equally inadequate as a way of dealing with the complex problems that are leading to demoralization of faculty and deterioration in the quality of education that all students are receiving.

Materialism

One final problem with the prevailing social paradigm is its tendency to concentrate on questions of resource allocation and to consign cultural issues to the margins. This strategy is understandable since questions about the distribution of resources are easier to manage, but it results in a truncated political life. Politics is not just about pocketbook issues, and one requirement for an adequate social paradigm is that it enable us to talk to each other intelligently about cultural issues. The inability of the current social paradigm to adequately accommodate people's concerns about things like family structure or education (which are not readily quantifiable) is an important reason why problems arising from the changing role of women have not been confronted more directly. And the marginalization of cultural issues is probably one reason why religious motivations appear in public life in displaced form—especially, of course, among liberals who officially hold that religion should be kept out of politics. When religion does appear, as it is bound to, it is treated as irrational and as something we hope will go away (a kind of return of the repressed).

The Shape of the New Paradigm

Before I address the role of the university, it is necessary to say something about what sort of paradigm of social life we ought to adopt. Certainly, an adequate social paradigm should be free of the erroneous assumptions discussed in the preceding section, but what are we to put in their place? This is not the place to develop a complete social philosophy, and what I have to say will necessarily be sketchy and unsupported by argumentation.

To the extent that it is within our power to shape our social institutions, we need most of all to keep our eyes on how well those institutions contribute to human flourishing. People have a wide range of distinctively human capacities—intellectual, moral, social, artistic, and spiritual—the cultivation of which is integral to human well-being. Friendship, self-esteem, or self-discipline, for example, are not things that can be distributed to and possessed by individuals like coffee or VCRs, but they are important to human well-being. This is why the sort of materialism and individualism underlying the prevailing paradigm misses the mark. Our distinctively human capacities require some sort of ongoing communal life for their development, and social institutions should be designed in such a way as to facilitate rather than hinder this sort of life.[26] Moreover, the promotion of human flourishing, and the overcoming of barriers to it such as racial discrimination and the legacy of slavery, is the task of all of our institutions and not just the federal government.

The sort of work people do should be regarded not primarily as a way of obtaining prestige and income, but as a way of using and developing their human capacities in a way that contributes to the common good. Marx said that "the free development of each is the condition for the free development of all."[27] No doubt the idea that everyone will spontaneously flourish in ways that complement and support the flourishing of everyone else is a utopian one, and some other mechanisms for allocating labor are needed. Not everyone can be a lawyer, for example. Nonetheless, every individual has talents that can be put to use for the common good, and we cannot afford to waste the talents of those who are presently falling through the cracks because of poverty, ignorance, addiction, or chronic unemployment.

If promoting human flourishing is at the heart of the new paradigm, universities will be particularly important because their mission directly involves the cultivation of the students' intellectual, moral, artistic, social, and sometimes spiritual capacities. Different schools will, of course, accord higher priority to some of these than others—for example, art schools or religious schools will differ from schools whose primary focus is on science or business administration. But every school will have some impact on how students develop in all these areas since to neglect something is to communicate the message that it is not important.

III. The Role of the University

Universities ought, first of all, to do their own proper job and do it well. Illusions of omnipotence and the temptation to use universities in the service of external political causes, even good ones, should be resisted, or at least kept at the margins; our own task is quite demanding enough.

Developing a New Social Paradigm

One task that it is altogether appropriate to assign universities is the development of a new social paradigm. It is widely acknowledged that welfare liberalism is in serious trouble. Conservatives are divided along numerous axes, and the communitarian alternative is as yet underdeveloped and timid. Developing and elaborating a coherent new paradigm is a genuine intellectual project that could unite scholars, reinvigorate universities, and provide a welcome alternative to the current debilitating combination of politics and therapy.

Affirmative action is usually justified in terms of the faulty social paradigm criticized above, and therefore reinforces it rather than encouraging us to think creatively about ways in which we might develop a better one. The situation in academia, however, is more complicated in that the multiculturalist model plays a more important and explicit role in justifying such policies than it does elsewhere. Is this model, perhaps, the new social paradigm we are seeking?

No doubt some of the insights of weak multiculturalists will be useful to those developing the new paradigm. But the strong multiculturalists criticized in Chapter 4 offer mainly slogans and symbolic gestures and have not yet given thought to how to resolve the grave problems that arise when free rein is given to tribalism and everything common is eroded—such as people being unwilling to pay taxes in the absence of any sense of the common good. And their way of thinking, at least as it comes into play in faculty appointments, tends to treat cultures as inhering in individuals atomistically conceived, to regard any cultures that do not dovetail well with careerism as cultures of victimization, and to nurture only a thin, homogeneous, elite sort of culture thought to be characteristic of each group while showing no interest in how most members of the group actually think or taking other cultures seriously enough to enter into dialogue with them.

The Advancement of Knowledge

It is also the job of universities to contribute to the expansion of knowledge—both theoretical and practical—across a wide range of subject areas. The various academic disciplines can be regarded as traditions in Alasdair MacIntyre's sense of the term. They involve an inherited set of practices with standards of excellence internal to them. Moreover, they are also living traditions insofar as those who take part in them maintain an ongoing argument concerning their ends and the best means to those ends.

To the extent that affirmative action involves overriding the professional judgments of search committee members who are trained in the discipline (or putting strong pressures on them to bend their professional standards) by outside persons not so trained, it interferes with their ability to hand on their tradition to the next generation of practitioners (a power traditionally accorded all the professions).[28] Having their professional judgment overridden in this way is demoralizing to those who have a strong sense of commitment to their discipline, and if it happens frequently it is likely to diminish the amount of good scholarly work being done in the field (both because of demoralization and because good, creative scholars get squeezed out).

Overriding the professional judgment of search committees also reflects and enhances the hegemony of number crunchers—something that in the long run could be fatal to the whole enterprise. The goal of university education is to help students become educated people, and being an educated person is not something that can be measured quantitatively. The idea that only what can be quantified is real is already too prevalent in our society, and this sort of thinking is particularly damaging to education.

Handing On Our Cultural Tradition

Universities should familiarize students with some of the main cultural and historical landmarks that have made America what it is. Failure to do so is serious since there is no other institution that can step in and do this job if universities do not. Students can neither carry on nor intelligently revise their cultural tradition if they do not know what it is. To the extent that affirmative action is motivated and guided by the multiculturalist model of education, it is likely to interfere with the ability of universities to do this task. Not teaching students about the American tradition will also undercut the attainment of the goals sought by affirmative action policies. For, if students are unaware of such things as the Declaration of Independence, the Civil War, and the speeches of Martin Luther King, they are unlikely to see anything wrong with racial discrimination of even the most blatant sort.

Imparting Basic Skills

The rather prosaic but often desperately difficult task of teaching students to write, speak, and think clearly is also very important. Affirmative action in the selection of faculty may have no effect on the teaching of these basic skills. But if, as a result of preferential appointments, students get teachers less able to teach these skills, or ones who regard clear thinking and writing as a manifestation of hegemonic white male culture, then it will have a negative impact.

Teaching the Art of Rational Dialogue

In the present cultural climate, one of the most valuable things universities can do is to teach students how to engage in courteous and intelligent discussion with people they disagree with—to try to appreciate their concerns, give them the benefit of the doubt, abstain from sneering and ad hominem arguments, and to defend their own views rationally. People often resort to vilifying opponents when they find themselves unable to defend their own positions rationally, so teaching students logical argumentation would in the long run greatly improve the quality of our public discourse. Affirmative action, when justified by strong multiculturalism, or when associated with a postmodern rejection of the possibility of reasoning about matters of truth, has been especially harmful here, as I have argued in Chapters 3 and 4.

Tutoring

Finally, universities can expand their educational mission to include tutoring programs that help disadvantaged children in nearby communities. Tutoring could stimulate their interest in learning, encourage them to remain in school, and help them attain the qualifications necessary for admission to college. Faculty as well as students might participate in such programs. Scholarships should be made available to talented students from impoverished homes, and schools that can afford need-blind admissions should adopt that policy.

IV. The Problem Redefined

Thinking about social problems using the paradigm criticized above made affirmative action look like a solution—a way of giving black people a temporary leg up in the race. In the early sixties when the economy was still growing at a healthy rate and when there was a relatively high level of social agreement, this way of thinking was perhaps less inadequate than it is now. But we now face a very different world in which we can no longer count on the stability of families and local communities. Fear, distrust of all public institutions, bitter factionalism, and the breakdown of communication are the norm rather than the exception. The growing rift among Americans along racial lines is cause for especially grave concern (although we are falling apart along other lines as well). We no longer seem to be one nation.

Implicit or explicit fear of race war is an important motivation for affirmative action policies. However, if our central problem is social fragmentation rather than the fact that some people are falling behind in an otherwise reasonably fair and orderly race, affirmative action in the university (especially in faculty appointments) is part of the problem rather than part of the solution.

If the problems are reforming our institutions so that they contribute more effectively to human flourishing and trying to increase social trust and communication, then investing in early education for the disadvantaged, teaching people the art of rational dialogue, and attempting to formulate a more adequate social paradigm will be ways the university can play a constructive role.

Affirmative action, as it has been practiced by those making faculty appointments, makes social trust and communication harder to attain. The postmodern rejection of the possibility of rational dialogue about what is true or right results in a failure to teach the required skills, and sends students out into the world unprepared to defend their own views rationally and therefore able only to wall out the views of people they disagree with or resort to ad hominem arguments. Those versions of the corrective argument that presume all white people are deeply and irremediably racists are certain to poison the atmosphere on both sides and make mutual trust harder to attain. I don't mean, of course, to deny that some white people are racists. But many are not. Furthermore the supposition that *only* white people can be racists is ridiculous.

If what we are threatened with is the disintegration of the United States into warring tribal groups, adopting policies that require students and faculty to identify themselves as members of competing tribes, and justifying them in ways that undercut everything that might keep them from flying apart into warring factions, is throwing fuel on a fire.

Notes

1. Tie-breaking, strictly understood, does not really occur in making faculty appointments since the appointment decision involves weighing and balancing different sorts of considerations in a way that cannot be quantified neatly. What I have in mind is discussed under remedies (section I), below.

2. See the discussion in Chapter 4, section II.

3. Pursuing it on the faculty as a whole has the effect of driving white men out of disciplines in which there are many female and minority candidates in order to balance the shortage of women and people of color in fields like the hard sciences and engineering.

4. See the argument in Chapter 4.

5. See the argument in Chapter 3 to the effect that the role model, mentor, and diversity arguments fail to justify demands for proportional representation of this sort.

6. People I know who have worked in administration have told me that administrators are under pressure from trustees to increase the number of female and minority faculty, but I also know that sometimes trustees oppose such policies. I honestly do not know how to determine just where the pressure originates; no doubt it differs some from school to school (and for the purposes of my argument it does not matter).

7. I find myself in partial agreement here with Judith Jarvis Thomson, who says that a private university is entitled to appoint whomever it likes so long as it "make[s] plain in its advertising that it is prepared to allow the owners' racial or religious or other preferences to outweigh academic qualifications in its teachers." "Preferential Hiring," *Philosophy & Public Affairs*, 2, 4 (1973), 273.

8. Cornel West, for example, seems to take this sort of position. *Race Matters* (Boston: Beacon Press, 1993), 64–65.

9. I am indebted for this idea to Mary Midgley and Judith Hughes, *Women's Choices: Philosophical Problems Facing Feminism* (New York: St. Martin's Press, 1983), 8–9, and 98–99. They remark that "for racial disputes there are in principle at least three possible solutions which do not depend on the parties understanding, accepting and learning to live with each others' distinctness. They are assimilation, apartheid and emigration. For sex, there are none" (98).

10. And if their husbands are (or perceive themselves to be) unemployed or underemployed as a result of affirmative action, such women become understandably quite angry, especially if they hear affirmative action defended as in the interests of women.

11. These include things like parental leaves, on-site child care, flexible hours for parents, and career sequencing. For a valuable introductory discussion of these issues and of how American policy differs from that of other major industrialized countries, see Sylvia Hewlett's books: *A Lesser Life* (New York: Morrow, 1986) and *When the Bough Breaks* (New York: Basic Books, 1992).

12. In *The Content of Our Characters: A New Vision of Race in America* (New York: St. Martin's Press, 1990), Shelby Steele provides an account of the psy-

chological dynamics of race relations in the United States that is particularly insightful about the powerful dialectic of guilt, innocence, and power that comes into play between white people and black people.

13. Although I am unsure how much to make of it, the fact that the victim sacrificed to atone for the sins of the community in the Jewish and Christian traditions had to be an unblemished young male is rather striking.

14. John Rawls, *A Theory of Justice* (Cambridge: Harvard University Press, 1971), 587. Note the admixture of Enlightenment, Christian, and stoic elements in this formulation.

15. For example, the concept of "public reason" developed by John Rawls, in *Political Liberalism* (New York: Columbia University Press, 1993), requires citizens to set aside such convictions, at least when discussing central constitutional issues.

16. Paraphrasing Marianne Moore.

17. I am in part indebted to Hewlett, *When the Bough Breaks*, for the suggestion that this might be a good way to unite Americans politically in support of constructive social programs.

18. Richard Rodriguez, in "Symposium: Affirmative Action," *Dissent* (Fall 1995), 473–74.

19. Rawls, *Theory of Justice*, 62. By contrast, Aristotle ranks friendship very highly, saying that "No one would choose to live without friends, even if he had all other goods." *Nichomachean Ethics*, Book VIII, 1155a5–6, Martin Ostwald, trans. (Indianapolis: Bobbs-Merrill, 1962), 214.

20. Thomas Hobbes, *The Elements of Law*, part I, ch. 9, para. 21.

21. A neighbor who is a nurse reports that in her unit five of the twenty nurses are mothers of small children who want to stay home with their children but whose husbands are unemployed or underemployed as a result of affirmative action. They have consequently been forced to work full time in order to obtain medical insurance.

22. Christopher Lasch, *The Revolt of the Elites and the Betrayal of Democracy* (New York: Norton, 1995), 79.

23. Criticisms have come from a number of directions, but communitarians like Mary Ann Glendon, Amitai Etzioni, Charles Taylor, and Michael Sandel come most readily to mind here.

24. I borrow the term "racial body count" from Stephen Halpern's *On the Limits of the Law: The Ironic Legacy of Title VI of the 1964 Civil Rights Act* (Baltimore: Johns Hopkins University Press, 1995), 301.

25. Halpern, *Limits*, 321.

26. So far the ideal is Aristotelean, except that we ought to think in terms of the development of all people and not just the elite as Aristotle did.

27. Karl Marx and Frederick Engels, *Collected Works* (New York: International Publishers, 1975), VI, 506.

28. I am puzzled by the fact that MacIntyre himself does not draw this conclusion. See "Some Sceptical Doubts" in Steven Cahn's *Affirmative Action and the University: A Philosophical Inquiry* (Philadelphia: Temple University Press, 1993).

Supplementary Essays

Affirmative Action in Faculty Appointments: A Guide for the Perplexed

George Rutherglen

To the uninitiated, the legal issues surrounding affirmative action constitute a confused mass of contradictory opinions, varying legal standards, and uncertain obligations. All of this confusion can be attributed to the deep and lasting controversy over affirmative action, which has led to as much collective indecision in the Supreme Court as it has in the public mind. Individual justices have taken definite positions, but when combined together, their views yield no consistent set of standards. The performance of Congress has been no better. When faced with a clear-cut decision whether or not to enforce affirmative action, as in the Civil Rights Act of 1991, it has answered with a definite maybe. To quote the words chosen by Congress itself: "Nothing in the amendments made by this title shall be construed to affect court-ordered remedies, affirmative action, or conciliation agreements, that are in accordance with the law."[1] Such delphic pronouncements, leaving open exactly what is "in accordance with the law," are all too typical of the law of affirmative action.

Or, to be precise, there is no law, not in the sense of definite legal rules. What we have, instead, are various standards whose meaning depends more on how they are applied than on the particular terms in which they are framed. Three such standards occupy center stage in the legal debate over affirmative action. The first is the constitutional standard for strict scrutiny of racial classifications. In other contexts, this standard has almost invariably resulted in a decision that racial classifications are unconstitutional. With respect to affirmative action, its meaning has become more flexible and less definite, as we shall see. The other two standards are derived from the principal federal statute that prohibits discrimination in employment, Title VII of the Civil Rights Act of 1964.[2] The first of these was offered as an interpretation of Title VII in the controversial decision in *United*

181

Steelworkers v. Weber.[3] It permits employers to engage in affirmative action if it is "designed to break down old patterns of segregation and hierarchy" and if it "does not unnecessarily trammel the interests of the white employees."[4] The second standard also was based on a controversial decision interpreting Title VII, *Griggs v. Duke Power Co.*,[5] but it has now been codified by the Civil Rights Act of 1991.[6] This standard prohibits employers from adopting personnel practices with disparate adverse impact upon minority groups or women, unless these practices can be justified as "job related for the position in question and consistent with business necessity."[7] As with the constitutional standard, the content of these statutory standards remains uncertain, an uncertainty heightened by the relationship between these two standards.

In fact, none of these three standards fits very well with the others, although the different coverage of each standard allows them to coexist together. The constitutional standard applies only to government action, while the standard under Title VII applies to private employment as well as to government employment. Additional standards can be found in other sources of law, from the constitutional standards for evaluating classifications on the basis of sex, to specialized statutes governing recipients of federal funds, to executive orders and regulations that apply only to federal contractors. The initial section of this chapter sorts out these various sources of law, leading to the conclusion that almost all colleges and universities in fact must conform to the standards from the Constitution and Title VII. The succeeding sections of this chapter then examine each of these standards, beginning with the abstract requirements of the Constitution and proceeding to the practically more significant standards under Title VII. The discussion of the latter standards suggests some practical steps that can be taken to comply with the increasingly strict review of affirmative action plans that appears to be imminent.

I. Coverage

All legal regulation of affirmative action derives from some source of law that has limited coverage. No one constitutional or statutory provision covers all of the many different varieties of affirmative action. And, in fact, this chapter will only examine affirmative action on the basis of race, national origin, and sex, and only in appointments and promotions in higher education. This restriction leaves out affirmative action with respect to students, mainly in making decisions on admissions and scholarships, and affirmative action on behalf of groups that, for one reason or another, have been less controversial than minorities and women. The latter include the disabled, veterans, and, curiously, Native Americans, whose racial identity has been deliberately ignored by judicial decisions that categorize them as quasi-sovereign tribes.[8] The arbitrariness of this last distinction gives some idea of how the law of affirmative action has avoided consistent adherence to principle.

The constitutional standards have been dominant in the legal debates over affirmative action, most fundamentally because the constitutional decision in *Brown v. Board of Education*[9] is the fountainhead of all of the modern law of civil rights. Constitutional prohibitions against discrimination on the basis of race and sex, however, apply of their own force only to government action. The Equal Protection Clause of the Fourteenth Amendment prohibits such discrimination by the states and the Due Process Clause of the Fifth Amendment does the same for the federal government.[10] Only the Thirteenth Amendment prohibits both public and private discrimination, and only in the extreme form of slavery. Otherwise, the Constitution prohibits only discrimination by the government. Specifically with respect to colleges and universities, the Constitution prohibits discrimination—and therefore regulates affirmative action—only by public institutions, not by private ones.

The Constitution nevertheless has exercised a profound influence over all forms of affirmative action, private as well as public. Partly, this influence arises from the breadth of government action directly covered by the Constitution. Thus, the executive orders that apply to federal contractors, to the extent that they require affirmative action, must meet constitutional standards. The same holds true of judicial decrees requiring affirmative action.[11] Moreover, even where the Constitution does not apply directly, it has been used as an explicit model for statutory prohibitions on discrimination.

To take the most salient example, Title VI of the Civil Rights Act of 1964 prohibits racial discrimination by the recipients of federal funds.[12] The purpose of Title VI was to extend to federally funded programs, such as federally subsidized loans and scholarships, the same prohibitions against racial discrimination that applied to the federal government.[13] (We may assume that the same is true for national origin, which has not been sharply distinguished from race in the constitutional decisions of the Supreme Court. For the sake of simplicity, the two will be subsumed under the term "race" for the remainder of this chapter.) Title VI does not itself apply to employment, illustrating another quirk of issues of coverage, this one the product of an explicit statutory exception. Nevertheless, several other statutory prohibitions against discrimination have been interpreted in the same way. The most important of these for higher education is Title IX of the Education Amendments of 1972, which prohibits sex-based discrimination by educational institutions that receive federal funds.[14]

Title IX, however, does not precisely track the constitutional prohibition against sex-based discrimination, which brings us to yet another form in which constitutional law has influenced other sources of law. Even in statutes that do not explicitly adopt constitutional standards, constitutional decisions on discrimination inevitably affect the meaning of statutory prohibitions that invoke the concept of discrimination. The constitutional prohibition is an open-ended standard that requires a party seeking to uphold a sex-based classification to establish an "exceedingly persuasive" justification for that classification by showing that it "serves important governmental objectives" and is "substantially related to achievement of those objectives."[15] Title IX, by contrast, simply prohibits sex-based discrimination in education unless it falls within designated exceptions, such as that for traditionally single-sex schools.[16]

Title VII follows the same model of a general prohibition subject to specific exceptions, but it expands on the constitutional prohibitions in several different ways. First, with respect to coverage, it reaches all forms of employment, private in addition to public. Second, it makes the prohibition against racial discrimination nearly absolute, allowing only narrow exceptions. For instance, Title VII explicitly allows affirmative action only on behalf of Native Americans and only in carefully defined circumstances.[17] Third, like Title IX, Title VII contains exceptions to its prohibition against sex discrimination that are of some significance. The most important of these is for jobs in which sex is a "bona fide occupational qualification."[18] And fourth, as the section on disparate impact discusses in more detail later, Title VII does not just prohibit intentional discrimination; it also prohibits neutral employment practices that have adverse effects on minority groups or women and that lack a sufficient business justification.

These detailed provisions in Title VII, and in other statutes, do not have any exact counterparts in constitutional law. The broad and abstract phrases of the Equal Protection and Due Process Clauses, even when elaborated through the process of judicial interpretation, do not have the same detailed texture as a statute. Nevertheless, the statutory provisions end up having much the same effect within their own sphere of operation as do the general constitutional prohibitions. And even when the statutory provisions lead to results different from those required by the constitutional standard, they still strike variations on the constitutional theme. These variations can be significant, as the discussion of disparate impact under Title VII illustrates, but they all derive from the common constitutional purpose of prohibiting discrimination.

In the end, only two sources of law, the Constitution and Title VII, account for all of the effective regulation of affirmative action in employment. Public institutions are subject to the Constitution of its own force and all colleges and universities must conform to Title VII because they meet the statutory definition of covered employers.[19] As we shall see, the Constitution imposes stricter requirements than Title VII on permissible forms of affirmative action on the basis of race and national origin. Or, at least, the law is currently at this somewhat unstable equilibrium. For affirmative action on the basis of sex, the situation is the reverse: Title VII imposes more significant restrictions than does the Constitution, mainly because Title VII contains a general prohibition against sex-based classifications while the Constitution has been interpreted to allow sex-based classifications that "substantially" serve "important government objectives." It follows that all forms of affirmative action in employment must meet at least the standards of Title VII. In higher education, all public institutions must also conform to the stricter constitutional standards for affirmative action on the basis of race and national origin.

This simple analysis of coverage leaves only the question of whether some private colleges and universities come under additional requirements which force them to conform to standards stricter than Title VII. The short answer to this question is no. The longer answer takes us through the statutes and regulations designed to extend the reach of the constitutional prohibitions to recipients of federal funds and to federal contractors. Title VI, as we have seen, accomplishes this result for race, but it does not apply to employment, which it leaves wholly to regulation under Title VII. Title IX of the Education Amendments of 1972 accomplished the same extension for sex-based discrimination in federally supported programs in education. Title IX also goes further than Title VI to reach employment, but in this respect it does not add to the prohibitions against sex-based discrimination in Title VII. Moreover, both Title IX and Title VII contain sections that disclaim any intent to require affirmative action.[20] As a practical matter, what is a permissible employment practice under Title VII is also a permissible employment practice under Title IX.

Executive Orders 11246 and 11375 also prohibit discrimination and require affirmative action by federal contractors.[21] Exactly what "affirmative action" means in these executive orders is spelled out in a complicated series of regulations.[22] These regulations stop short of requiring absolute racial, ethnic, and sexual balance in a contractor's workforce, but they do impose a general obligation to remedy "under-utilization" of minorities and women. They also impose significant reporting requirements, over and above the minimal requirements imposed by Title VII. All of these obligations become more onerous for employers with larger contracts. In recent years, however, the executive orders have been enforced more with a view to ending discrimination than to requiring stronger forms of affirmative action on the basis of race or sex.

The protean character of the term "affirmative action" permits exactly this kind of equivocation, just because it means nothing except as a piece of legal jargon. More specific terminology, on the other hand, means altogether too much. It ends up expressing the speaker's favorable or unfavorable attitude towards the practice in dispute. Where a form of affirmative action is regarded as illegal or questionable, it is condemned as a "quota"; where it is thought to be permissible or desirable, it is accepted as a combination of "goals and timetables." In legal usage, affirmative action embraces a range of practices from encouraging applications by members of particular groups, to providing them with training, to explicitly favoring them in the process of making employment decisions. In the executive orders, these ambiguities have been largely resolved in favor of the least controversial enforcement policies, addressed primarily to prohibiting discrimination and, where affirmative action is concerned, limiting it to agreements negotiated with federal contractors to improve their recruiting practices. For instance, the Clinton administration has interpreted the most recent decision of the Supreme Court on affirmative action, *Adarand Constructors v. Pena*,[23] to severely limit the scope of affirmative action plans adopted or required by the government.[24] The latter development illustrates again the far-reaching influence of constitutional law.

A final source of regulation is state law, illustrated by the action recently taken by the Board of Regents of the University of California to eliminate affirmative action in admissions. The California Civil Rights Initiative would more broadly prohibit all forms of affirmative action by state government.[25] Despite an early decision to the contrary, almost all such actions under state law are likely to be held constitutional. Neither the Constitution nor any federal statute requires affirmative action, except in the rare instances when it has been shown to be the only effective remedy for proven past discrimination. State law that is more restrictive of affirmative action than federal law falls within the general category of state law not preempted by the exercise of federal power. Title VII makes this principle explicit. It preempts only state law "which purports to require or permit the doing of any act which would be an unlawful employment practice under this title."[26] Since Title VII does not require employers to engage in affirmative action, apart from the exceptional cases mentioned earlier, it follows that states can require the opposite: that employers *not* engage in affirmative action. This simple argument has some complicated ramifications discussed later in the section on disparate impact, but these complications remain largely hypothetical. Just as Title VII, broadly speaking, follows the Constitution, state law follows Title VII. Actions and proposals, such as those in California, only illustrate the power of the state to act like any employer covered by Title VII. So long as it is only regulating its own employment practices, a state is only acting like any private employer in taking action permitted by the statute.

A close analysis of questions of coverage again confirms the central role of the Constitution and Title VII in regulating affirmative action. Of these two sources of law, the Constitution has received far more attention, mainly because constitutional decisions cannot be revised by Congress, whereas decisions interpreting a statute, like Title VII, can. Constitutional decisions also interpret broadly phrased provisions, such as the Equal Protection Clause, whereas statutory decisions often turn on the details of statutory language and legislative history. As we shall see, however, the two sources of law are intimately related, and in particular, the technical question of how employers can comply with Title VII profoundly influences the scope of affirmative action that they can engage in under the Constitution.

II. Constitutional Decisions

The earliest and the latest of the Supreme Court's decisions on affirmative action accurately frame the current constitutional law on this subject. The first decision, *Regents of the University of California v. Bakke*,[27] held unconstitutional an affirmative action plan that reserved a definite number of places in professional school for members of minority groups. Any such attempt to earmark specific positions for members of identified groups has been prohibited since the decision in *Bakke*. Nevertheless, the decision also allowed other plans that took race into account in a more flexible way. It was this second holding that was viewed as an endorsement of a range of affirmative action plans, even though it was rendered without any agreement by the justices on a majority opinion. The latest decision, *Adarand Constructors, Inc. v. Pena*,[28] examined a federal program that gave preferential treatment to minority contractors and held that it had to satisfy the most exacting standard of constitutional review: strict scrutiny. Justice O'Connor, who wrote the decisive opinion, interpreted strict scrutiny to require proof that the racial classifications at issue were "narrowly tailored" to serve a "compelling governmental interest."[29] Again, the Supreme Court was closely divided, and again, it could not agree on a majority opinion. Indeed, it did not even hold the federal program at issue unconstitutional, leaving that question to be resolved by the lower federal courts. Nevertheless, its decision has been widely viewed as casting doubt on a wide range of affirmative action plans.

As these decisions demonstrate, the Supreme Court has been unable, over a span of almost two decades, to produce a majority opinion that sets forth the general constitutional standards for evaluating affirmative action plans. Although some intervening cases were actually decided by a single majority opinion, these cases have not proved to be of lasting significance. In the absence of agreement on general standards, the decisions have varied depending on the facts of each case. Each decision has been accompanied by the expectation that it will resolve the constitutionality of affirmative action once and for all, yet each has turned on the details of the affirmative action plan in question. The difference between *Bakke* and *Adarand* depends more on how the standards are applied than on how they are articulated. It also depends upon the difference between admissions to professional school—which are usually decided according to regular procedures— and preferences for government contracts—which often have been treated as the spoils of political victory. Moreover, neither *Bakke* nor *Adarand* concerned affirmative action in employment, so it is necessary to exercise additional caution in applying them in that context.

Keeping these qualifications in mind, the language of the opinions reveals a trend toward stricter examination of affirmative action plans. Between them, *Bakke* and *Adarand* address three critical issues: first, what standard is to be applied to assess the constitutionality of affirmative action plans; second, the purposes, or "governmental interests" that those plans can serve; and third, how closely, or how "narrowly tailored," the plans must be to serve those purposes. The trend over the last two decades, neglecting only a few decisions that have since been narrowed or overruled, has been to increase the hurdles that affirmative action plans must surmount. How much higher these hurdles are is anybody's guess, but the trend is unmistakable.

There has been the least change on the first issue, but it is only at the superficial level of how the standard of constitutional review is articulated. In his decisive opinion in *Bakke*, Justice Powell applied a standard of strict scrutiny, which he interpreted to require proof that racial classifications were necessary to accomplish a substantial governmental purpose.[30] His formulation of the standard was slightly weaker than the formulation that Justice O'Connor later adopted in *Adarand*. In particular, he required only a "substantial" governmental interest, not a "compelling" governmental interest. This slight change in terminology marks a significant difference in attitude, revealed by Justice Powell's willingness to uphold affirmative action plans that considered race to be one factor among others. Justice O'Connor offered no such comfort to advocates of affirmative action in her opinion in *Adarand*. Exactly what either justice meant by "strict scrutiny" remains a matter of controversy, but they are both closer to each other than to more liberal justices who would have adopted an entirely different standard of review.

In *Bakke*, the liberal justices jointly authored an opinion which applied a standard of "intermediate scrutiny," midway between the "rational basis" review accorded to economic legislation under the Due Process Clause and the "strict scrutiny" applied by Justices Powell and O'Connor. This standard applies to classifications on the basis of sex and typically is formulated in the following terms: the disputed classification "must serve important governmental objectives and must be substantially related to achievement of those objectives."[31] For a brief time, this standard was applied to affirmative action plans enacted or approved by Congress,[32] but it was precisely this holding that was overruled in *Adarand*.[33] The consequence of applying intermediate scrutiny would have been to uphold affirmative action plans based on a wider range of more speculative justifications, but with its rejection, affirmative action plans must meet the more exacting requirements of strict scrutiny. Although we cannot say what "strict scrutiny" means as applied to affirmative action, we can say easily—but somewhat unhelpfully—what it does not mean: it does not mean intermediate scrutiny.

The difficulty in clarifying precisely what strict scrutiny means lies in the departure, initially by Justice Powell and more recently by Justice O'Connor, from the usual application of that standard in constitutional law. Gerald Gunther exaggerated only slightly when he said, in a widely quoted phrase, that review under this standard was "strict in theory but fatal in fact."[34] For neither of these justices is the standard always fatal. Combined with the views of more liberal justices, who would apply some form of intermediate scrutiny, their views have defined the minimum requirements for any constitutional form of affirmative action. In *Bakke*, Justice Powell endorsed flexible forms of affirmative action that took race into account to further the academic interest in diversity.[35] In *Adarand*, Justice O'Connor simply denied that strict scrutiny always leads to a judgment of unconstitutionality, but unlike Justice Powell in *Bakke*, she did not identify any example of a permissible affirmative action plan.[36] It is how the standard of strict scrutiny is applied, rather than how it is formulated, that defines the minimum requirements imposed by the Constitution.

Application takes us to the second of the issues addressed in these cases: the "governmental interests" or purposes that can be served by affirmative action. On this issue, *Bakke* and *Adarand* differ dramatically, although for the paradoxical reason that Justice Powell also differed dramatically from all of his colleagues. Alone among the justices in *Bakke*, he held that diversity in higher education was a sufficient justification for considering race in admissions decisions. No other justice took issue with his position, but none endorsed it either. His views on diversity have become influential only because his opinion was decisive; not because it commanded widespread—or indeed, any—support.

Nor has diversity fared any better in subsequent opinions of the Supreme Court. Partly this development can be attributed to the absence of any further cases on affirmative action in higher education. The most recent decision concerned employment practices by a local school district, but yields contradictory implications for affirmative action in higher education. On the one hand, employing teachers to serve as role models for students cannot serve as a justification for affirmative action.[37] On the other hand, diversity in higher education might be different, at least according to Justice O'Connor.[38] In any event, that case concerned preferences in avoiding layoffs, a topic on which the Supreme Court has never allowed any consideration of race.[39] As this point illustrates, the shift from admissions to employment raises a whole new set of issues, not least the diminished role assigned to diversity under Title VII, a topic taken up in the next section.

A further reason that diversity has not received much attention, either favorable or unfavorable, is that it must compete with the indisputably fundamental goal of eliminating the consequences of past discrimination. The liberal justices in *Bakke* found this purpose entirely sufficient to justify the preference in that case.[40] They differed with Justice Powell, just as the liberal justices in *Adarand* differed with Justice O'Connor, over the third issue. The goal of eliminating the consequences of past discrimination becomes controversial at this point: in establishing the connection between the purpose served by an affirmative action plan and the plan itself. Justice Powell, of course, recognized the importance of remedying the effects of past discrimination, as has Justice O'Connor,[41] but he rejected the preference in *Bakke* because it was not narrowly tailored to serve that interest.[42] Using a constitutional standard of intermediate review, the liberal justices consistently have imposed less stringent requirements for connecting affirmative action with past discrimination. Other justices have required a stronger connection.

Again, however, precision has proved elusive. Exactly how strong the connection must be to satisfy a majority of the Supreme Court remains a vexed question. With the passage of time, this question might become less difficult, but at the expense of most forms of affirmative action. As blatant forms of discrimination fade further and further into the past, it becomes increasingly difficult to trace any disadvantage suffered by the beneficiaries of affirmative action to any particular acts of discrimination, let alone acts committed by the institution that has established the affirmative action plan. In a decision that preceded *Adarand*, a majority of justices rejected general "societal discrimination" as a sufficient justification for affirmative action.[43] Instead, racial classification must be "narrowly tailored" to remedy the effects of past discrimination in the market (or similar segment of society) covered by the affirmative action plan.[44] This limitation to the relevant market bears a striking resemblance to doctrines developed under Title VII, as explained in the next section.

On this issue, as on the others addressed in *Bakke* and *Adarand*, the consistent trend has been toward more exacting judicial review of affirmative action plans. If "strict scrutiny" has not been applied with full force, it certainly has been applied with increasing strictness. For university administrators, the lesson is clear: affirmative action plans of all kinds must be more carefully justified, more narrowly defined in scope, and more cautiously applied in practice in order to survive judicial review. Of course, a plan that conforms as closely as possible to existing law also will deter the complaints and lawsuits that lead to judicial review. Whatever the outcome of the current debate, the fact that it is occurring should be warning enough that the era of routine—and routinely approved—affirmative action is over. The recent decision in *Hopwood v. Texas*,[45] which held unconstitutional a separate admission procedure for African American and Hispanic students, just confirms what should be obvious. If a college or university seeks to engage in any form of affirmative action, elaborate precautions are necessary, and with respect to employment, Title VII provides some guidance about what precautions to take. Title VII does not require preferences, but it does impose significant restrictions on voluntary preferences. Colleges and universities cannot afford any longer to ignore these restrictions.

III. Affirmative Action Under Title VII

Title VII allows a greater range of affirmative action plans than the Constitution, but only in order to remedy the effects of past discrimination. As interpreted in the leading decision, *United Steelworkers v. Weber*,[46] Title VII permits voluntary forms of affirmative action "designed to break down old patterns of racial segregation and hierarchy" so long as they do not "unnecessarily trammel the interests of the white employees." This standard has none of the implications of strict review under the Constitution. It seems to allow evidence of societal discrimination to prove "old patterns of racial segregation and hierarchy" and it does not require proof that an affirmative action plan has been "narrowly tailored," only that it is not unnecessarily harsh. The statutory standard is more restrictive than the constitutional standard in only one respect: in not allowing diversity as a justification for affirmative action, except perhaps as lack of diversity might contribute to proof of "old patterns of racial segregation and hierarchy."

Interpretations of Title VII, however, cannot escape the influence of constitutional law. First, the scope of the statutory standard is narrower than it first appears to be. Although Title VII applies to all forms of employment, public or private, it overlaps with the Constitution as applied to all forms of affirmative action involving any form of government action. These include plans adopted by government employers and plans imposed by administrative or judicial order. With respect to those plans, only the stricter constitutional standard makes a difference. The lenient statutory standard only makes a difference in a case like *Weber* itself, in which a private employer adopted an affirmative action plan, with only minimal involvement by the government. Whether the government's involvement really was minimal was disputed in *Weber* itself,[47] as it was in a subsequent decision that applied the same standard to consent decrees accepted by employers but subject to judicial approval.[48]

The second, and more significant, influence of the constitutional standard on Title VII can be found in the convergence of results under these ostensibly different standards. To take the most obvious case, mentioned earlier, racial preferences in layoffs are allowed neither under the Constitution nor under Title VII.[49] Decisions under both sources of law hold that an affirmative action plan cannot concentrate its adverse effects on employees who are entirely deprived of their jobs. Likewise, affirmative action judged under either constitutional or statutory standards must meet the same requirements of flexibility and, in particular, of limiting the burden that affirmative action places on any small group of individuals.[50] Thus, Title VII, like the Constitution, prohibits affirmative action plans that "unnecessarily trammel the interest of the white employees," a requirement that from the beginning has been interpreted to preclude preferences in layoffs.[51]

A more general pattern of convergence emerges in the gradual tightening of the requirements for proof of "old patterns of racial segregation and hierarchy." The decision that initiated this trend, like others on affirmative action, is fundamentally ambiguous. In *Johnson v.*

Transportation Agency,[52] the Supreme Court upheld an affirmative action plan in favor of women, applying the same standard to sex-based classifications as it had already applied to race-based classifications. This holding was entirely unexceptional since Title VII prohibits sex discrimination in the same terms as racial discrimination, apart from a few limited exceptions, none of which were applicable. Nor was the decision problematic in its result. The facts of the particular case concerned the promotion of a woman to a position that had never been occupied by a woman before. For that reason alone, the case presented a compelling inference that affirmative action was necessary to correct the effects of past discrimination.

What made the decision problematic—and certainly confusing—was the discussion of how much evidence was necessary to establish past discrimination. The opinion in *Johnson* equivocated on this subject, relying on technicalities about the proof of disparate impact, discussed in the next section of this chapter. The general problem can be set forth more plainly: To what extent can an employer engage in affirmative action in order to protect itself from future charges of discrimination? Statistics that show a significant imbalance in the employer's workforce can be used to establish a violation of Title VII by a variety of means: as background evidence supporting a claim of intentional discrimination against a particular individual; as evidence supporting an inference of general discriminatory practices; or as evidence of a disparate impact on minorities or women caused by the employer's personnel practices and not justified by a sufficient business purpose. Whatever the use of statistical evidence under Title VII, employers are entitled to take any steps necessary to protect themselves from liability, and in particular to correct past violations or to prevent future violations. This principle holds true, not just as a matter of statutory interpretation, but also as a matter of constitutional law. Preventing future discrimination or eliminating the effects of past discrimination constitutes a plainly sufficient justification for any form of affirmative action, provided that no other remedies will do.

The proviso, of course, is crucial and goes directly to the question of what connection must be established between affirmative action and the goal of remedying discrimination. In the clearest case, in which an individual victim of discrimination obtains compensatory relief, the remedy is so closely connected to the wrong that it is not even recognized as a form of affirmative action. Yet it is based on race or sex just as much as the underlying discrimination that gave rise to the victim's claim. Standard forms of affirmative action differ from this simple case only in the increasingly approximate nature of the remedy. As the remedy becomes less closely tied to any proven wrongdoing, the disjunction increases between the victims of discrimination and the beneficiaries of affirmative action. It becomes increasingly likely that the affirmative action plan does not compensate any victim of past discrimination, let alone past discrimination committed by the employer who established the affirmative action plan.

Some approximation plainly is necessary even in a remedial scheme that seeks to award individual relief. Familiar legal devices, such as the burden of proof, recognize the degree of uncertainty that attends any process that seeks to identify and remedy past wrongdoing. Other devices, such as class actions, seek to distribute the benefits of adjudication over a class of likely victims or, by means of injunctive relief, prevent discrimination against future victims. Still other remedial principles, such as those awarding back pay, seniority, damages for emotional distress, and punitive damages, inevitably remain only approximate.

Affirmative action as a remedy for discrimination only carries the debate over appropriate legal approximations one step further: to the question whether classifications on the basis of race and sex can be used to devise approximate remedies. This question, in the first instance, is one of kind: Can such classifications be used at all? This question has been answered by all but the most conservative judges in favor of allowing some forms of affirmative action. For example, in the cases upholding court-ordered affirmative action plans, solid majorities have upheld the use of race to remedy "particularly longstanding or egregious discrimination."[53] The difficult question is one of degree: How close a connection is needed between the wrong of past discrimination and the remedy of affirmative action?

Under Title VII, this question usually arises in the following form: How much evidence of a violation of the law must an employer present to justify an affirmative action plan? On the one hand, employers cannot be expected to submit conclusive evidence that they have violated the law. In doing so, they would only succeed in defending their affirmative action plans from claims of reverse discrimination at the risk of generating claims of direct discrimination.[54] On the other hand, the employers must be required to submit sufficient evidence to distinguish the use of race or sex to remedy past discrimination from the use of these characteristics simply to allocate benefits on these grounds. The stronger the evidence required of a past violation, the closer the statutory standard for permissible preferences comes to the constitutional standard. Evidence of a past violation of Title VII establishes exactly the kind of compelling government interest necessary to justify a racial classification in constitutional law. The decision in *Johnson* requires almost this much evidence, and in particular, evidence that approaches the showing needed to establish a claim of disparate impact under Title VII. Exactly what constitutes a claim of disparate impact, however, remains a subject of continuing controversy, partly because it is so closely related to the issue of affirmative action. The next section of this chapter turns to a discussion of this theory of liability under Title VII.

IV. Disparate Impact Under Title VII

An air of paradox has always surrounded claims of disparate impact. As a theory of liability, it permits a plaintiff to prove illegal discrimination without proving discriminatory intent. More familiar claims of discrimination, for instance, under the Constitution, require the plaintiff to prove that the defendant acted with such intent, that the defendant considered race or sex in making a decision adverse to the plaintiff. Claims of disparate impact under Title VII dispense with the need to prove discriminatory intent. They instead require only proof of discriminatory effects. Exactly what this means—how it is proved by the plaintiff and how it may be rebutted by the defendant—has been a source of continuing controversy, most recently in the Civil Rights Act of 1991.

In a claim of disparate impact, a plaintiff can recover by proving that an employment practice has a disparate impact on persons of a particular race, national origin, sex, or religion. If the plaintiff proves disparate impact, then the burden of proof shifts to the defendant to prove that the employment practice is justified by "business necessity" or is "related to job performance."[55] These two elements of a claim of disparate impact have been almost as controversial as affirmative action itself. The first element emphasizes effects in exactly the same way as affirmative action, but instead of using effects to allow affirmative action, it uses effects to require the employer, through the second element, to justify the failure to eliminate the disparate effects. For an employer who decides to engage in affirmative action, the first element is the more important, since it defines the level of proof necessary to infer a violation of Title VII. An employer can take reasonable steps to reduce its exposure to liability, the most direct being affirmative action that eliminates any inference of disparate impact. The second element defines the consequences of failing to eliminate disparate impact. It effectively imposes a penalty, in the form of the burden of proof, upon employers who have not engaged in affirmative action and who then must justify the disputed personnel practices that gave rise to the disparate impact.

The principal question raised by disparate impact as a theory of liability is how far it goes in requiring, as opposed to simply encouraging, employers to engage in affirmative action. The Supreme Court has taken different views on this question, as it has on affirmative action generally. An important provision in Title VII disclaims any implication that the statute requires affirmative action.[56] Relying on this provision, the Supreme Court has interpreted the theory of disparate impact simply to be a modest addition to liability for intentional discrimination. On this view, the theory of disparate impact reduces the burden of proof on the plaintiff and shifts part of it to the defendant.[57] In other decisions, however, the Supreme Court has taken a broader view of the theory of disparate impact, treating it as an entirely independent basis for liability, designed to discourage employers from using employment practices with an adverse impact upon historically disfavored groups.[58] This view creates incentives for employers to engage in affirmative action, but stops short of imposing an outright requirement that they do so.

Congress rejected the first, narrower view of disparate impact when it amended Title VII in the Civil Rights Act of 1991. Whether Congress accepted the second, broader view, however, is another question. The provisions that were enacted as amendments to Title VII now equivocate on exactly what an employer must prove in order to justify personnel practices with disparate impact.[59] Not surprisingly, the Civil Rights Act of 1991 also equivocates on its overall approach to affirmative action. It left untouched the disclaimer of any intent to require preferences and it specifically prohibited one form of affirmative action—adjusting the scores of different groups on standardized tests.[60] The Act also contained the delphic provision, mentioned earlier, that allows existing affirmative action plans to remain in effect, so long as they are "in accordance with the law."[61]

Despite these uncertainties, the Civil Rights Act of 1991 made only modest changes in the method that the plaintiff must use to prove disparate impact, and none at all that have any direct bearing on the justification that can be offered for affirmative action plans. The method of proving disparate impact depends upon an economic analysis of the labor market for the jobs in question. With respect to an affirmative action plan, first, the labor market for the jobs covered by the plan must be defined; then the proportion of a particular group among those in the labor market must be ascertained; next the proportion of that group among those holding covered jobs must be determined; then the two proportions must be compared by statistical means to determine the probability that any difference between them resulted solely by chance; and finally, any statistically significant difference must be examined to determine whether it is large enough to be practically significant.[62] These steps are necessary, despite their complexity, because they establish the essential predicate for affirmative action: the existence of continuing discrimination or the continuing effects of past discrimination, as defined by the theory of disparate impact.

For example, a university that sought to establish an affirmative action plan for women in its mathematics department would, first, define the relevant labor market. If the plan covered all tenured and tenure-track positions, and a doctoral degree was a prerequisite for these positions, then the labor market would consist of all holders of this degree available for and interested in employment at the university. Next the proportion of women among that group would be ascertained. This figure can often be approximated by the proportion of women among those who actually apply for the position in question. Whether this correlation exists depends upon whether the employer's recruiting practices yield an unbiased sample of the labor market, without underrepresenting women, for instance, by recruiting at predominantly male colleges, or overrepresenting them, for example, by engaging in affirmative action.

The employer would then determine the proportion of women in the tenure and tenure-track positions who had been appointed in the department. If the gap between the proportion of women recently appointed and the proportion of women in the labor market was large enough to be statistically and practically significant, then an affirmative action plan would be justified. It would still, of course, have to be sufficiently flexible so as to minimize the burden that it placed on male applicants for these positions, a requirement usually satisfied by making the preference for female applicants only one factor among others considered in the appointments process. Diluting the preference in this way diminishes its effectiveness in increasing the representation of women in the department, but it also enables men who possess plainly superior qualifications to the female applicants to compete for every position open in the department. The crucial step in justifying the preference, however, is usually the first: establishing that the representation of women in the department was less than their representation in the relevant labor market over the relevant time period.[63]

In my experience, few colleges and universities and fewer selection committees undertake an analysis along these lines, at least in advance of any claim of reverse discrimination. The cost of a detailed analysis of the labor market, not to mention the need to do it repeatedly as the labor market and the composition of the workforce change, no doubt dissuade them from doing so. If so, they would be well advised to reconsider. The trend toward increasingly strict review of all forms of affirmative action now justifies the expense and inconvenience of the necessary statistical analysis. Some such analysis must usually be undertaken anyway by all employers with 100 or more employees, who must file annual reports with the EEOC describing the composition of their workforce, broken down by type of job and by race and sex.[64] An approximate analysis is better than none at all, especially if it reveals a substantial disparity. Statistics on the racial and sexual composition of the labor market usually can be obtained from national associations, either in the form of those seeking jobs, those actually employed, or those recently receiving degrees. Establishing the disproportion between a group in the labor market and a group in positions with the employer establishes the risk of liability for continuing discrimination under the theory of disparate impact. As explained earlier, evidence of past discrimination creates a sufficient justification for an affirmative action plan, under either the Constitution or Title VII.

Of course, any analysis of the labor market might be disputed on the facts of any particular case, but an extended inquiry into each particular aspect of the labor market is not needed and should not be required. In order to justify an affirmative action plan, it should only be necessary to establish the risk of liability. The analysis of the labor market for this purpose has raised only one issue of general significance: Which qualifications for the jobs covered by the affirmative action plan should be considered in defining the relevant labor market? The more qualifications that are considered, the more narrowly the labor market will be defined. And as it is defined more narrowly, the proportion of minorities or women in the labor market will tend to fall. This tendency follows, at least in part, from the deterrent effect of past exclusionary practices. If a group historically has been excluded from particular jobs, then its current members are less likely to have gained the training or experience necessary for those jobs precisely because the group as a whole has been excluded in the past.

Under a strict analysis, sufficient to impose liability for disparate impact, all of the undisputed qualifications for the jobs must be taken into account.[65] This narrow definition of the relevant labor market is necessary to support the inference that the employer's personnel practices—not the undisputed qualifications for the job—have caused the low proportion of minorities or women in its workforce. In justifying an affirmative action plan, however, a narrow definition of the relevant labor market has the opposite effect. Instead of relieving the employer of liability for direct discrimination, it imposes liability for reverse discrimination. A limited proportion of minorities or women in the labor market supports a finding of no disproportion in hiring which, in turn, leads to a finding of liability for reverse discrimination. A narrow definition of the relevant labor market moves the law from avoiding regulation of direct discrimination to increasing regulation of affirmative action.

A further complication concerns the figures used from the employer's workforce: whether the comparison should be between the composition of the labor market and the current composition of the employer's workforce—likely to reflect hiring decisions made over many years—or the composition of the pool of recently hired employees—reflecting hiring decisions only over the years in which minorities and women have entered the labor market in significant numbers. The first of these figures exaggerates the effect of tenure in depressing the proportion of minorities or women in departments in which they have not traditionally sought advanced degrees. In the example given earlier, a low proportion of women among tenured faculty in the mathematics department might have resulted from the low proportion of women receiving doctorates in mathematics over a period extending back over several decades. The second figure, limited to hiring decisions over the last few years, more closely approximates the comparison that would be used to determine the existence of direct discrimination, but it impairs the effectiveness of affirmative action to remedy "traditional patterns of segregation and hierarchy" recognized in *Weber*. Again, in our example, using this figure would limit the comparison to tenure-track faculty appointed in the recent past. Without directly addressing this particular issue, the trend in the recent cases has been to require stronger evidence of past discrimination to justify affirmative action plans.[66]

From the employer's perspective, the effect of requiring a stronger showing of past discrimination tends to force them to convict themselves of direct discrimination under the theory of disparate impact in order to avoid liability for reverse discrimination. As a consequence, they would stand to gain nothing by engaging in voluntary affirmative action; any benefit from avoiding liability for reverse discrimination would expose them to liability for direct discrimination. It follows that enforcing absolute neutrality in employment practices—a currently popular conservative position—conflicts with the goal of minimizing the role of government in regulating employment—a traditionally conservative position. Conservatives, as much as liberals, must recognize that government may not be able to accomplish all the goals that they hold dear. At any rate, arguments along these lines led to the uncertainty in *Johnson v. Transportation Agency*, discussed in the previous section, about exactly what must be proved to establish "old patterns of racial segregation and hierarchy." Something less than proof of discrimination by the employer is necessary, but how much remains open to dispute.

One way to resolve these disputes might be to rely on regulations promulgated by the Equal Employment Opportunity Commission (EEOC).

Because the EEOC has not been delegated the power to issue substantive regulations with the force of law,[67] its regulations on the theory of disparate impact are only "guidelines." They represent the EEOC's view of how it will exercise its discretion to enforce the statute, but they are not binding upon the courts. In fact, the Supreme Court has taken different attitudes towards the EEOC's guidelines, ranging from "great deference"[68] to no deference at all.[69] The version of the guidelines that now applies to the theory of disparate impact, the Uniform Guidelines on Employee Selection Procedures,[70] departs from the case law on proof of disparate impact in simplifying the plaintiff's burden of proof and in complicating the defendant's.[71] Neither of these changes, however, have much effect on an employer who wants to engage in affirmative action and seeks a justification for doing so. These regulations, like the theory of disparate impact which they seek to interpret, go to contested issues in actually determining liability, not to the existence of a sufficient risk of liability to justify affirmative action.

At various points, however, the Uniform Guidelines do endorse affirmative action,[72] an issue that is taken up in detail in an entirely different set of guidelines devoted to this issue.[73] Unlike other substantive guidelines, the Guidelines on Affirmative Action purport to do more than state the EEOC's position on the exercise of its discretion to enforce Title VII. These guidelines invoke a provision in Title VII that confers a complete defense on employers who conform to official interpretations or opinions of the EEOC.[74] The guidelines state that any affirmative action plan that conforms to their requirements constitutes a complete defense to any claim of reverse discrimination.[75]

The Guidelines on Affirmative Action theoretically confer a broad immunity on any reasonably based affirmative action plan, yet no decision has upheld any defense on these grounds. The Supreme Court has cited the guidelines favorably on only a single occasion and only for the innocuous proposition that Title VII favors settlement over litigation of employment discrimination claims. In the course of its brief discussion of the guidelines, the Supreme Court pointedly remarked that they "do not have the force of law."[76] This conclusion follows not so much from a technical reading of Title VII as from the sense that the legitimacy of affirmative action plans should not be determined conclusively through an obscure set of regulations.

V. Conclusion

Anyone who turns to the judicial decisions on affirmative action for definite answers to precisely defined legal questions is doomed to disappointment. The decisions are heavily dependent on the facts of the precise case before the court, the particular sources of law invoked by the parties, and more often than not, by the alignment of the views of individual judges. More depends on the attitude that the judges bring to affirmative action plans than on the arguments that they have articulated in their opinions. This uncertainty in the law only reflects uncertainty in society as a whole and may, for that reason, amount to a justifiable exercise of judicial indecision.[77] This chapter has not attempted a theoretical defense of existing law on this, or any other, ground. Instead, it has sought to describe the main elements of the different sources of law that bear on affirmative action in employment, with particular reference to employment decisions in higher education. This task does not demand justification, so much as exposition and explanation. Those who seek to justify or criticize the law, or who simply try to anticipate and conform to its requirements, must first understand what it is and how it came to be that way. This chapter has offered an initial answer to these preliminary questions.

Notes

1. Civil Rights Act of 1991, Pub. L. No. 102–166, 105 Stat. 1079, § 116 (1991).
2. 42 U.S.C. § 2000e et seq. (1994).
3. *United Steelworkers v. Weber*, 443 U.S. 193 (1979).
4. Id. at 208–09.
5. 401 U.S. 424 (1971).
6. Pub. L. No. 102–166, 105 Stat. 1071 (1991).
7. 42 U.S.C. § 2000e-2(k)(1)(A)(i) (1994).
8. *Morton v. Mancari*, 417 U.S. 535, 552 n. 12 (1975) (upholding the federal statute that grants employment to Native Americans if they have one-fourth or more degree of Indian blood and have membership in a federally recognized tribe).
9. 347 U.S. 483 (1954).
10. *Bolling v. Sharpe*, 347 U.S. 497, 500 (1954).
11. *Local 28 of Sheet Metal Workers International Association and Local 28 Joint Apprenticeship Committee v. EEOC*, 478 U.S. 421, 480 (1986) (opinion of Brennan, J.); id. at 484 (Powell, J., concurring in part and concurring in the judgment).
12. 42 U.S.C. § 2000d et seq. (1994).
13. *Regents of the Univ. of Cal. v. Bakke*, 438 U.S. 265, 284–87 (1978) (opinion of Powell, J.); id. at 328–41 (Brennan, White, Marshall, Blackmun, JJ., concurring in the judgment in part and dissenting).
14. 20 U.S.C. § 1681 et seq. (1994).
15. *United States v. Virginia*, 116 S. Ct. 2264, 2275 (1996); *Mississippi University for Women v. Hogan*, 458 U.S. 718, 724 (1982).
16. 20 U.S.C. § 1681(a)(3)-(9) (1994).

17. § 703(i), 42 U.S.C. § 2000e-2(i) (1994).

18. 42 U.S.C. § 2000e-2(e)(1) (1994).

19. 42 U.S.C. § 2000e(b) (1994). Colleges and universities run by the federal government may fall within the equivalent prohibitions of 42 U.S.C. § 2000e-16(a) (1994).

20. 20 U.S.C. § 1681(b) (1994); 42 U.S.C. § 2000e-2(j) (1994).

21. Reprinted following 42 U.S.C. § 2000e (1994).

22. 41 C.F.R. pts. 60-1 to 60-60 (1995).

23. 115 S. Ct. 2097 (1995).

24. In 1995, the Clinton administration informed executive departments and agencies that any affirmative action program that creates a quota, preferential treatment for unqualified individuals, or reverse discrimination, or continues after its equal opportunity purposes have been achieved must be eliminated or reformed. President Clinton's Memorandum on Affirmative Action for Heads of Executive Departments and Agencies, July 19, 1995, 68 Fair Employ. Prac. Cas. (BNA) No. 6 at S-45, (Aug. 7, 1995); Federal Agencies Get Guidance Under *Adarand*, 151 Lab. Rel. Rep. (BNA), Analysis/News and Background Information 316 (Mar. 11, 1996). However, the Clinton administration noted that executive orders fall outside the *Adarand* decision because they only require contractors to set up goals and timetables, not quotas. Enforcement at the Agencies, 68 Fair Empl. Prac. Cas. (BNA) No. 6 at S-19 (Aug. 7, 1995). Reading between the lines in these statements, the Clinton administration seems determined to enforce the executive orders in ways that avoid an insistence on rigid forms of affirmative action that would raise constitutional questions about their validity.

25. Proposed Cal. Const. amend II (introduced Dec. 5, 1994).

26. 42 U.S.C § 2000e-7 (1994).

27. 438 U.S. 265 (1978).

28. 115 S. Ct. 2097 (1995).

29. Id. at 2117 (opinion of O'Connor, J.).

30. *Bakke*, 438 U.S. at 290–91 (separate opinion of Powell, J.).

31. Id. at 359 (opinion of Brennan, White, Marshall, Blackmun, JJ.).

32. *Metro Broadcasting, Inc. v. FCC*, 497 U.S. 547, 564–65 (1990).

33. 115 S. Ct. at 2114–17.

34. Gerald Gunther, "The Supreme Court, 1971 Term—Foreword: In Search of Evolving Doctrine on a Changing Court: A Model for a Newer Equal Protection" 86 *Harv. L. Rev.* 1, 8 (1972).

35. *Bakke*, 438 U.S. at 312–20.

36. *Adarand*, 115 S. Ct. at 2117.

37. *Wygant v. Jackson Bd. of Educ.*, 476 U.S. 267, 291–94 (1978) (opinion of Powell, J.).

38. Id. at 286 (O'Connor, J., concurring in part and concurring in the judgment).

39. *See Firefighters Local Union No. 1784 v. Stotts*, 467 U.S. 561, 580–81 (1984) (reversing modification of consent decree to favor blacks in avoiding layoffs); *United Steelworkers*, 443 U.S. 193, 208–09 (1979) (upholding affirmative action plan partly because whites were not bumped out of their jobs).

40. *Bakke*, 438 U.S. at 362–79 (opinion of Brennan, White, Marshall, Blackmun, JJ.).

41. *Adarand*, 115 S. Ct. at 2117.

42. *Bakke*, 438 U.S. at 307–10.

43. *City of Richmond v. J. A. Croson Co.*, 488 U.S. 468, 485, 496 (opinion of O'Connor, J.); id. at 520–21 (Scalia, J., concurring in the judgment).

44. Id. at 498–99.

45. 84 F.3d 720 (5th Cir. 1996), *cert. denied*, 116 S. Ct. 2581 (1996). The fact that the Supreme Court denied certiorari in this case has no precedential significance. It indicates only that the Supreme Court did not find this case appropriate for addressing the general validity of affirmative action plans in higher education, as Justice Ginsburg suggested in her separate statement accompanying the denial of certiorari.

46. 443 U.S. 193, 208 (1979).

47. Or at least so the majority construed the record. Id. at 201. The dissent found that the plan in that case was adopted to forestall enforcement of the executive orders requiring affirmative action by government contractors. Id. at 225–26 (Rehnquist, J., dissenting).

48. *Local No. 93, International Association of Firefighters v. City of Cleveland*, 478 U.S. 501 (1986).

49. *See* note 39 supra.

50. *See Local 28 of Sheet Metal Workers International Association & Local 28 Joint Apprenticeship Committee v. EEOC*, 478 U.S. 421, 479 (1986) (opinion of Brennan, J.); *id.* at 485 (Powell, J., concurring in part and concurring in the judgment).

51. *Weber*, 443 U.S. at 208.

52. 480 U.S. 616 (1987).

53. *Sheet Metal Workers*, 478 U.S. 421, 448–50 (1986) (opinion of Brennan, J.); *id.* at 483 (Powell, J., concurring in part and concurring in the judgment); *id.* at 499–500 (White, J., dissenting).

54. *United Steelworkers v. Weber*, 443 U.S. 193, 209–11 (1979) (Blackmun, J., concurring).

55. *Griggs v. Duke Power Co.*, 401 U.S. 424, 431 (1971).

56. 42 U.S.C. § 2000e-2(j) (1994).

57. *Wards Cove Packing Co. v. Atonio*, 490 U.S. 642, 659 (1989).

58. *Griggs*, 401 U.S. at 432–33; *Albemarle Paper Co. v. Moody*, 422 U.S. 405 (1975).

59. In particular, if the plaintiff proves that a particular personnel practice resulted in disparate impact, the employer must now "demonstrate that the challenged practice is job related for the position in question and consistent with business necessity." 42 U.S.C. § 2000e-2(k)(1)(A)(i) (1994). This language was derived from prior opinions of the Supreme Court, but it is not clear either what those opinions required or what the newly combined phrases now mean.

60. 42 U.S.C. § 2000e-2(l) (1994).

61. Pub. L. No. 102–166, 105 Stat. 1079, § 116 (1991).

62. *Hazelwood School District v. United States*, 433 U.S. 299 (1977).

63. In theory, the same analysis could be applied to affirmative action in promotions. In a college or university, however, these decisions tend to be controversial only when they result in a denial of tenure and loss of a job. If a woman or a member of a minority group is granted tenure, no plaintiff has standing to challenge the decision. On the other hand, if a white male is denied tenure, the denial cannot legally be based on a preference for someone of a different race or sex. The Supreme Court has repeatedly made clear that affirmative action cannot be grounds for discharging employees outside the preferred group. See note 39 supra.

64. 29 C.F.R. § 1602.7 (1995).

65. *Hazelwood*, 433 U.S. at 309; *International Brotherhood of Teamsters v. United States*, 431 U.S. 324, 328 (1977).

66. *In re Birmingham Reverse Discrimination Employment Litigation*, 20 F.3d 1525, 1539–41 (11th Cir. 1994); *Edwards v. City of Houston*, 37 F.3d 1097, 1111 (5th Cir. 1994).

67. 42 U.S.C. § 2000e-12(a) (1994).

68. *Albemarle Paper Co. v. Moody*, 422 U.S. 405, 431 (1975); *Griggs v. Duke Power Co.*, 401 U.S. 424, 433–34 (1971).

69. *International Brotherhood of Teamsters v. United States*, 431 U.S. 324, 346 n.28 (1977).

70. 29 C.F.R. pt. 1607 (1995).

71. 29 C.F.R. § 1607.4 (1995).

72. 29 C.F.R. §§ 1607.4E, .6A, .13, .17 (1995).

73. 29 C.F.R. pt. 1608 (1995).

74. 42 U.S.C. § 2000e-12(b) (1994).

75. 29 C.F.R. § 1608.4(d) (1995). These requirements are that the plan be dated, in writing, and that it is reasonable in the following respects: it is based on a reasonable analysis of the employer's personnel practices, which provides a reasonable basis for finding intentional discrimination, disparate impact, or uncorrected effects of past discrimination; and that the employer takes reasonable action to correct these problems. Id. § 1608.4(a), (b), (c) (1995).

76. *Local No. 93, Int'l Ass'n of Firefighters v. Cleveland*, 478 U.S. 501, 517 (1986).

77. See J. Wilkinson, *From Brown to Bakke, the Supreme Court and School Integration: 1954–78*, at 298–306 (1979); Guido Calabresi, "*Bakke* as Pseudo-Tragedy," 28 *Cath. U. L. Rev.* 427, 427–31 (1970); Paul J. Mishkin, "The Uses of Ambivalence: Reflections on the Supreme Court and the Constitutionality of Affirmative Action," 131 *U. Pa. L. Rev.* 907, 916–18 (1983).

Are Quotas Sometimes Justified?*

James Rachels

Of the many kinds of policies that have been devised to combat discrimination, quotas are the most despised. Almost no one has a good word to say about them. Even those who defend other varieties of preferential treatment are eager, more often than not, to make it known that they do not approve of quotas. In an area in which there is little agreement about anything else, there is a remarkable consensus about this.

Why are quotas thought to be so objectionable? The key idea seems to be that justice is blind, or at least that it should be blind where race and gender are concerned. Jobs should go to the best qualified applicants, regardless of race or sex; anything else is unacceptably discriminatory. A race- or gender-based quota contradicts this fundamental principle. A hiring quota seems to involve—necessarily—the idea that a less qualified black or woman may be hired ahead of a better qualified white male. But if it is wrong to discriminate against blacks and women, how can it be right to discriminate against white men? This point seems to many people to be so obviously correct that quotas are ruled out peremptorily. It is no wonder that the very word has acquired a bad smell.

With so many other issues still unresolved, it may seem perverse to question the one thing about which there is agreement. Nevertheless, I believe that the prevailing consensus concerning quotas is misguided. There is nothing wrong with a quota used in the right circumstances and for the right reason. It needs to be emphasized, however, that there are significant differences in the ways that quotas may be used. They may be imposed in various sorts of circumstances and for various purposes. In what follows I describe a set of circumstances in which I believe the imposition of a quota is justified. I do not conclude from this that the imposition of quotas is in general a good thing or

*This essay originally appeared in *Affirmative Action and the University: A Philosophical Inquiry*, edited by Steven M. Cahn. Copyright © 1993 by Temple University. Reprinted by permission of Temple University Press.

that they should be widely used. If only because they cause such resentment, they should be used sparingly. But I do conclude that the near-universal condemnation of quotas is misguided. It is wrong to think they should never be used.

Suppose you are the dean of a college—let us say that it is a good college, but not one of the most prestigious in the country—and you are concerned that only the best qualified scholars are hired for your faculty. Your college uses the standard procedure for selecting new faculty: The relevant department solicits applications, reviews them, and then recommends the best qualified to you. You then authorize the formal offer of employment. Your role is mainly that of an overseer; so long as everything seems to be in order, you go along with the departments' recommendations.

In your philosophy department, there are vacancies almost every year. You notice, however, that women are almost never hired to fill them. (One woman was hired years ago, so there is a token female. But that's as far as it has gone.) So you investigate. You discover that there are, indeed, lots of female philosophers looking for jobs each year. And you have no reason to think that these women are, on average, any less capable than their male counterparts. On the contrary, all available evidence suggests that they are equally as good. So you talk to the (male) chairperson of the philosophy department and you urge him to be careful to give full and fair consideration to the female applicants. Being a good liberal fellow, he finds this agreeable enough—although he may be a little offended by the suggestion that he is not already giving women due consideration. But your admonition has little apparent effect. Each time there is a vacancy in the philosophy faculty, and candidates are being considered, he continues to report, with evident sincerity, that in the particular group under review a male has turned out to be the best qualified. And so, he says each year, if we want to hire the best qualified applicant we have to hire the man, at least this time.

This is repeated annually, with minor variations. One of the variations is that the best female philosopher in the pool may be listed as the department's top choice. But when, predictably enough, she turns out to be unavailable (having been snapped up by a more prestigious university), no women in the second tier are considered to be good alternatives. Here you notice a peculiar asymmetry: namely, that although the very best males are also going to other universities, the males in the second tier are considered good alternatives. Momentarily, then, you consider whether the problem could be that philosophical talent is distributed in a funny way: While the very best women are equal to the very best men, at the next level down the men suddenly dominate. But that seems unlikely.

After further efforts have been made along these lines, without result, you might eventually conclude that there is an unconscious prejudice at work. Your department, despite its good intentions and its one female member, is biased. It isn't hard to understand why this could be so. In addition to the usual sources of prejudice against women—the stereotypes, the picture of women as less rational than men, and so forth—an all-male or mostly male group enjoys a kind of camaraderie that might seem impossible if females were significantly included. In choosing a new colleague the matter of how someone would "fit in" with the existing group will always have some influence. This will work against females, no matter what their talents as teachers and scholars.

Finally, then, you reach two conclusions. First, you are not getting the best qualified scholars for your faculty. Better qualified women are being passed over in favor of less qualified men. Second, this problem is unlikely to be corrected if the "standard" procedure of permitting the philosophy department to choose its own new members is continued.

Therefore, you issue a new instruction: You tell the philosophy department that it *must* hire some additional women, in numbers at least in proportion to the number of women in the applicant pool. (Why that number? Because, if talent is equally distributed among men and women, that is the number most likely to result in the best qualified individuals being hired.) The department's reaction is easily predictable. It will be objected that this policy could result in hiring a less qualified woman over a better qualified man. That would be unfair. Faculty should be hired, it will be said, according to their qualifications and not according to their gender.

But you agree that the best qualified should be hired. That is precisely what you are trying to achieve. You are not out to give women a special break. You are not trying to redress the injustices they have suffered in the past; nor are you trying to provide "role models" for female students. You may be pleased if your policy has these effects, but the purpose of your new instruction is not to achieve them. Your only purpose is to get the best qualified scholars for your faculty, regardless of gender. The question is simply what selection procedure will best serve that purpose. The fact of unconscious prejudice makes the usual system of simply allowing your experts—the philosophy department—to exercise their judgment an ineffective method. Allowing them to exercise their judgment within the limits of a quota, on the other hand, might be more effective because it reduces the influence of unconscious prejudice. The department's objection, along with all the other usual objections to quotas, misses the point.

That's the argument. It is worth emphasizing that this argument takes into account a feature of the selection process that is often ignored when "preferential treatment" is discussed. Often, the question is put like this: Assuming that X (a white man) is better qualified than Y (a black or a woman), is it justifiable to adopt a policy that would permit hiring or promoting Y rather than X? Then the debate begins, and various reasons are produced that might justify such a policy, such as that it redresses wrongs or that it helps to combat racism or sexism. The debate focuses on whether such reasons are sufficient, and the critical issue appears to be justice versus social utility: Justice argues for hiring X, while reasons of social utility weigh in on behalf of hiring Y.

When the issue is approached in this way, a crucial point is overlooked. People do not come prelabeled as better or worse qualified. Before we can say that X is better qualified than Y, someone has to have made that judgment. And this is where prejudice is most likely to enter the picture. A male philosopher, judging other philosophers, might very well rate women lower, without even realizing he is doing so. The argument we are considering is intended to address this problem, which arises before the terms of the conventional discussion are even set.

Of course, this argument does not purport to show that any system of quotas, applied in any circumstances, is fair. It implies nothing at all about whether schools should establish quotas for the admission of minority students, for example; nor does it imply anything about whether a certain number of government contracts should be set aside for minority businesses. Those remain separate issues. Moreover, the argument does not even say that hiring quotas should be used for all academic appointments. The argument is only a defense of quotas used in a certain way in certain particular circumstances.

But the type of circumstances I have described is not uncommon. Actual quota systems, of the sort that have been established and tested in the courts in recent years, often have just this character. They are instituted to counter the prejudice, conscious or otherwise, that corrupts judgments of merit. When Federal District Court Judge Frank Johnson ordered the Alabama State Police to hire black officers—an order that was widely condemned as just another objectionable "quota"—he was not attempting to redress past injustices or anything of the sort. He was, instead, attempting to curb present injustices against blacks whose qualifications were being systematically underrated by white officials. University people are likely to feel superior to the Alabama police officers: *They* may be guilty of bias, it will be said, but *we* are not. But of course it is almost always a mistake to think oneself an exception to tendencies that are well-nigh universal among human beings. Few of us are saints.

To summarize: Our argument envisions the imposition of a quota as a corrective to a "normal" decision-making process that has gone wrong. We may define a "normal" process as follows: (1) The goal of the process is to identify the best qualified individuals for the purpose at hand. (2) The nature of the qualifications is specified. (3) A pool of candidates is assembled. (4) The qualifications of the individuals in the pool are assessed, using the specified criteria, and the candidates are ranked from best to worst. (5) The jobs, promotions, or whatever are awarded to the best qualified individuals.

This process may go wrong in any number of ways, of course, some of them not involving prejudice. We are not concerned here with all the ways in which things can go wrong. We are concerned only with this possibility: First, we notice that, as the selection process is carried out, individuals from a certain group are regularly rated higher than members of another group. Second, we can find no reason to think that the members of the former group are, in fact superior to the members of the latter group—on the contrary, there is reason to think the members of the two groups are, on average, equally well qualified. Moreover, the distribution of qualifications within the two groups seems normal, from top to bottom. And third, there is reason to think that the people performing the assessments are prejudiced against members of the latter group. These are the circumstances in which our argument says the imposition of a quota may be justified, if other corrective steps cannot do the job. The quota is justified as an effective method for making sure that the best qualified win out, despite the prejudices that inescapably operate against them. The quota does not introduce a new element of prejudice. It merely cancels out an old one.

In deciding what should be done, the policies that have the best reasons on their side should come out on top. In this area, however, emotions run so high that reason often takes second place, and arguments are adduced only to support views to which people are already viscerally committed. I cannot say for certain that the argument I have presented does not contain some flaw that has escaped my notice. But even if it is unassailable, I am pessimistic about whether it will make much difference in the public debate. The emotions that surround this whole subject are too powerful, and the lines that have been drawn are too firmly in place, to allow much optimism on behalf of reason. Nevertheless, if this argument is sound, it does show that the prevailing consensus against quotas does not have reason on its side, no matter how powerful are the emotions that sustain it.

"Minority Student"*

Richard Rodriguez

I.

Minority student—that was the label I bore in college at Stanford, then in graduate school at Columbia and Berkeley: a nonwhite reader of Spenser and Milton and Austen.

In the late 1960s nonwhite Americans clamored for access to higher education, and I became a principal beneficiary of the academy's response, its programs of affirmative action. My presence was noted each fall by the campus press office in its proud tally of Hispanic-American students enrolled; my progress was followed by HEW statisticians. One of the lucky ones. Rewarded. Advanced for belonging to a racial group "underrepresented" in American institutional life. When I sought admission to graduate schools, when I applied for fellowships and summer study grants, when I needed a teaching assistantship, my Spanish surname or the dark mark in the space indicating my race—"check one"—nearly always got me whatever I asked for. When the time came for me to look for a college teaching job (the end of my years as a scholarship boy), potential employers came looking for me—a minority student.

Fittingly, it falls to me, as someone who so awkwardly carried the label, to question it now, its juxtaposition of terms—minority, student. For me there is no way to say it with grace. I say it rather with irony sharpened by self-pity. I say it with anger. It is a term that should never have been foisted on me. One I was wrong to accept.

In college one day a professor of English returned my term paper with this comment penciled just under the grade: "Maybe the reason you feel Dickens's sense of alienation so acutely is because you are a minority student." *Minority student.* It was the first time I had seen the expression; I remember sensing that it somehow referred to my race.

*This essay originally appeared as a chapter entitled "Profession" in *Hunger of Memory* by Richard Rodriguez. Copyright © 1982 by Richard Rodriguez. Reprinted by permission of David R. Godine, Inc.

Never before had a teacher suggested that my academic performance was linked to my racial identity. After class I reread the remark several times. Around me other students were talking and leaving. The professor remained in front of the room, collecting his papers and books. I was about to go up and question his note. But I didn't. I let the comment pass; thus became implicated in the strange reform movement that followed.

The year was 1967. And what I did not realize was that my life would be radically changed by deceptively distant events. In 1967, their campaign against southern segregation laws successful at last, black civil rights leaders were turning their attention to the North, a North they no longer saw in contrast to the South. What they realized was that although no official restrictions denied blacks access to northern institutions of advancement and power, for most blacks this freedom was only theoretical. (The obstacle was "institutional racism.") Activists made their case against institutions of higher education. Schools like Wisconsin and Princeton long had been open to blacks. But the tiny number of nonwhite students and faculty members at such schools suggested that there was more than the issue of access to consider. Most blacks simply couldn't afford tuition for higher education. And, because the primary and secondary schooling blacks received was usually poor, few qualified for admission. Many were so culturally alienated that they never thought to apply; they couldn't even imagine themselves going to college.

I think—as I thought in 1967—that the black civil rights leaders were correct: Higher education was not, nor is it yet, accessible to many black Americans. I think now, however, that the activists tragically limited the impact of their movement with the reforms they proposed. Seeing the problem solely in racial terms (as a case of *de facto* segregation), they pressured universities and colleges to admit more black students and hire more black faculty members. There were demands for financial aid programs. And tutoring help. And more aggressive student recruitment. But this was all. The aim was to integrate higher education in the North. So no one seemed troubled by the fact that those who were in the best position to benefit from such reforms were those blacks least victimized by racism or any other social oppression—those culturally, if not always economically, of the middle class.

The lead established, other civil rights groups followed. Soon Hispanic-American activists began to complain that there were too few Hispanics in colleges. They concluded that this was the result of racism. They offered racial solutions. They demanded that Hispanic-American professors be hired. And that students with Spanish surnames be admitted in greater numbers to colleges. Shortly after, I was "recognized" on campus: an Hispanic-American, a "Latino," a Mexican-American, a "Chicano." No longer would people ask me, as I had been asked before, if I were a foreign student. (From India? Peru?) All of a sudden everyone seemed to know—as the professor of English had known—that I was a minority student.

I became a highly rewarded minority student. For campus officials came first to students like me with their numerous offers of aid. And why not? Administrators met their angriest critics' demands by promoting any plausible Hispanic on hand. They were able, moreover, to use the presence of conventionally qualified nonwhite students like me to prove that they were meeting the goals of their critics.

In 1969, the assassination of Dr. Martin Luther King, Jr., prompted many academic officials to commit themselves publicly to the goal of integrating their institutions. One day I watched the nationally televised funeral; a week later I received invitations to teach at community colleges. There were opportunities to travel to foreign countries with contingents of "minority group scholars." And I went to the financial aid office on campus and was handed special forms for minority student applicants. I was a minority student, wasn't I? the lady behind the counter asked me rhetorically. Yes, I said. Carelessly said. I completed the application. Was later awarded.

In a way, it was true. I was a minority. The word, as popularly used, did describe me. In the sixties, *minority* became a synonym for socially disadvantaged Americans—but it was primarily a numerical designation. The word referred to entire races and nationalities of Americans, those numerically underrepresented in institutional life. (Thus, without contradiction, one could speak of "minority groups.") And who were they exactly? Blacks—all blacks—most obviously were minorities. And Hispanic-Americans. And American Indians. And some others. (It was left to federal statisticians, using elaborate surveys and charts, to determine which others precisely.)

I was a minority.

I believed it. For the first several years, I accepted the label. I certainly supported the racial civil rights movement; supported the goal of broadening access to higher education. But there was a problem: One day I listened approvingly to a government official defend affirmative action; the next day *I* realized the benefits of the program. I was the minority student the political activists shouted about at noontime rallies. Against their rhetoric, I stood out in relief, unrelieved. *Knowing*: I was not really more socially disadvantaged than the white graduate students in my classes. *Knowing*: I was not disadvantaged like many of the new nonwhite students who were entering college, lacking good early schooling.

Nineteen sixty-nine. 1970. 1971. Slowly, slowly, the term *minority* became a source of unease. It would remind me of those boyhood years when I had felt myself alienated from public (majority) society— *los gringos*. *Minority*. *Minorities*. *Minority groups*. The terms sounded in public to remind me in private of the truth: I was not—in a *cultural* sense—a minority, an alien from public life. (Not like *los pobres* I had encountered during my recent laboring summer.) The truth was summarized in the sense of irony I'd feel at hearing myself called a minority student: The reason I was no longer a minority was because I had become a student.

Minority student!

In conversations with faculty members I began to worry the issue, only to be told that my unease was unfounded. A dean said he was certain that after I graduated I would be able to work among "my people." A senior faculty member expressed his confidence that, though I was unrepresentative of lower-class Hispanics, I would serve as a role model for others of my race. Another faculty member was sure that I would be a valued counselor to incoming minority students. (He assumed that, because of my race, I retained a special capacity for communicating with nonwhite students.) I also heard academic officials say that minority students would someday form a leadership class in America. (From our probable positions of power, we would be able to lobby for reforms to benefit others of our race.)

In 1973 I wrote and had published two essays in which I said that I had been educated away from the culture of my mother and father. In 1974 I published an essay admitting unease over becoming the beneficiary of affirmative action. There was another article against affirmative action in 1977. One more soon after. At times, I proposed contrary ideas; consistent always was the admission that I was no longer like socially disadvantaged Hispanic-Americans. But this admission, made in national magazines, only brought me a greater degree of success. A published minority student, I won a kind of celebrity. In my mail were admiring letters from right-wing politicians. There were also invitations to address conferences of college administrators or government officials.

My essays served as my "authority" to speak at the Marriott Something or the Sheraton Somewhere. To stand at a ballroom podium and hear my surprised echo sound from a microphone. I spoke. I started getting angry letters from activists. One wrote to say that I was becoming the *gringos'* fawning pet. What "they" want all Hispanics to be. I remembered the remark when I was introduced to an all-white audience and heard their applause so loud. I remembered the remark when I stood in a university auditorium and saw an audience of brown and black faces watching me. I publicly wondered whether a person like me should really be termed a minority. But some members of the audience thought I was denying racial pride, trying somehow to deny my racial identity. They rose to protest. One Mexican-American said I was a minority whether I wanted to be or not. And he said that the reason I was a beneficiary of affirmative action was simple: I was a Chicano. (Wasn't I?) It was only an issue of race.

It is important now to remember that the early leaders of the northern civil rights movement were from the South. (The civil rights movement in the North depended upon an understanding of racism derived from the South.) Here was the source of the mistaken strategy—the reason why activists could so easily ignore class and could consider race alone a sufficient measure of social oppression. In the South, where racism had been legally enforced, all blacks suffered discrimination uniformly. The black businessman and the black maid were undifferentiated by the law that forced them to the rear of the bus. Thus, when segregation laws were challenged and finally defeated, the benefit to one became a benefit for all; the integration of an institution by a single black implied an advance for the entire race.

From the experience of southern blacks, a generation of Americans came to realize with new force that there are forms of oppression that touch all levels of a society. This was the crucial lesson that survived the turbulence in the South of the fifties and sixties. The southern movement gave impetus initially to the civil rights drives of nonwhite Americans in the North. Later, the black movement's vitality extended to animate the liberation movements of women, the elderly, the physically disabled, and the homosexual. Leaders of these groups described the oppression they suffered by analogy to that suffered by blacks. Thus one heard of sexism—that echo of racism, and something called gray power. People in wheelchairs gave the black-power salute. And homosexuals termed themselves "America's last niggers." As racism rhetorically replaced poverty as the key social oppression, Americans learned to look beyond class in considering social oppression. The public conscience was enlarged. Americans were able to take seriously, say, the woman business executive's claim to be the victim of social oppression. But with this advance there was a danger. It became easy to underestimate, even to ignore altogether, the importance of *class*. Easy to forget that those whose lives are shaped by poverty and poor education (cultural minorities) are least able to defend themselves against social oppression, whatever its form.

In the era of affirmative action it became more and more difficult to distinguish the middle-class victim of social oppression from the lower-class victim. In fact, it became hard to say when a person ever *stops* being disadvantaged. Quite apart from poverty, the variety of social oppressions that most concerned Americans involved unchangeable conditions. (One does not ever stop being a woman; one does not stop being aged—short of death; one does not stop being a quadriplegic.) The commonplace heard in the sixties was precisely this: A black never stops being black. (The assertion became a kind of justification for affirmative action.)

For my part I believe the black lawyer who tells me that there is never a day in his life when he forgets he is black. I believe the black business executive who says that, although he drives an expensive foreign car, he must be especially wary when a policeman stops him for speeding. I do not doubt that middle-class blacks need to remain watchful when they look for jobs or try to rent or when they travel to unfamiliar towns. "You can't know what it is like for us," a black woman shouted at me one day from an audience somewhere. Like a white liberal, I was awed, shaken by her rage; I gave her the point. But now I must insist, must risk presumption to say that I do not think that all blacks are equally "black." Surely those uneducated and poor will remain most vulnerable to racism. It was not coincidence that the leadership of the southern civil rights movement was drawn mainly from a well-educated black middle class. Even in the South of the 1950s, all blacks were not equally black.

All Mexican-Americans certainly are not equally Mexican-Americans. The policy of affirmative action, however, was never able to distinguish someone like me (a graduate student of English, ambitious for a college teaching career) from a slightly educated Mexican-American who lived in a barrio and worked as a menial laborer, never expecting a future improved. Worse, affirmative action made me the beneficiary of his condition. Such was the foolish logic of this program of social reform: Because many Hispanics were absent from higher education, I became with my matriculation an exception, a numerical minority. Because I was not a cultural minority, I was extremely well placed to enjoy the advantages of affirmative action. I was groomed for a position in the multiversity's leadership class.

Remarkably, affirmative action passed as a program of the Left. In fact, its supporters ignored the most fundamental assumptions of the classical Left by disregarding the importance of class and by assuming that the disadvantages of the lower class would necessarily be ameliorated by the creation of an elite society. The movement that began so nobly in the South, in the North came to parody social reform. Those least disadvantaged were helped first, advanced because many others of their race were more disadvantaged. The strategy of affirmative action, finally, did not take seriously the educational dilemma of disadvantaged students. They need good early schooling! Activists pushed to get more nonwhite students into colleges. Meritocratic standards were dismissed as exclusionary. But activists should have asked why so many minority students could not meet those standards; why so many more would never be in a position to apply. The revolutionary demand would have called for a reform of primary and secondary schools.

To improve the education of disadvantaged students requires social changes which educational institutions alone cannot make, of course. Parents of such students need jobs and good housing; the students themselves need to grow up with three meals a day, in safe neighborhoods. But disadvantaged students also require good teachers. Good teachers— not fancy electronic gadgets—to teach them to read and to write. Teachers who are not overwhelmed; teachers with sufficient time to devote to individual students; to inspire. In the late sixties, civil rights activists might have harnessed the great idealism that the southern movement inspired in Americans. They might have called on teachers, might have demanded some kind of national literacy campaign for children of the poor—white and nonwhite—at the earliest levels of learning.

But the opportunity passed. The guardians of institutional America in Washington were able to ignore the need for fundamental social changes. College and university administrators could proudly claim that their institutions had yielded, were open to minority groups. (There was proof in a handful of numbers computed each fall.) So less thought had to be given to the procession of teenagers who leave ghetto high schools disadvantaged, badly taught, unable to find decent jobs.

I wish as I write these things that I could be angry at those who mislabeled me. I wish I could enjoy the luxury of self-pity and cast myself as a kind of "invisible man." But guilt is not disposed of so easily. The fact is that I complied with affirmative action. I permitted myself to be prized. Even after publicly voicing objections to affirmative action, I accepted its benefits. I continued to indicate my race on applications for financial aid. (It didn't occur to me to leave the question unanswered.) I'd apply for prestigious national fellowships and tell friends that the reason I won was because I was a minority. (This by way of accepting the fellowship money.) I published essays admitting that I was not a minority—saw my by-line in magazines and journals which once had seemed very remote from my life. It was a scholarship boy's dream come true. I enjoyed being—not being—a minority student, the featured speaker. I was invited to lecture at schools that only a few years before would have rejected my application for graduate study. My life was unlike that of any other graduate student I knew. On weekends I flew cross country to say—through a microphone—that I was not a minority.

Someone told me this: A senior faculty member in the English department at Berkeley smirked when my name came up in a conversation. Someone at the sherry party had wondered if the professor had seen my latest article on affirmative action. The professor replied with arch politeness, "And what does Mr. Rodriguez have to complain about?"

You who read this act of contrition should know that by writing it I seek a kind of forgiveness—not yours. The forgiveness, rather, of those many persons whose absence from higher education permitted me to be classed a minority student. I wish that they would read this. I doubt they ever will.

II.

When civil rights leaders first demanded the admission of minority students to higher education, academic officials could have challenged their critics to seek the more important reform of primary and secondary education. Academics might have agreed to commit themselves to the goal of helping more nonwhite students enter college. But they should have simply acknowledged (the truth) that higher education is out of the reach of minorities—poorly schooled, disadvantaged Americans. That admission would have taken great courage to make. But more than courage was lacking. When educators promised to open their schools, it was partly because they couldn't imagine another response; their schools were rooted in the belief that higher education should be available to all. (This democratic ideal had made possible the post–World War II expansion of higher education.) Academics would have violated their generation's ideal of openness if they had said that their schools couldn't accommodate disadvantaged Americans. To have acknowledged the truth about their schools, moreover, academics would have had to acknowledge their own position of privilege. And that would have been difficult. The middle-class academy does not deeply impress on students or teachers a sense of social advantage. The campus has become a place for "making it" rather than a place for those who, relatively speaking, "have it made." Even academics on the Left who criticized the "elitism" of higher education seemed not to recognize how different they themselves were from the socially disadvantaged. Many supported affirmative action, assuming that only access kept minority Americans out of college.

So it happened: Academia accepted its so-called minority students. And after the pool of "desirable" minority students was depleted, more "provisional" students were admitted. But the academy was prepared to do little more for such students. (Getting admitted to college was for many nonwhite students the easiest obstacle to overcome.) The conspiracy of kindness became a conspiracy of uncaring. Cruelly, callously, admissions committees agreed to overlook serious academic deficiency. I knew students in college then barely able to read, students unable to grasp the function of a sentence. I knew nonwhite graduate students who were bewildered by the requirement to compose a term paper and who each day were humiliated when they couldn't compete with other students in seminars. There were contrived tutoring programs. But many years of inferior schooling could not be corrected with a crowded hour or two of instruction each week. Not surprisingly, among those students with very poor academic preparation, few completed their courses of study. Many dropped out, most blaming themselves for their failure. One fall, six nonwhite students I knew suffered severe mental collapse. None of the professors who had welcomed them to graduate school were around when it came time to take them to the infirmary or to the airport. And the university officials who so diligently took note of those students in their self-serving totals of entering minority students finally took no note of them when they left.

On every campus, on every faculty, there were exceptions—remarkable professors who took it upon themselves to act as tutors, advisors, friends. Rare women and men, always well known to nonwhite students needing help. More common, however, were those faculty members who simply passed their provisional students. Teachers confronted with evidence of a student's inadequate comprehension found it easiest to dispense a grade that moved a student toward meaningless graduation. The new minority students had been treated with such generosity before. That is how many of them had passed through twelve years of grammar and high school, in the end still needing to be considered culturally disadvantaged.

My experience was different. No professor simply passed me. None treated me with condescension. I was well schooled. Ironically, it was because of what I was so well taught in the classroom that my unease over affirmative action deepened. I was instructed to hear in the Renaissance poet's celebration of pastoral life the reminder of his reader's own civic responsibility and power. I learned how a popular novelist like Dickens, writing for a middle-class audience, makes his readers aware of their ability to effect social reform. Teachers made me aware of D. H. Lawrence's felt separation from his working-class father. And I was made to listen to George Orwell's admission that, as a literate man, he would never be able to imagine what it is like to be one of the uneducated poor.

The odd thing was that in the classroom teachers reminded me of both my public identity and power as a student of literature. But outside of class few were willing to recognize that I was, at best, paradoxically named a minority student. Professors I'd approach would usually

defend affirmative action. (Perhaps they felt they had to. Perhaps they
intended to help me, to relieve my disquiet.) I was told not to worry so
much. "It's possible to be too conscientious about these matters." One
of my best teachers in graduate school seemed surprised that I always
brought up the subject. I was not like "the others," he confided, as a
kind of compliment. Why then did all this minority business concern
me so incessantly? Why spend so much valuable time writing and arguing about affirmative action? he wondered. And I saw deluxe editions of
Spenser and Dryden ranged on a bookshelf behind him. Now then, he
smiled, when was I going to give him that paper comparing Marx and
Wordsworth that sounded so promising?

III.

Officially the academy never lost its enthusiasm for affirmative action
during the years I was a student. But in the early 1970s I remember
hearing professors quietly admit their alarm over various aspects of
what was then called the Third World Student Movement.

Faculty members were understandably troubled, though most
seemed unwilling to make their concern public. As more and more
nonwhite students arrived on campus, less well prepared, many of
them chose to believe that they were, in some cultural sense, minorities. They imagined themselves belonging to two very different societies. What campus officials had implied about them—through the
policy of affirmative action—the students came to believe, seizing
upon the idea of belonging at once to academia and to the society of
the disadvantaged. Modern-day scholar-workers, indulging in clownish display, adopted ghetto accents and assumed costumes of the rural
poor. The students insisted they still were tied to the culture of their
past. Nothing in their lives had changed with their matriculation. They
would be able to "go home again." They were certain, as well, that their
enrollment implied a general social advance for many others of their
race off campus. (The scholar remained united with his people.)

For some students perhaps these ideas provided a way of accepting
benefits suddenly theirs, accruing simply to race. For others these
ideas may have served as a way of accommodating themselves to the
life of a campus so culturally foreign. Especially in the early years of
the Movement, one often heard nonwhite students complain of feeling
lost on the campus. There were demands for separate dormitory facil-
ities, clubhouses, separate cafeteria tables, even for soul-food menus.
And in the classroom: "We can't relate to any of this."

Nonwhite activists began to complain that college and university
courses took little account of the lives of nonwhite Americans. Their

complaint was well founded. And it implied a startling critique of the academy's tendency toward parochialism. Ultimately, it led to the establishment of ethnic studies departments where courses were offered in such fields as nineteenth-century black history and Hispanic-American folk art. The activists made a peculiar claim for these classes. They insisted that the courses would alleviate the cultural anxiety of nonwhite students by permitting them to stay in touch with their home culture.

The perspective gained in the classroom or the library does indeed permit an academic to draw nearer to and understand better the culture of the alien poor. But the academic is brought closer to lower-class culture because of his very distance from it. Leisured, and skilled at abstracting from immediate experience, the scholar is able to see how aspects of individual experience constitute a culture. By contrast, the poor have neither the inclination nor the skill to imagine their lives so abstractly. They remain strangers to the way of life the academic constructs so well on paper.

Ethnic studies departments were founded on romantic hopes. And with the new departments were often instituted "community action" programs. Students were given course credit for work done in working-class neighborhoods. Too often, however, activists encouraged students to believe that they were in league with the poor when, in actuality, any academic who works with the socially disadvantaged is able to be of benefit to them only because he is culturally different from them.

When, for example, Mexican-American students began to proclaim themselves Chicanos, they taught many persons in the barrios of southwestern America to imagine themselves in a new context. *Chicano*, the Spanish word, was a term lower-class Mexican-Americans had long used to name themselves. It was a private word, slangish, even affectionately vulgar, and, when spoken by a stranger, insulting, because it glibly assumed familiarity. Many Mexican-Americans were consequently shocked when they heard the student activist proclaim himself and his listeners Chicanos. What initially they did not understand was that the English word—which meant literally the same thing (Mexican-American)—was a public word, animated by pride and political purpose. "¡Somos Chicanos!" the student activist proclaimed, his voice enlarged through a microphone. He thereby taught his listeners to imagine their union with many others like themselves. But the student easily coined the new word because of his very distance from *Chicano* culture.

Let the reader beware at this point: I am not the best person to evaluate the Third World Student Movement. My relationship to many of the self-proclaimed Chicano students was not an easy one. I felt threatened by them. I was made nervous by their insistence that they still were allied to their parents' culture. Walking on campus one day with my mother and father, I relished the surprised look on their faces when they saw some Hispanic students wearing serapes pass by. I needed to laugh at the clownish display. I needed to tell myself that the new minority students were foolish to think themselves unchanged by their schooling. (I needed to justify my own change.)

I never worked in the barrio. I gave myself all the reasons people ever give to explain why they do not work among the disadvantaged. I envied those minority students who graduated to work among lower-class Hispanics at barrio clinics or legal aid centers. I envied them their fluent Spanish. (I had taken Spanish in high school with *gringos*.) But it annoyed me to hear students on campus loudly talking in Spanish or thickening their surnames with rich baroque accents because I distrusted the implied assertion that their tongue proved their bond to the past, to the poor. I spoke in English. I was invited to Chicano student meetings and social events sponsored by *La Raza*. But I never went. I kept my distance. I was a scholarship boy who belonged to an earlier time. I had come to the campus singly; they had come in a group. (It was in the plural that they often referred to themselves—as minority students.) I had been submissive, willing to mimic my teachers, willing to re-form myself in order to become "educated." They were proud, claiming that they didn't need to change by becoming students. I had long before accepted the fact that education exacted a great price for its equally great benefits. They denied that price—any loss.

I was glad to get away from those students when I was awarded a Fulbright Fellowship to study in London. I found myself in the British Museum, at first content, reading English Renaissance literature. But then came the crisis: the domed silence; the dusty pages of books all around me; the days accumulating in lists of obsequious footnotes; the wandering doubts about the value of scholarship. My year in Britain came to an end and I rushed to "come home." Then quickly discovered that I could not. Could not cast off the culture I had assumed. Living with my parents for the summer, I remained an academic—a kind of anthropologist in the family kitchen, searching for evidence of our "cultural ties" as we ate dinner together.

In late summer, I decided to finish my dissertation and to accept a one-year teaching assignment at Berkeley. (It was, after all, where I belonged.)

What I learned from my year at the British Museum and from my summer at home, other academics have learned; others have known the impossibility of going home, going back. Going back to Berkeley, however, I returned to a campus where I was still officially designated a minority—still considered by university officials to be in touch with my native culture. And there were minority students to face.

In my department that year there were five black graduate students. We were the only nonwhite students in a department of nearly three hundred. Initially, I was shy of the black students—afraid of what they'd discover about me. But in seminars they would come and sit by me. They trusted the alliance of color. In soft voices—not wanting to be overheard by the white students around us—they spoke to me. And I felt rewarded by their confidences.

But then one afternoon a group of eight or ten Hispanic students came to my office. They wanted me to teach a "minority literature" course at some barrio community center on Saturday mornings. They were certain that this new literature had an important role to play in helping to shape the consciousness of a people lacking adequate literary representation. I listened warily, found myself moved by their radiant youth. When I began to respond I felt aged by caution and skepticism: . . . that I really didn't agree with them. I didn't think that there *was* such a thing as minority literature. Any novel or play about the lower class will necessarily be alien to the culture it portrays. I rambled: . . . the relationship of the novel to the rise of the middle class in eighteenth-century Europe. Then, changing the subject to Alex Haley's *Roots*: That book tells us more about his difference from his illiterate, tribal ancestors than it does about his link to them. More quickly: The child who learns to read about his nonliterate ancestors necessarily separates himself from their way of life. I saw one of my listeners yawn. Another sort of smiled. My voice climbed to hold their attention. I wanted approval; I was afraid of their scorn. But scorn came inevitably. Someone got up while someone else thanked me for my "valuable time." The others filed out of the room; their voices turned loud when they got out in the hall. Receded. Left me alone at my desk.

After that I was regarded as comic. I became a "coconut"—someone brown on the outside, white on the inside. I was the bleached academic—more white than the *anglo* professors. In my classes several students glared at me, clearly seeing in me the person they feared ever becoming. Who was I, after all, but some comic Queequeg, holding close to my breast a reliquary containing the white powder of a dead European civilization? One woman took to calling me, with exaggerated precision, *Miss-ter Road-ree-gas*, her voice hissing scorn. (The students sitting around her seemed unaware of her message.)

Still, during those months, Berkeley faculty members continued to assure me that—they were certain—I would be able to work as a special counselor to minority students. The truth was that I was a successful teacher of white middle-class students. They were the ones who lined up outside my door during office hours, the ones who called me at night. Still, I continued to receive invitations to conferences to discuss the problems of the disadvantaged. Envelopes found their way to my apartment addressed to *Señor* Ricardo Rodriguez. I heard myself introduced at conferences as a "Chicano intellectual." (And I stood up.)

IV.

I remember my minority student years in graduate school and need to remember them also as years of white student protests. I was at Columbia during the student riots of 1968 and later at Berkeley during the Cambodian invasion. Powerful images stay from those days: The rock-shattered window discloses a slow-drifting Vietcong flag against the Greco-Roman facade of the university library; campus policemen with bulbous insectlike helmets are chasing students past the open door of my classroom. It is spring.

With most students and teachers I knew, I was opposed to America's Vietnam War. (For me there were deferments and then, when I was vulnerable to the draft, a high lottery number.) I signed petitions and wrote letters to United States senators. I marched up Fifth Avenue in New York, and I joined demonstrations outside the Oakland Induction Center in California. But I was not a very active participant in that season of protest. I never "occupied" a school building. Or heaved a rock. I slept soundly through a riotous night at Columbia while students and sirens screamed outside my dormitory window. I walked through picket lines to study in libraries. There seemed to me something sadly unserious about the militancy. Student demonstrations at Berkeley always blossomed when the weather turned fine. Many students who demanded that the university be "shut down" were careful to check with instructors to be certain they would get course credit at the end of the quarter. Too often the engagement with violence seemed playful. Students rushed to assume, without irony, the role of society's victims.

Victims. At Berkeley, that institution which symbolizes middle-class opportunity, students complained about the impersonal life on the campus—they were being reduced to IBM numbers. But they seemed not to realize that the reason most of them could receive higher education was that universities as vast as Berkeley existed, replacing more private (more exclusionary) institutions of higher learning. White women on campus proclaimed their sisterhood with working-class women. "We all are oppressed," they insisted. Then went on to demand the "solution" of affirmative action, thereby repeating the mistake of claiming benefits for the relative few because of the absence of the many. Students gathered at lunchtime in front of Low Library at

Columbia or on Sproul Plaza at Berkeley to hear student radicals claim their union with "the people." And nobody laughed.

It was one thing for poorly schooled nonwhite students to claim that they were minorities. It was ludicrous for white middle-class students to claim social oppression. They were not victims. They were among the fortunate ones, America's favored children. They were the ones with the opportunity for higher education. It is true that as more and more persons were graduating from college in the sixties, the diploma's value on the job market diminished. Nevertheless, college students were different from those in America's underclass. Many college graduates were forced to work as cabbies or waitresses after graduation, but they retained the confidence of a public identity. They knew how to survive in institutional America. (Students certainly knew how to deal with their draft boards. It wasn't any coincidence that most of those drafted to fight in Vietnam were working-class teenagers, out of high school.)

I was at Berkeley in 1974 when the romantic sixties came to an end. A more pragmatic time succeeded it. Reporters for *Time* and for CBS informed the nation that a new mood of careerism had seized the campus. ("Suddenly . . .") Suddenly students in my classes admitted to being ambitious for good grades. Freshmen had already mapped the progress that would lead them to business or law school. (Professional schools were the only places which dispensed diplomas promising jobs.) Students would come to my office to challenge the grade of *B* they had received. ("Couldn't you please reconsider, Professor Rodriguez? I need an *A*-minus for my transcript.") They would sit in the back rows of my classes surreptitiously reading biochemistry textbooks, while I lectured on Spenser or Dickens, insisting that the reader of literature is made mindful of his social position and privilege. In such classrooms, before students who were so anxious and uncertain of their social advancement, the enlarging lessons of the humanities seemed an irrelevance.

I cannot say now whether I was more comfortable on the campus of the sixties or the campus of the seventies. I'm not sure that they were such different places. The two eras were not so much in opposition as they were complementary developments, indicative of a single fact: Students at the new middle-class campus lacked deep appreciation of their social advantages. What had been lost in the postwar expansion of higher education was the sense that higher education implied privilege. Thus, for a few years, students could be lured by a romantic idea of their victimization. And after a few years students could embrace mean careerism. In either case, self-pity was triumphant.

White students in the seventies frequently complained to me about affirmative action. They said that the reason they couldn't get admitted to business school or the reason their fellowship application had been rejected was the minorities. I tried to sympathize with the convenient complaint. I was on record as being opposed to affirmative action. But I was increasingly annoyed by the fact that the white students who complained about affirmative action never bothered to complain that it was unfair to lower-class whites. What solely concerned them was that affirmative action limited *their* chances, *their* plans.

I would tell fellow graduate students about my outrageous good fortune. Smiling at my irony, I would say that I had been invited to join "minority leaders" on trips to distant Third World countries. Or I would mention that I had been awarded a thousand dollars for winning an essay contest I had not even entered. Or I would say that I had been offered a teaching job by an English department. Some listeners smiled back, only to say: "I guess they need their minority." The comment silenced me. It burned. (It was one thing for me to say such a thing; oddly hard to hear someone else say it.) But it was true, I knew.

In the seventies, as more and more Americans spoke out against affirmative action, university presidents were forced to take the defense. They spoke for the necessity of creating a nonwhite leadership class. But their argument was challenged by a man named Allan Bakke—a man of the new university, a man ambitious for his future, caught in the furious competition for professional school. He suggested a middle-class hero of a sort as he struggled for success and asserted his rights. I supported his claim. I continued to speak out in opposition to affirmative action. I publicly scorned the university presidents' call for a nonwhite leadership class. This defense seemed to me to belong to an earlier time, before World War II, when higher education could ensure positions of social power and prominence. I did not yearn for that older, more exclusive (less open) type of school. I wanted, however, something more from the new middle-class institution than either the decadent romanticism of the sixties or the careerism of the seventies. I wanted students more aware of their differences from persons less advantaged. I wanted university presidents to encourage students to work to improve the condition of disadvantaged Americans. To work, however, not as leaders but in order that the socially disadvantaged could lead their own lives.

My thoughts on the issue were printed. But by the late seventies the debate over affirmative action concerned itself only with the rights of white middle-class students. Opinions came from both sides. One heard from politicians and social activists and editorial writers. Finally, the justices of the Supreme Court rendered their judgment in the case of *Bakke v. University of California*. (Bakke was admitted to medical school.) But no one wondered if it had ever been possible to make higher education accessible to the genuinely socially disadvantaged.

V.

In 1975, I was afraid of the success I knew I would have when I looked for a permanent teaching position. I accepted another one-year appointment at Berkeley in an attempt to postpone the good fortune awaiting me and the consequent issue it would finally force. But soon it came time: September, October, November—the traditional months of academic job-searching arrived. And passed. And I hadn't written to a single English department. When one of my professors happened to learn this, late in November, he was astonished. Then furious. He yelled at me over the phone. Did I think that just because I was a minority, the jobs would come looking for me? Didn't I realize that he and several other faculty members had already written letters on my behalf to various schools? Was I going to start acting like some other minority students he knew? They struggled for academic success and then, when they almost had it made, they chickened out. Was that it? Had I decided to fail?

I didn't want to respond to his questions. I didn't want to admit to him—thus to myself—the reason for my delay. I agreed to write to several schools. I wrote: "I cannot claim to represent socially disadvantaged Mexican-Americans. The very fact that I am in a position to apply for this job should make that clear." After two or three days, there were telegrams and phone calls inviting me to job interviews. There followed rapid excitement: a succession of airplane trips; a blur of faces and the murmur of soft questions; and, over somebody's shoulder, the sight of campus buildings shadowing pictures I had seen, years before, when as a scholarship boy I had leafed through Ivy League catalogues with great expectations. At the end of each visit, interviewers would smile and wonder if I had any questions for *them*. I asked if they were concerned about the fact that I hadn't yet finished my dissertation. Oh no, they said. "We regularly hire junior faculty members who complete their dissertation during their first year or two here." A few times I risked asking what advantage my race had given me over other applicants. But that was an impossible question for them to answer without embarrassing me. They rushed to assure me that my ethnic identity had given me no more than a foot inside the door, at most a slight edge. "We just looked at your dossier with extra care, and, frankly, we liked what we saw. There was never any question of our having to alter our standards. You can be certain of that."

In the first part of January their offers arrived on stiff, elegant stationery. Most schools promised terms appropriate for any new assistant professor of English. A few made matters worse by offering more: an unusually large starting salary; a reduced teaching schedule; free university housing. As their letters gathered on my desk, I delayed my decision. I started calling department chairmen to ask for another week, another ten days—"more time to reach a decision"—to avoid the decision I would have to make. (One chairman guessed my delay to be a bargaining ploy, so he increased his offer with each of my calls.)

At school, meanwhile, I knew graduate students who hadn't received a single job offer. One student, among the best in the department, did not get so much as a request for his dossier. He and I met outside a classroom one day, and he asked about my prospects. He seemed happy for me. Faculty members beamed at the news. They said they were not surprised. "After all, not many schools are going to pass up the chance to get a Chicano with a Ph.D. in Renaissance literature." Friends telephoned, wanting to know which of the offers I was going to take. But I wouldn't make up my mind. Couldn't do it. February came. I was running out of time and excuses. I had to promise a decision by the tenth of the month. The twelfth at the very latest. . . .

February 18. The secretaries in the English department kept getting phone calls; there were messages left on yellow slips of paper: Where was I? What had I decided? Have Professor Rodriguez return my call (*collect*) this evening. Please tell Richard Rodriguez that we must have a decision from him immediately because budget estimates for next year are due at the end of the week.

Late afternoon: In the office at Berkeley I shared with several other lecturers and teaching assistants, I was grading some papers. Another graduate student was sitting across the room at his desk. At about five, when I got up to leave, he looked over to tell me in a weary voice that he had some very big news. (Had I heard?) He had decided to accept a position at a faraway state university. It was not the job he especially wanted, he said. But he needed to take it because there hadn't been any other offers. He felt trapped and depressed, since the job would separate him from his young daughter, who would remain in California with her mother.

I tried to encourage him by remarking that he was lucky at least to have found a position. So many others hadn't. . . . But before I finished, I realized that I had said the wrong thing. And I anticipated what he would say next.

"What are your plans?" he wanted to know. "Is it true that you've gotten an offer from Yale?"

I said that it was. "Only, I still haven't made up my mind."

He stared at me as I put on my jacket. And then stretching to yawn, but not yawning, he asked me if I knew that he too had written to Yale. In his case, however, no one had bothered to acknowledge his letter with even a postcard. What did I think of that?

He gave me no chance to reply.

"Damn!" he said, and his chair rasped the floor as he pushed himself back. Suddenly it was to *me* that he was complaining. "It's just not right, Richard. None of this is fair. You've done some good work, but so have I. I'll bet our records are just about even. But when we go looking for jobs this year, it's a very different story. You're the one who gets all the breaks."

To evade his criticism, I wanted to side with him. I was about to admit the injustice of affirmative action. But he continued, his voice hard with accusation. "Oh, it's all very simple this year. You're a Chicano. And I am a Jew. That's really the only difference between us."

His words stung anger alive. In a voice deceptively calm, I replied that he oversimplified the whole issue. Phrases came quickly: the importance of cultural diversity; new blood; the goal of racial integration. They were all the old arguments I had proposed years before—long since abandoned. After a minute or two, as I heard myself talking, I felt self-disgust. The job offers I was receiving were indeed unjustified. I knew that. All I was saying amounted to a frantic self-defense. It all was a lie. I tried to find an end to my sentence; my voice faltered to a stop.

"Yeah, yeah, sure," he said. "I've heard all that stuff before. Nothing you say, though, really changes the fact that affirmative action is unfair. You can see that, can't you? There isn't any way for me to compete with you. Once there were quotas to keep my parents out of schools like Yale. Now there are quotas to get you in. And the effect on me is the same as it was for them. . . ."

At the edge of hearing, I listened to every word he spoke. But behind my eyes my mind reared—spooked and turning—then broke toward a reckless idea: Leave the university. Leave. Immediately the idea sprang again in my bowels and began to climb. Rent money. I pictured myself having to borrow. Get a job as a waiter somewhere? I had come to depend on the intellectual companionship of students—bright students—to relieve the scholar's loneliness. I remembered the British Museum, a year in the silence. I wanted to teach; I wanted to read; I wanted this life. But I had to protest. How? Disqualify myself from the profession as long as affirmative action continued? Romantic exile? But I had to. Yes. I found the horizon again. It was calm.

The graduate student across the room had stopped talking; he was staring out the window. I said nothing. My decision was final. No, I would say to them all. Finally, simply, no.

I wrote a note to all the chairmen of English departments who had offered me jobs. I left a note for the professor in my own department at Berkeley who was in charge of helping graduate students look for teaching positions. (The contradictions of affirmative action have finally caught up with me. Please remove my name from the list of teaching job applicants.)

I telephoned my mother and father. My mother did not seem to hear exactly what I was trying to tell her. She let the subject pass without comment. (Was I still planning on coming for dinner this Sunday?) My father, however, clearly understood. Silent for a moment, he seemed uncertain of what I expected to hear. Finally, troubled, he said hesitantly, "I don't know why you feel this way. We have never had any of the chances before."

We, he said. But he was wrong. It was *he* who had never had any chance before.

Index

Sandel, Michael, 76n11, 77n25,
121n50
segregation, 182, 191–92, 212
seniority provisions, 11, 14, 34,
40n21
set–asides, 30, 156
sex discrimination, 40n20,
42n41, 45n109, 46n111, 182,
184; compared with race discrimination, 18–20, 25, 161,
193; prohibited by Title IX,
184 and sex roles, 161;
sex roles, 20, 36, 97, 160–62, 170
sexism, 72, 74, 86, 144, 148, 215;
analogy of sexism with racism
criticized, 160–62. *See also*
hermeneutics of suspicion
Sher, George, 75n7
Simon, Robert, 4n1, 76n20
slavery, 47–54, 57, 61–63, 70–73,
75n4, 75n9, 77n28, 162, 166,
171, 183
Smith, Howard, 18–19
Sowell, Thomas, 40n11, 121n56
standards, 3, 56, 79, 83, 89, 91,
101, 104, 117, 121n52, 123–25,
138–47, 169, 176n7; androcentric bias in, 128–35; concern
over declining, 37–38; misperceptions of, 140, 144–46,
205–9; postmodernist critique
of, 124–28; pressure to bend,
156, 173
state universities, 55, 92, 123,
157, 183
statistics, 7, 30–31, 102; collection of, 140; placement,
140–41; and proof of discrimination, 30, 129, 135–47, 156;
reliance on connected with
atomistic understanding of
society, 166–7; statistical arguments, 6, 135–47, 193

Steele, Shelby, 53, 76n12, 177n12
stereotypes, negative, 81, 92, 104,
107, 120n43, 144–45, 156–57
strict scrutiny, 2, 30, 181,
187–91. *See also* intermediate
scrutiny
students, 182; demands for affirmative action by, 46n121;
impact of affirmative action
on, 38–39, 105–7, 111–15, 123,
156–57, 173–74. *See also* role
models and mentors
Students for a Democratic
Society (SDS), 9–10
symbolic politics, 101–2, 110–11,
117, 164–66

taxpayers, 35–36, 38, 47, 92, 123,
172
terminology, choice of, 4. *See
also* inclusive language
*Texas et al v. Cheryl Hopwood, et
al.*, 2, 26, 32, 44n71, 191
textbooks, controversy over, 36
Third World, 64, 220–21
Thomas, Clarence, 38
Thomson, Judith Jarvis, 54–56,
61, 64, 68–72, 134, 176n7
tie-breaking, 46n110, 56, 64, 69,
79, 88, 104, 153, 176n1. *See
also* ice-breaking affirmative
action
Title VI and Title VII. *See* Civil
Rights Act of 1964
Title IX (Education
Amendments, 1972), 10,
12–13, 24, 184–85
tort law, 49–51, 53, 57, 71–72,
153, 163
tribalization, 39, 46n123, 80,
89–91, 109, 116, 175; and
multiculturalism, 98, 104, 109,
172

About the Author and Contributors

CELIA WOLF-DEVINE is associate professor and chair of the philoso-
phy department at Stonehill College. She is the author of *Descartes on
Seeing: Epistemology and Visual Perception* (*Journal of the History of
Philosophy* Monograph Series, 1994), co-editor of *Sex and Gender: A
Spectrum of Views* (under contract with Jones & Bartlett), and of vari-
ous articles and essays, including "Abortion and the Feminine Voice,"
(*Public Affairs Quarterly*, July 1989). She received a B.A. from Smith
College and a Ph.D. from the University of Wisconsin, Madison, and
has taught previously at Simmons College and Tufts University.

JAMES RACHELS is University Professor of Philosophy at the
University of Alabama at Birmingham and the author of *The Elements
of Moral Philosophy* (1986), *The End of Life: Euthanasia and Morality*
(1986), and *Created from Animals: The Moral Implications of
Darwinism* (1980). He has previously taught at the University of
Richmond, New York University, Duke University, and the University
of Miami.

RICHARD RODRIGUEZ is the author of *Days of Obligation* and
Hunger of Memory. He works as an editor at the Pacific News Service
in San Francisco, where he currently resides, and is a contributing editor for *Harpers* and the Sunday "Opinion" section of *The Los Angeles
Times*. He appears on *The Newshour with Jim Lehrer* as an essayist.

GEORGE RUTHERGLEN is the O. M. Vicars Professor of Law at the
University of Virginia School of Law. He is the author of *Major Issues
in the Federal Law of Employment Discrimination* (now in its 3rd edition), and of numerous articles on affirmative action and discrimination in employment. His contribution was originally written for this
volume.